The African Voice
in Southern Rhodesia

.T. MARY'S COLLEGE OF MARYLAND
ST. MARY'S CITY, MARYLAND

053200

The African Voice
in Southern Rhodesia
1898–1930

T. O. RANGER

Professor of African History
University of California
Los Angeles
Formerly Professor of History
University College
Dar es Salaam

NORTHWESTERN UNIVERSITY PRESS · *EVANSTON*

ISBN 0-8101-0320-6

© T. O. Ranger 1970
First published 1970

Printed in the United Kingdom

To John Conradie
who was to have shared
in the making of this book

Contents

Introduction

This book is one of six to be published in the African Voice series. The intention of the series is to present readers with the evidence of what Africans in East and Central Africa were thinking and saying during the long period between 'primary' resistance and the emergence of modern nationalist movements. Whites often said, and some of them complained, that during this period there was no African voice at all. Conservative whites maintained that Africans were silent because they were contented. Liberal whites complained that African inability to speak for themselves left the heavy responsibility of acting as spokesmen for African interests to missionaries and philanthropists. In reality, as the books in this series set out to show, Africans were saying a very great deal.

This study of the African Voice in Southern Rhodesia is the first to be published. Further volumes on Kenya, Uganda, Tanganyika, Malawi and Zambia are being prepared. It is hoped that when all are published, readers will be able to compare and contrast these vital middle years in the six territories concerned and so to understand something more of their contrasting recent history. It is the general intention of the series to present a series of documents to the reader with only that amount of editorial introduction and comment necessary for understanding. In this way the African Voice is to be allowed to speak for itself.

This book does not follow the general pattern of the series, however. It does not take the form of a series of edited documents. For this there are two reasons. The first is that so little has been written about African politics in Southern Rhodesia that it is more necessary to present a narrative and analytical account of them than is the case for Kenya, where the reader can be referred to the work of Nottingham and Rosberg, or for Malawi and Zambia, where the reader can be referred to the work of Rotberg. The second reason is that I was refused permission by the National Archives of Rhodesia in Salisbury to have full copies made of the documents selected for this book. Indeed, since my application was made a number of the most important files upon which I have relied in writing this book have been withdrawn from public access altogether. I have had to depend upon my own notes which are rarely full enough to allow for the complete reproduction of the texts. This book, therefore, takes an unusual, though I hope not a bastard, form. It has much more analysis and comment than the other volumes in the series but it reproduces and cites documents at greater length than is customary in a work of analytical or narrative history.

A number of other explanations and apologies are also necessary. This book ends at the year 1930. Most of the other volumes in the series have a significantly later terminal date and for Southern Rhodesia also it would be ideally suitable to end at 1945 or at least 1939. The reason for this early terminal date is a simple one. When I left Southern Rhodesia in 1963 as a prohibited immigrant I had been able to see records up to 1930. I have had no subsequent opportunity to work further in the Rhodesian archives. It has seemed to me that given the difficulties of pursuing research on African politics in Southern Rhodesia today and given the withdrawal of much of the material it is better to carry the story up to 1930 than not to tell it at all.

Since I left Rhodesia and had the opportunity to work in the challenging environment of the University College, Dar es Salaam, I have become more conscious of two other deficiencies of this book. One is its almost complete reliance on archival sources and overwhelmingly on archival sources produced or collected by the Rhodesian government. I have realized in Tanzania the wealth of documentary material which exists for this period in African hands; I have also realized the great value of oral testimony for the middle years of African political history. I have no doubt at all that the documentary material in African hands in Southern Rhodesia is as rich if not richer and that a scheme of directed student collection of oral reminiscence similar to those carried out in Tanzania would yield very rewarding results. But as it is this book continues to rely on white archival sources for its account of the African Voice.

Finally I have become increasingly interested in the social and economic background to African politics. I have tried to raise in this book some of the sort of questions that are being asked and answered for East African political history. But I am aware that neither my own evidence nor the supporting secondary material available for Southern Rhodesia allows any definite or final answer to them. To take one example – we have no study of the work of any of the missionary societies in Southern Rhodesia; no study of any of the key African schools. Again there are no regional political studies for Southern Rhodesia comparable to those which have been carried out in Tanzania and Kenya. There is no alternative at the moment but to talk about 'the Ndebele' or 'the Shona', unsatisfactory though this is.

For me personally this book is not only set in the context of the African Voice series but in the context of a frustrated trilogy on African politics in Southern Rhodesia. It follows on after my *Revolt in Southern Rhodesia 1896–7* and was to have been followed by a book on the rise and dilemma of mass nationalism. By comparison with a book on the risings of 1896 and 1897 the attempt to recapture African thinking and speaking in the middle period poses difficult problems. The events of the risings impose a shape in themselves. No-one can deny the impact of the risings or their significance. But African politics in the middle period, and still more the movements of African opinion in the rural areas, are very unfocused; and they appear very insignificant. In a recent review Mr Gann has commented that the African political associations of this period were small in numbers, unrepresentative, ineffective, and that they have no real connection with the later flowering of nationalism. Much of what Mr Gann says is perfectly true. Many of the groups discussed in this book were certainly small in numbers and ineffective and the extent to which they were representative is problematical. If one were to write history solely in terms of what pressures were effective at the time then most of the men and movements discussed in this book would find no place in it.

There are a number of reasons why it seems to me nevertheless to be worth looking at these men and movements. The first is that history is increasingly concerning itself not only with the making of policy at the centre but with the impact of policy and of the total, partly planned, largely unplanned, situation upon the people of a territory. This book deals with the impact of the colonial situation in Southern Rhodesia upon the African people of that colony. It sets out to see Rhodesian history in the years between 1898 and 1930 from the bottom up. Seen in this way the emphases tend to be rather different. Policies are not seen as reflected in the polished professions of the policy makers but as mirrored by the reactions, and often the protests, of Africans. This is particularly true of land policy, and especially the policy of Land Apportionment which is in many ways the central theme of this book.

Secondly I do not agree with Mr Gann that there is no connection between the political history of this middle period and later African political movements. This book does not only deal with the impact of colonial policy upon Africans; it does not only deal with Africans as passive victims or subjects. To use the language of Edward Thompson in his great book on the making of the English working class it seeks also to study Africans as *agents*, as helping to make their own history, as helping to make themselves. Upon what Africans were made during this period; upon what they made themselves, later African politics is based. I try to examine, therefore, the various ways in which Africans sought to retain pride; the various ways in which they sought to mould their own lives whether this involved independent churches or trade union movements. I also try to set out in some detail the case for a series of connections between the politics of this period and the development of later mass nationalism.

Finally, there have been some topics upon which even the most conventional of historians has admitted that the African view is worth noting. A classic case is once again that of Land Apportionment. Most historians who have written about the evolution of the principle of possessory segregation and its eventual enactment have given us their version of what Africans thought of it. Most often we are told that in general Africans approved of Land Apportionment. If the views of Africans are worth noting it will be conceded that they are worth noting accurately. I shall try to show in this book that the African response to Land Apportionment at its various stages was significantly different from what is normally supposed.

I owe thanks to many people. In particular I am very grateful to those of my colleagues in Dar es Salaam who were once, like myself, members of the staff of the University College in Salisbury. Dr Arrighi has allowed me to see drafts of portions of his forthcoming economic history of Southern Rhodesia; Roger Woods has made available to me his knowledge of the Native Purchase Areas; Nathan Shamuyarira has been a constant source of stimulating comment and criticism. It will be obvious also that I have drawn heavily upon the work of a group of younger historians who were products of the first History Honours group in Salisbury. I owe much to the work of Keith Rennie on missionary history, of Robin Palmer on the history of land policy, and of Rachel Whitehead on the history of the philanthropic Rhodesian lobby. I am also very grateful to Mr Martinus Daneel for the opportunity to read his drafts on the history of the Zionist and Vapostori movements. I have profited a great deal from the conversation and published work of a number of colleagues who have been working in the field of twentieth century African politics, in particular from Professor Jaap Van Velsen, Dr John Lonsdale and Dr John Iliffe. Finally, since this book is in many ways an extended debate with and criticism of Mr Lewis Gann's interpretation of Southern Rhodesian history, I should acknowledge here how valuable it is for anyone working on some more limited aspect of the Rhodesian twentieth century to have Mr Gann's *A History of Southern Rhodesia* to rely upon for some matters and to quarrel with for others.

I must also thank the staff of the National Archives of Rhodesia for many kindnesses received while I was collecting material for this book. All file references in its footnotes are to material in the National Archives of Rhodesia unless otherwise stated.

Dar es Salaam 1969   *T. O. Ranger*

ONE

Mashonaland
after the Rebellions
1898–1918

The risings of 1896–7 had seen the almost total commitment of most of the Shona in the greater part of the province of Mashonaland to armed resistance against the whites. Shona chiefs, who a few years previously had been fighting each other, came together in the risings. The spirit mediums, who were believed to be possessed by the spirits of dead kings, and the Mwari priests, who interpreted the commands of an oracular high god, combined to preach a gospel of wider African unity. The Shona religious and secular leaders refused to surrender when offered terms at the end of 1896 and the rising was bloodily suppressed throughout 1897. This great uprising was to condition Shona attitudes to politics for decades after its suppression. In the long run the memory of it could be used to gain support for the mass nationalist movements of the late 1950s and 1960s. But immediately the collapse of the risings brought greater disunity instead of the greater unity which was its aspiration; a collapse of morale instead of triumphant self assertion.

In 1898 the 'rebel' areas of Mashonaland presented a picture of demoralization, fear and famine. White suppression of the risings had been slow and piecemeal and very destructive; strongholds had been blasted with dynamite; crops had been systematically destroyed; many Shona peoples had fled from their homes to take refuge in the high lands and some never again returned to settle in their old areas. These experiences left very many Shona with a profound sense of white power and white ruthlessness. The leaders of the rising had in the end surrendered unconditionally and in 1898 many of them were brought to trial and hanged, including the mediums of the Kagubi and Nehanda spirits who had been the chief religious leaders of the Shona rising. Everywhere the hunt went on for those leaders who had evaded capture. For their followers, too, it was a time of great anxiety and much suffering. There was widespread famine. Within each tribal group the tension between ex-rebels and 'loyalists' ran high. Often the new chief, placed in office as a reward for 'loyalty' during the risings, commanded the respect of only a small proportion of his people, and there were areas in Mashonaland where the new chiefs were harassed by the fugitive sons of the deposed rebel paramount.

Gradually, of course, conditions improved; the trials stopped; crops grew; with whatever reluctance the Shona peoples accepted the new chiefs. But the legacy of disunity and disintegration remained; so too did the frustration caused by the feeling that the tribal political authorities were not true representatives of their peoples' interests and grievances. It was to be a long time before self-confidence returned to the mass of the Shona people.

Even in those areas of Mashonaland which had not been involved in the risings the effect of their suppression was felt. Disarmament was general. Many people in the settled areas of the south and east, which had kept out of the risings, had gone to join the fight against the whites and now returned with stories of the suppression. To the north and north-east, where before 1896 regular white administration had hardly existed, Shona peoples felt the impact of white patrols in search of rebel fugitives. Soon these patrols were followed up by regular administrative officers, by disarmament, hut tax and labour recruitment.

The problem for the Shona people was how, if at all, to respond to the pressures of the post-rebellion period. During the 1896–7 risings there had been such a wholesale commitment of the prestige of the Shona secular and religious authorities and such an effective appeal to the Shona past that few institutions and persons and memories in the area of the revolt had survived the collapse unscathed. Armed resistance seemed to have been disastrous. The new chiefs did not promise effective secular leadership. The religious authorities, spirit mediums and Mwari priests alike, seemed to have been crushingly defeated in what had increasingly come to seem like a war between two religious systems. How, then, were the Shona people to find effective forms of political activity, of protest, of appeal?

In this period there were broadly three responses. One was to cling, despite everything, to the idiom of Shona resistance, an idiom which stretched back, after all, to the revolts and wars against the Portuguese. It was possible to find explanations for the defeat of the risings; they had taken place at a time when the white factions of southern Africa were united or at least not fighting amongst themselves; a better chance would come when they once again made war upon each other. The religious leaders, it could be argued, had been betrayed by followers reluctant to observe in full their commands and prohibitions. Unity might again be possible to achieve through the spirit mediums and Mwari priests. The whites might impose 'loyalist' chiefs but they could hardly impose 'loyalist' spirit mediums. The best the administration could do was to harry the mediums, perhaps drive them underground. And if a great medium called once again for revolt there were men in each paramountcy who could provide a focus of opposition to the new chiefs. There were even surviving secular leaders of the 1896 risings, like chief Kunzwi-Nyandoro, who was widely regarded as the real leader of the central Shona. All this enabled dreams of armed resistance to survive.

A second response was to turn inwards to the local situation. The wider alliance of the Shona paramountcies had collapsed with the defeat of the risings; even the old contact of rivalry and inter-paramountcy war was no longer possible; in many cases white settlement interposed a geographical barrier between different Shona groups. Yet reduced in power and prosperity though they were the Shona chieftaincies were still a focus of political ambition. There was still plenty of life in the politics of the Shona paramountcies. Struggle for the chiefship, struggle for positions of influence as headmen or councillors, struggle for prestige at the village level, all this absorbed a great deal of Shona political energy.

A third response was to accept that defeat in the risings was not merely one additional episode in the long history of Shona clashes with whites but that it marked a turning point. There were some men who saw no future in plans of renewed violent resistance but who were not satisfied to accept the parochial concentration upon the internal politics of the paramountcies. Christianity, they thought, had been victorious; now its potentialities must be explored. At first in humble apprenticeship to the white religion, later in attempts to master and to use its sources of power, they sought new ways after 1898.

The Tradition of Shona Resistance and the Mapondera Rising

It is easier to understand the long hold over the imaginations of the Shona people exercised by the tradition of old-style armed resistance if we remember that the very first Shona voice to be raised to any effect after the suppression of the risings was that of a resister. Into the demoralized and uncertain Mashonaland of the post-rebellion years there burst a self-confident hero out of the old Shona mould, the Rozwi chief Mapondera of Mazoe. His story bears telling in some detail because it catches so much of the quality of the Shona world upon which colonialism was making its impact and because it illustrates why men went on thinking in terms of this sort of action.

Kadungure Mapondera could trace his descent from the Rozwi Changamire Mambos, rulers of Zimbabwe, who had long ago sent their emissaries into the Mazoe area. His father, Gorajena Negomo, was a famous warrior, husband of many wives, father of many children. Of all these Mapondera 'took over Gorajena's spirit of war'. Today his descendants tell stories of his prowess; of his wonderful war medicines; his alliance with the great Shona chief Makombe of Barwe, in what is now Mozambique; his defeats of Ndebele raiding parties. Mapondera was the very symbol of pre-colonial Shona independence. When the hunter Selous visited his area in 1889 he made gifts to Mapondera in return for a concession. In this document Mapondera and his brother described themselves as 'chiefs of a free and independent nation, as was their father Nigoma before them, paying no tribute, nor being subject in any way, either to Lobengula . . . or to the Portuguese Government.'[1]

When the Pioneer Column and the British South Africa Company administration arrived in 1890, the proud Mapondera found the closeness of the white men intolerable. Between 1890 and 1894 there were a series of incidents in his part of the Mazoe valley and one of his brothers was jailed for the killing of a white man. In 1894 Mapondera totally refused the Company demand for tax. He took his immediate following out of the Mazoe valley and went to Mozambique to assist his ally, Makombe, in his war with the Portuguese.

Mapondera was not, therefore, involved in the 1896-7 risings. But his reputation increased during his absence. Before 1896, while most Shona paramounts were compelled to observe the Pax Britannica, Mapondera gained new laurels in war. In 1896, as the Mazoe Shona prepared to rise against the whites, they sent to Mapondera in Barwe to ask him for war medicine.

This, then, was the formidable figure who suddenly re-entered the politics of Mashonaland in 1900. Mapondera had reason to hate the Rhodesian administration. 'When he left his kraal and lived in the bush,' runs a press report of his testimony at his trial in 1904, 'a Native Commissioner took all his cattle away . . . He was asked to return to his kraal but declined because his children and his cattle had been killed. 'During the rising of 1896 he was in Portuguese territory. He then went to Chiutsi's country and said he had been driven from his own land.' 'Why he became aggressive towards Europeans,' writes his grand-daughter, 'was because they had caused the death of his eldest son, Chivarange. What happened is

---

[1] Agreement between F. C. Selous and Mapondera, 25 September 1889, CT 1/6/8. I am much indebted to the surviving members of Mapondera's family who have given me accounts of his life and in particular to his granddaughter, Mrs E. Mwendapole, who has compiled a manuscript history of him.

that he had remained alone at home when the administrators came to attack his father's village, and when the messengers wanted to arrest him he reversed his own gun against himself. It was loaded so it triggered and killed him. This angered Mapondera . . . He was revenging his son.'[1]

In April 1900 Mapondera returned to Rhodesia for his revenge. He raided into his old country of South Mazoe but found the people there too crushed by the suppression of the risings to rally to him. He then retreated northwards into Korekore country where the recent establishment of the administration and attempts at disarmament had created much discontent. Mapondera encouraged the Korekore not to pay hut-tax; in June 1900 he ambushed a police patrol near his kraal on the Dande river. But he was at once followed up by a force which more or less ended Korekore resistance. On July 16th Mapondera was attacked and defeated by a patrol of seven officers and seventy-nine men of the Imperial Yeomanry, twenty-seven white police and sixty black, together with 'friendlies'.

But Mapondera persisted. He moved north once more and made contact with the last titular Mwene Mutapa, Chioko, who lived on the border of Rhodesian and Portuguese Tavara country. Mutapa Chioko had a force of soldiers well armed with rifles; he rejected Portuguese authority over the Tavara country and encouraged refusal to pay tax in Rhodesian Hutavara. With Chioko's support Mapondera made a plan to invade Rhodesia, wipe out the administrative post at Mount Darwin and regain northern Mashonaland.

The prestige of the Mutapa and his senior spirit mediums had not been called upon during the 1896 risings when it was rather to the memory of the Rozwi Mambo that the rebels had appealed. But the Mutapa proved still to have a surprisingly extensive influence; sufficient in combination with Mapondera's reputation as a warrior to raise a large force from a wide area. In February 1901 Mapondera entered Rhodesia at the head of this force.

He entered in intransigent mood. 'On the fifth morning', testified an African policeman, 'we were attacked by some natives. . . . They shouted that the whites had killed one of Mapondera's sons and that they were going to drive the whites out of the country.' After the police had retreated Mapondera captured the 'loyalist' chief Chimanda. 'He wanted me to guide them to (Native Commissioner) Kenny's camp,' testified Chimanda. 'He said that Kenny was my "father" . . . He said that he was going to kill all the white people at Darwin, then at Mazoe, establishing himself at the latter place.' 'I am glad to see you, Chimanda,' Mapondera concluded. 'I

[1] Mapondera's statement, *Rhodesia Herald*, 4 May 1904.

will kill you the day I kill Kenny, placing Kenny's body on top of yours.'[1]

Mapondera's invasion was in fact forestalled by white counter-attack. On 4 March a force of Mashonaland Native Police under white command launched a surprise attack on Mapondera's camp. We may quote two accounts of the last military engagement on Rhodesian soil until modern times. 'We attacked the impi at dawn,' reported Native Commissioner Kenny. 'They were sheltered in scherms. We fired on the impi which returned the fire. Fighting lasted about two hours. We retreated about one and-a-half miles followed by the impi; we there took up a position and drove the enemy off . . . I heard several cries, among others, "We are Mapondera's people". They were singing the praises of their leader.' 'When the first shot was fired', remembers Mpanduki Gotora Mapondera, 'some ran away. But the fighting soon started in earnest. I saw Chiutsi fall and I myself fired and the bullet hit a rock, the chip from which flew and cut Kenny on the nose. There was fierce fighting there on that day and even today bones lie scattered about.'[2]

There had been a moment in the battle when the Mashonaland Native Police, who suffered heavy casualties, had nearly broken. But the fight ended with Mapondera's defeat. Thereafter he abandoned ideas of invading Rhodesia in force. For another year he carried out guerrilla activity along the border, raiding white prospectors and 'loyal' chiefs. In June 1902 he returned to Barwe to help his ally Makombe against the renewed Portuguese assault. But his time was running out. Both Makombe and Chioko were defeated by the Portuguese; white administration was beginning to be a reality on both sides of the border and the world of the old Shona warrior was shrinking to almost nothing.

Mapondera decided to return to his own country, not as a conqueror but as a defeated man. 'Kadungure was then running away from Rhodesia,' his grandson Alexander tells us. 'He went on and one day he walked a whole day without covering an inch of ground. He was still in one place and when he thought he had sighted a place where to spend the night it was only to discover that it was the same place where he started.' The local spirit medium 'ordered Kadungure to go no further . . . Kadungure then told his son that he was going back to die.'[3]

Mapondera moved back towards Mazoe. On 30 August 1903 he sent in to the Native Commissioner, South Mazoe, offering to surrender. Mean-

---

[1] Evidence of Chimanda, 22 February 1904; evidence of Chikwa, 28 March 1904; D 3/5/10.

[2] Evidence of Kenny, 14 March 1904, D 3/5/10; interview with Mpanduki Gotora Mapondera, 16 January 1963.

[3] Interview with Alexander Mapondera, 21 January 1963.

while police learnt of his presence from informers. That night, 'Surrounding the place as much as my party would permit, entering I found Mapondera at the fire and arrested him. By his manner he seemed surprised. The following appeared to be his sixteen wives. He had a Martini Henry rifle lying across his knee and four rounds of ammunition in an old stocking.' The Mapondera family tradition maintains to the last the mythical quality of the old hero. 'Kadungure was taken out whereupon he flew all over the place until he was tired and gave himself up.'[1]

So ended Mapondera's protest. In May 1904 he was put on trial in Salisbury charged with murder and sedition. He was found guilty of sedition. It had been, said the judge, 'the prisoner's intention to wipe out the whole white population in the neighbourhood of Mount Darwin. This was a serious offence and he would have to pass such a sentence as would prevent the recurrence of such acts. The prisoner was an old man and he would take that into consideration . . . it was improbable that even in view of the sentence that was to be passed upon him he would come out of jail again. The sentence of the court was seven years hard labour.'[2]

This outcome at first pleased the indomitable old man, 'for after he left court he danced like a child and said he fully expected to have been hanged.' The judge was right, however. Mapondera never left prison, but died there after a hunger strike. His family remained in intransigent bitterness. Enoch Mapondera, the youngest son, 'was the only child who managed to get education. The rest being bitter about what had happened to the old man in prison never liked to be in contact with a white man.'[3]

In some ways Mapondera's story reveals Shona disunity. The administration was able to raise a force against him from the paramounts of the old rebel areas, largely because they remembered and resented the lack of assistance that the Korekore and Tavara had given them in 1896. Nevertheless it also reveals how much the heroic world of the pre-colonial Shona past was still a living reality in the first years of the twentieth century. And Portuguese administration was still sufficiently tenuous after the military campaigns of 1902 to enable Shona opposition in western Mozambique to take militant forms for another decade after Mapondera's imprisonment. In the old heartland of the Mutapa empire it did not seem impossible to emulate Mapondera's march on Mount Darwin.

We may take as an example the career of the spirit medium, Kamota, who

[1] Goodyear to Commandant, Salisbury, 4 September 1903, RC 3/3/8; interview with Alexander Mapondera, 21 January 1963.
[2] *Rhodesia Herald*, 4 May 1904.
[3] Letter from Mrs E. Mwendapole to the author, 12 December 1963.

was believed to be possessed of the spirit of an eighteenth century Mutapa. Kamota lived in Mozambique but on three occasions he crossed into Rhodesia to challenge white rule. In 1910 he entered the Mrewa district 'to put his people right'; he was promptly deported. In July 1915, stimulated by the difficulties of the British and Portuguese in the German East African campaign, he again entered Rhodesia and told the Tavara people to buy guns and to store food in readiness for a rising. In 1917 Portuguese administration in the Zambezi valley broke down in the face of a major Shona uprising that ran all along the Rhodesian frontier from Zumbo to the province of Barwe. The main leader of the rising was the claimant to the title of Makombe in Barwe but the Kamota medium took a leading role in Portuguese Hutavara. He took command of the rebel impis there together with the medium of Dzivaguru, the greatest of all Tavara spirits and the leading religious figure of the old Mutapa empire; he led his men to the siege of the Portuguese post at Kachomba. Before he left the border he sent messages to all the chiefs and mediums in Rhodesian Hutavara. He called on them to cross the border and join in the fight against the Portuguese. When the Portuguese were beaten the impis would march on Darwin, Bindura and Salisbury. Kamota himself, it was announced, would come over the frontier and set himself up at the Muti Muchena shrine, which had been the chief religious centre of the Mutapa empire but which had been harassed and driven underground by the Rhodesian administration.[1]

This renewed invasion of Rhodesia never took place since Kamota's impis were defeated by the Portuguese and the medium himself had to flee into Rhodesia to escape capture. Nevertheless the dramatic events of 1917 did attract a number of Rhodesian Tavara across the border to fight the Portuguese. The Rhodesian administration were anxious for fear that the last resistance of the Shona of Barwe would encourage some of the Shona tribes in the old rebel areas of Rhodesia to throw off the authority of their imposed 'loyalist' chiefs. Right up to 1917, then, the tradition of Shona resistance was very much alive on the borders and in Portuguese East Africa.

This was the situation in the unsettled frontier areas of the northeast. What of the settled and tightly administered areas of Mashonaland? The great mediums of the Rozwi complex – the Chaminuka medium, the Nehanda medium and the rest – remained influential; some trusted chiefs had survived the risings, in particular chief Kunzwi-Nyandoro who was

[1] T. O. Ranger, 'The last days of the empire of Mwene Mutapa', *Conference on the History of the Central African People*, Lusaka, 1963.

looked to as a natural leader by ex-rebels from areas well outside his para-mountcy. Moreover, the grievances of the settled areas were greater; the colonial pressure more hardly felt. White settlement, land alienation, total disarmament, taxation – all these things were deeply resented. Yet at the same time they bespoke an effective white presence which made any sort of armed resistance virtually impossible. What happened, then, in the greater part of Mashonaland was that people dreamed and planned but did not act in the same idiom upon which Mapondera and the Kamota medium had drawn.

Even though none of these dreams and plans ever came to anything it is worthwhile looking at some of the instances of them. Our information comes from government spies and must be used with caution. But it demonstrates at least a fundamental refusal to accept the colonial régime as permanent or legitimate and garbled though it is in the sources available to us it represents an important African voice.

In 1900, for example, the year of Mapondera's return, rumours were spreading in central Mashonaland about the events of the Boer War. African messengers reported that the following things were being an-nounced to the people by the spirit mediums:

'That the Mashonas are being cheated by the English when they say that the Boers have been defeated. We are told this because the English think that if they are beaten by the Boers we will turn on the English.'

'That the Portuguese under "Guveya", Matabeles and Mashonas have fought the English and have been beaten by them. The Dutch are now beating the English and the above named will join them against the English.'

'That when the Boers come they will come from the south-west and drive Salisbury towards us (the Mashonas): we must all be on the *qui vive*.'

The centre of these rumours was the country of the old rebel paramount, Kunzwi-Nyandoro. In March 1900 an African spy overheard a conversa-tion at the kraal of one of Kunzwi's headmen, Mparadzi. Mparadzi's son told his father:

'that he had come from Kunzwi's and that Kunzwi had been called by the Acting Native Commissioner. He then went on to say that he had heard that the English were cheating and that the Mrenga (the name of the chief spirit involved in 1896) is going to rise a second time! Kunzwi told me that when the grain was ripe to store it under ground. The English have taken our country, we don't get sufficient food, the English won't allow us to drive out witches; before the English came we were allowed to drive out all evil-doing persons and consequently did not die at the high rate that we now do.'

Another African policeman was given a warning:

'The Mashonas don't like you Police: you had better leave the whites. We hear that all the English have been finished by the Boers and that the Boers are coming up to Salisbury from the south.'[1]

In 1903 there were again widespread rumours, this time among the whites, that the Shona were planning to rebel in protest against the increased hut tax. 'There is no doubt but that there is in many parts of Mashonaland an unusual activity amongst the witch-doctors . . . and that communications are passing between chiefs in the territory regarded as more or less disaffected.' So when a medium of the great spirit, Chaminuka, appeared in the Hartley district the Native Department were quick to send spies to discover what she was saying. In December 1903 the medium summoned chiefs from western and central Mashonaland to her kraal. The Chief Native Commissioner's messenger, 'one-eyed Jack', also turned up but was excluded from the meeting. The Department had therefore to rely upon the emissary of the loyalist chief Samuriwo. According to him the medium said:

'I am Chaminuka. I know everything. I am all powerful. I caused the downfall of the Barozwi and the Matabele and I will cause the white man to leave the country. Nothing is impossible to me. Follow my instructions. Makombe is coming soon. Why, he is one of my children. He will not stay away.'

'She told Samuriwo's representative,' reported Native Commissioner Morris, 'that she was very pleased to see that Samuriwo had returned to the true faith and that he was not to go to anyone else but to come to her again, when she would give him further advice. She also told him that Nyandoro had sent to her three times and that he and Mangwende had been advised when the white man would leave the country.' The medium was at once arrested and interrogated in an attempt to implicate Kunzwi-Nyandoro but she committed suicide before either could be brought to trial.[2]

Three years later, in 1906, a female medium appeared in Mazoe for the spirit of Nehanda. She was the first medium to appear since the execution of the Nehanda medium who led the 1896 rising in Mazoe and the administration were understandably anxious about her. In April an African spy was sent to find out what line she was taking. The spy reported the

[1] ANC Salisbury to CNC, 2 April 1900, N 3/1/18.
[2] N. C. Marendallas to CNC, 12 December 1903, A 11/2/12/11.

Africans in Mazoe were expecting a message from the north in the middle of the year, the Nehanda medium having told them that 'the great Chaminuka' had predicted that 'the Mondoro (spirit) who was ultimately to come and look after the Mashonas and free them would come from these directions'. The medium asked the spy if he knew her. 'I am Nehanda, the former spirit who was in Chiweshe's country, and I am now come to take care of all the Mashonas again.' Detecting his true role she told him that he must call the Native Commissioner, Mazoe, and the Chief Native Commissioner to come to visit her because 'she had risen to look after the people'. This news was considered sufficiently important for the Native Commissioner to visit the medium and to send her to Salisbury to see the CNC. The local chiefs were cautioned and a close watch was kept on the medium's activities.[1]

The outbreak of the first world war naturally produced a further crop of rumours among both blacks and whites. Once again some persistent Shona hoped that events would give them a chance to throw off white rule. Once again the reports centred around the spirit mediums. Early in 1915 a whole series of reports came in that the Nehanda medium – still the same woman as in 1906 – was in touch with the Mwari priests of the Matopos hills in Matabeleland and through them with the Ndebele. Spies said that she had told the Shona chiefs to wait for a message from Matabeleland; later it was reported that messengers had indeed come to say that the Germans were beating the British and that 'the Ndebele were ready to attack Bulawayo if the Shona would attack Salisbury'.[2]

Similar though all these reports are over a period of some fifteen years it is possible to detect a change in their character. To begin with the Native Department took them very seriously. They were haunted by the memory of the risings of 1896 and of their complete failure to predict them. Underneath the apparent humility and acceptance shown by the Shona the Department detected hidden reserves and hidden purposes; in 1903 experienced officers believed that the whites were in for a second rising which would dwarf the first; and right up to the war some members of the Department believed that the spirit mediums and the Mwari priests still possessed enough influence to raise the country against the whites if they acted in conjunction. It was difficult then and impossible now to tell whether they were right to take such reports so seriously. But what is plain is that by the 1920s they had ceased to do so. The early reports give the feeling of men ready to seize an opportunity for action should one present

[1] Statement of the spy Patrick, 21 April 1906, N 3/31/4.
[2] Statement of the spy Patrick, April 1915, N 3/14/5.

itself. The later reports reveal a deeply-rooted dislike of white rule but also a growing fatalism. The Native Department was no doubt correct in believing that any possibility of a rising had passed.

In 1915, despite the dramatic reports of the spies, it was this fatalism more than anything else which marked the Nehanda episode. Chief Chiberu testified, for example, that the messengers from Matabeleland had not urged a rising. They had certainly discussed the war as well as cattle dipping fees. But they did not see the war as offering them any chance of action; their speculations about it were entirely passive. 'We wonder who will win? In the event of the Germans winning would they treat us as well as the British? In the event of the British being beaten and driven out of the country would they first kill off the natives? Would Germans enforce compulsory dipping?'[1]

And this note of passively awaiting the outcome of white men's struggles is stronger still in a 1923 report. In October of that year, at a point when the first settler Responsible Government was about to take over, it was reported from Belingwe, a Shona area of eastern Matabeleland, that the Mwari priests were ordering people to store grain and kill cattle in readiness for a fight between the British and the Boers. 'There appears to have been talk of anticipated fighting between the Europeans (English and Dutch) . . . It is probable that this is due to the change of Government.'[2]

But no one thought in 1923 that Africans might be able to exploit white dissension. The unreality of the Shona dream of resistance had become plain. The Portuguese had at long last broken Shona opposition in the Zambezi valley and Barwe. The British had won the war and seemed in unchallenged control of Southern Africa. There is no doubt that there was serious discontent in 1923 but it had ceased to take the form of an intention or a hope of armed resistance. Instead there was what the Native Commissioner, Insiza, described as 'a passive resistance among the natives'. The Superintendent of Natives, Gwelo, analysed the frame of mind of the Belingwe Shona. They resented the demands made upon them for tax, rent, and so on. But they did not respond with aggressive protest. 'The older men show signs of despondency. The younger men show indifference amounting almost to passive acceptance of the penalties incurred by failure to fulfil their obligations.'[3]

The Superintendent was not deceived by the passivity and fatalistic acceptance into which much of Shona society seemed to have passed now

[1] N. C. Charter to CNC, 19 May 1915, N 3/14/5.
[2] S/N/Gwelo to CNC, 10 October 1923, N 3/14/5.
[3] S/N/Gwelo to CNC, 10 October 1923, N 3/14/5.

that dreams of successful rebellion had ended. It was 'fertile soil prepared for any seditious seed' and there was great need for 'tactful and careful handling of the natives'. But it seemed that the traditional religious authorities had lost, at least for the moment, their power to sow such seditious seeds. The great question was in what direction the Shona could move out of passivity and fatalism and towards some other expression of their grievances and aspirations.

Turning Inwards and the Economy of the Reserves

During the whole period 1898 to 1918, in fact, 'passive resistance' was more important as a Shona response to colonialism than were the rumours, dreams and plans of a rising. This passive resistance took the form of a general refusal to become involved in the new colonial labour and wage system. The Shona, as an administrative officer wrote, are 'essentially agriculturalists. They are of the earth, earthy. Agriculture to the Native is not an occupation or a trade. It is a mode of life.'[1]

This mode of life was threatened by white requirements of labour for the mines, for the urban communities and for European farms. Before 1896 whites pressganged labour. After 1898 the pressures upon the Shona were economic ones. Through the imposition of hut tax it was hoped that Shona men would be forced to enter the labour market in order to earn the cash to meet the tax. This hope was not realized to any significant extent in the period before the first world war. Dr Giovanni Arrighi, whose forthcoming history of the Southern Rhodesian economy will enable us to understand African political history very much better, has cited statistics to show the relatively low rate of Shona participation in the labour market. 'The proportion of able-bodied Mashona men in the age group eighteen to forty in wage employment for at least three months was 12·8 per cent and 20 per cent in the years ended 31 March 1903 and 31 March 1904, respectively. The corresponding percentages for Matabeleland were 48·5 and 50.' The discrepancy was not so great in subsequent years but up to the war 'the Matabele consistently showed a significantly greater rate of participation in the labour market than the Mashona'.

No doubt it is true that the Shona clung stubbornly to their way of life in this period. But it is also true that they were enabled to do so by the general economic circumstances. Dr Arrighi has pointed out that in pre-colonial times Shona agriculture involved the energies of both men and women and normally produced a surplus. The coming of colonial rule, despite the alienation of land and the upheavals of the risings, did not undermine the

[1] E. D. Alvord, *Agricultural Demonstration Work on Native Reserves*, Department of Native Development, Occasional Paper No. 3, 1930.

Shona rural economy; indeed it may even have involved 'a considerable increase of the surplus-generating capacity of the Mashona economy. Not only the surplus previously appropriated by the Matabele was to remain at the disposal of the Mashona, but also the drain on the latter's more productive human resources due to the raids was stopped.' In most areas of Mashonaland the period up to 1918 was not one of land shortage. The pressure of human and animal population resources upon available land did not yet constitute a major problem. Provided that there was a market for it the combined labour of Shona men and women could produce a sizeable agricultural surplus.

And in these years there was a market for such a surplus. Dr Arrighi writes:

'Before 1906, European farming in Rhodesia was insignificant and it was only in the middle 1910s that it got off the ground on a large scale. Throughout this period the mines relied almost entirely on African produce to supply their labourers with mealies . . . In 1903 it was estimated that the annual amount received by Africans for sale of grain, other produce and stock was £350,000 or well over twice the total wage bill earned by indigenous African labour in Rhodesia . . . African participation in the money economy was not limited to the sale of traditional produce: in certain districts maize soon displaced the traditional grains, and, in the vicinity of towns, vegetable gardening was introduced and the produce marketed regularly. The production for the market of green vegetables, potatoes, wheat, groundnuts and tobacco was either introduced or expanded . . . European trade with African tribesmen spread very rapidly and before 1906–7 it represented the major economic European activity, at least from the standpoint of profitability. These traders had their principal stores on mines and townships and other trading stations scattered about the country, thus spreading over a large portion of the population the opportunity of participating in the money economy through the sale of produce. The differential between the returns from self-employment and wage employment was very large. In 1903 for example it was reckoned that an African by cultivating one or two acres could make as much money in a month as he could in three months of wage employment . . . The Mashona could largely rely on the produce market for their cash requirements.'[1]

Resistance to entering the labour market, then, did not take the form of refusal to pay hut tax, even though there was widespread discontent when

[1] G. Arrighi, 'Labour Supplies in Historical Perspective: the Rhodesian case' University College, Dar es Salaam, September 1967, mimeo.

it was raised and even though later on there *was* a general refusal to pay rents to the Company for permission to 'squat' on unalienated land. The hut tax was paid, but in this period the cash was raised largely from the sale of agricultural surplus and stock. The consequences of this were complicated. In some ways, of course, the sale of crops and stock to European traders brought the tribesmen into the modern cash economy. Passive resistance is hardly an adequate term to use for the initiative displayed by those peasants who grew new crops or who developed market gardening near the towns. At the same time, however, the economic opportunity did enable the Shona to turn inwards to their own local situation. Shona 'traditional' life and ways were at least an economic success in this period even if there had been a collapse of military institutions and a serious erosion of political. This economic success averted the total demoralization of Shona rural society. It is worth noting that the despondency and fatalism recorded from Belingwe came in 1923 when the economic situation was radically different; when European agriculture was supplying the bulk of the needs of the modern economy; when prices for African cattle and crops had fallen; and when the pressures of tax and rent and dipping fees had to be faced without the support of a relatively prosperous African agriculture. The discontent of the Belingwe Shona, it was reported, 'may be attributed mainly to the difficulty experienced in meeting their financial obligations such as Government taxes, repayments for famine relief grains, dipping funds, and, on farms, rent. They have no market for their cattle and the older men show signs of despondency. The younger men show indifference amounting almost to passive acceptance of the penalties incurred by failure to fulfil their obligations.'

The Christian Solution
In the period up to 1918 relative agricultural prosperity enabled the great majority of Shona to continue their 'traditional' rural life. In the same period relative agricultural opportunity enabled a number of Shona to experiment with new crops, new techniques and new ideas. Slowly there developed a handful of men who aspired to farm commercially on the European model; to own land individually and to farm it 'progressively'. This development linked up with the spread of the influence of Christian teaching and the Christian way of life. Some of the early African teachers and preachers, drawn largely from South Africa, became themselves individual land-owners or leasers and demonstrated the connection in their own minds between Christianity, economic progress and modern farming. The opportunities existing before 1918 went some way to support the idea

that Africans could make their own fortunes by adopting the Christian virtues of discipline, responsibility and readiness to acquire modern skills.

After the suppression of the risings there had been something of a rush to the missions. No detailed study has been made of these early Shona converts and schoolboys; no study has been made of the first Shona catechists and teachers, nor even of the important mission schools which now began to prepare the future African teachers and clerks and clergy. This is, indeed, one of the major gaps in Rhodesian historiography, especially by comparison with the careful studies which have been made of the same problems in Malawi and East Africa. Without such work we are at a loss to document the beginnings of what was to become a very important process for the African political history of Rhodesia. In the 1930s the products of this Christian education emerged to take over the leadership of African political movements in Rhodesia. But we have little information about this early period and few expressions of the views and attitudes of the men of the Christian solution in the time of formation.

It is plain that the process of Christian education was slow in getting under way. In 1908 there were still only fifty recognized schools for Africans in Southern Rhodesia with a total of some 4,319 pupils. By 1913 there were 193 recognized schools with 15,723 pupils. By 1918 there were 648 schools with 41,874 pupils. But most of the increase had taken place with the so-called third-class schools. First-class schools – that is to say boarding schools under European supervision where a range of technical skills was taught – increased much less rapidly. In 1908 there were ten first-class schools with 755 pupils. In 1913 there were twenty-three such schools with 1,505 pupils. In 1918 there were only twenty-one first-class African schools in Southern Rhodesia with a total of 1,453 pupils. Meanwhile third-class schools had increased from thirty-three in 1908 to 553 in 1918, by which year they had some 35,000 pupils. This kind of educational development was not likely to produce a numerous educated élite. It is important to remember throughout this book, indeed, the smallness in numbers of the indigenous teachers and clerks and clergy in the 1910s and 1920s.

Nevertheless the men who were committed to the Christian solution were important. We can get something of the feeling of their careers by taking a couple of individual examples of Christian commitment in this period. There is the story of John Kapuya, for example. Kapuya was the son of Mtambira Kapuya, a famous diviner, and of Kuwana, niece of chief Mangwende of Nohwe. He was the first pupil of the Anglican catechist, Bernard Mizeki, and has given a fascinating account of his conversion and of how he hoped that through it he might come into direct contact and relationship with God. He served Bernard and the white missionaries as cook, carrier, messenger, interpreter, translator. Before the risings of 1896 he was sent away from his own home area because of the threats of Mchemwa, chief Mangwende's son and later the leader of the rising in Nohwe. Mchemwa 'said that I was being made into a European'. When the rising broke out Mizeki was killed on Mchemwa's orders but Kapuya managed to escape to Umtali. A month after Mizeki's death, in July 1896, he was baptized. He then returned to his home area with the white troops who were clearing the road between Umtali and Salisbury and watched them shell the strongholds of Mangwende's people, in which his own family had taken refuge. He was sent to be trained as a catechist to Isandhlwana College in Zululand. In 1900 he returned to Rhodesia to serve as catechist and teacher. Later he entered the service of the Native Department. In 1925 he was clerk to the Native Commissioner at Hartley and gave evidence in that year to the Carter Commission on land, in which he spoke up for the importance of individual land ownership and progressive farming.[1]

Another example is that of Michael Chivero. Chivero was one of the handful of Africans baptized at the Jesuit Mission at Chishawasha before the risings of 1896. He remained loyal to the missionaries through the risings and was a key figure in their exploitation of the favourable situation which developed after them. 'He is one of that first batch of Christians who took their baptismal promises very seriously and spent their lives teaching catechism, building schools and churches, walking and cycling thousands of miles.' For many years Chivero lived at Mhondoro, where he built the Catholic church. In 1945 he was elected Chief Chivero and has served as chief ever since. His grandson is a Catholic priest.[2]

What did such men expect of their acceptance of Christianity and of their alliance with the whites? It is clear from a story like John Kapuya's that some of them expected spiritual gains which we cannot discuss here. It is clear from the careers of both Kapuya and Chivero that many were content to serve the whites in church and state. It is plain that many linked their acceptance of Christianity with the acceptance of a whole series of social and economic attitudes, with what came to be called the 'progressive' position – concentration upon education and self-improvement, adoption of European standards of dress and housing, a desire to enter into European-style

[1] For John Kapuya see, Jean Farrant, *Mashonaland Martyr, Bernard Mizeki and the Pioneer Church*, Cape Town, 1966, especially pp. 127–42.

[2] W. Smulders, S. J., 'Chief Chivero' *Jesuit Missions* Vol. XIV, No. 136, Autumn 1968.

economic enterprise. In all these ways men of the Christian solution turned away from the values of their own societies. They had no sympathy with the whole tradition of Shona resistance; they were not content with an in-ward-turning concentration upon communal agriculture. But with all their commitment to the whites some of them did see themselves as men in training for the leadership of their own people.

In this they were encouraged by some missionaries. There were mis-sionaries, it is true, who shared the aims expressed by Van Buren Shumaker of the Apostolic Church Mission: 'We desire only . . . to aid the officials of Anglo-Saxon Governments, to control with authority the native and bid him attain to a place of usefulness as a servant people.' But there were others, like Wilder and Thompson of the American Board Mission, who did not wish 'to settle down to the work of attempting to develop a race of Christian slaves.'

Such men were worried about the lack of leadership among the African population, or at any rate leadership competent to understand the modern world. Thompson wrote in 1907:

'We may in a general way press the difference between Africa and other mission fields, by saying that Africa is *More Remote from Modern Civilization* both in *Time and Space* and *intellectually and spiritually*. There may be as many who seem densely ignorant and degraded in other countries but they have leaders of intelligence to represent them. Knowledge is nearer to them. More people die of famine in India than in Africa but there may be famines in Africa of which the world never hears and those who die know not of the relief that might be theirs. Those who are robbed and abused in other lands have a means of appeal thru their governments to the Court of the World. The African has none – perhaps does not suspect that he is wronged . . . The profound ignorance of the people and their consequent absence of national life makes them the pray [sic] of the injustice, greed and lust of all civilized nations. There is no Native African Nation in the political sense. The native inhabitants are helpless to resist encroachments of unscrupulous men . . . It is generally conceded that the bulk of the work must be done by leaders raised up from among the natives themselves. Our work is to produce these leaders. But it is not enough in Africa that these leaders be Christian and superior to their fellows, so as to be able to meet the opposition of heathenism. They must reach the point of being able to cope with the adverse forces of civilization also, if they are to stand alone, for these are here in full force. And since the adverse forces of civilization are various, we must produce leaders of various qualifications including the ability to lead in civilized industry and the professions as well as in religion; otherwise they will be (at the mercy of) the unscrupulous.'[1]

Thompson's programme was a statement of the Christian solution to the problems of leadership and articulation of grievances at its fullest and most ambitious. He stressed the importance of maintaining links *between the Leaders and the lowest of the community*. He envisaged a first-rate Mission school with a thousand African pupils; a self-supporting Industrial Department; a first-class Medical Department; a missionary legal adviser to teach the African leaders how to defend their interests and 'protect the weak and ignorant'.

Needless to say nothing like this programme was achieved by the American Board missions or by anyone else. Thompson himself blamed the inefficiency, waste, diffusion of effort of the missionaries themselves. But in addition there was the hostility of the whole Rhodesian environment to plans of this sort. In East Africa the German administration was running its own schools in order to produce enough African clerks and administrators to staff its system of government; in Malawi the Scottish missions were turning out pupils with academic and industrial skills. But in Rhodesia there was no need felt for African participation in administration at any but the lowest levels; nor was there need felt for African craftsmen to take their place in the incipient industries of Rhodesia. As for African leaders with legal training and capable of taking up the cases of their fellows nothing was less likely to be encouraged or tolerated. Moreover, although in the years before the first world war there was something of a boom in Shona agriculture, and peasant farmers were able to sell food on the European market, there was little opportunity for the development of individual commercial farming by 'modern' farmers on a freehold or leasehold basis.

All this meant that the Christian products of the Missions would obtain a severely restricted training and enter a severely restricted field of opportunity. Employment by the Native Department or by the churches was for most the best they could aspire to. Yet in this period there were few rebels against this state of affairs. There was some progress, after all. Men were obtaining education and with it status. Most were content to act as patient and submissive apprentices, committed to the Christian solution and neither disgruntled enough to challenge it nor self-confident enough to speak out in its name.

[1] Shumaker to CNC, 16 February 1929, S 84/A/264; 'Our Policy', reproduced as Appendix 11 in J. K. Rennie 'Settlers and Missionaries in South Melsetter, 1893–1925', mimeo., Salisbury, 1966. I am much obliged to the United Church Board for World Ministers for permission to quote from this document.

Matthew Zwimba and the Church of the White Bird

As it happens the one African Christian voice which does sound out clearly in this early period is that of a thoroughly unrepresentative man; a rebel where nearly everyone was conforming. It was the voice of a man who had committed himself to the Christian solution; had broken with the missionaries over their interpretation of it; had founded his own church and attempted to use the Christian idiom for directly African ends. In all this he was a lonely figure in the period before 1918. But he was not an insignificant one. The voice of this rebel illuminates the situation of the conformists. And he became something of a legend in his own right, his career having some effect on both later political and later religious movements among the Shona.

The name of this man was Matthew Chigaga Zwimba. He was the son of paramount chief Chigaga of Zwimba Reserve who had been imposed upon the tribe after the risings as a 'loyalist'. Matthew and his brother Mishek began their careers in the service of the triumphant new forces of Christianity and white administration. Matthew went to a Wesleyan Methodist school where he learnt, according to a hostile white witness, 'to ape the white man by wearing European clothes', to speak English and to type. He became a catechist and teacher for the Methodists and established the first mission school in Zwimba Reserve.

Up to this point Matthew was perfectly happy with his role in the new dispensation. His ambition was to bring the Christian solution to Zwimba under his own leadership. He saw himself as the educated adviser of the chief; he and his brother Mishek derived their names, he said, 'from the Bible where Matthew and Mishek were advisers to King David.' No doubt Matthew was very much in search of prestige in all this but at the same time he was in his way genuinely striving after something of the sort of leadership that Thompson had envisaged. So long as he remained in Zwimba Reserve there would be natural links between himself as leader 'and the lowest of the community'. Moreover Matthew intended to use his knowledge of public events to protect the legal interests of the Zwimba people and to act as their spokesman. Thus it was a severe blow to him when he was transferred by the church to Gatooma, where he had no family connections and where he was constantly under white supervision.

There were a series of disputes and clashes with his white supervisors which ended with Matthew's dismissal as teacher and catechist in 1907. He returned home in resentment and confusion; there was now no use to which he could put his skills in Zwimba; and he drifted into a series of clashes

with the administration one of which at least led to a term of imprisonment. Then in 1915 it at last came to him that it was possible to set up as a
preacher and teacher on his own account. At first he settled at Kanyemba,
outside the Zwimba Reserve. But in August 1915 he returned to Zwimba,
drove out the Methodist teacher and catechist, took over the station and
announced to Reverend Loveless, the local white superintendent, that he
had better send his catechist 'to another Mission Station. For Zwimba
Mission Station was commenced by me to do the missionary work and I am
going to commence the same work on it.'

Matthew now founded the very interesting Original White Bird Mission
or Shiri Chena Church, the first of the Shona independent churches. It was,
indeed, very explicitly a Shona church. The White Bird of its title was not
only the dove of the Holy Ghost but also the traditional messenger of the
High God, Mwari, to mankind; Matthew drew up lists of those who had
been killed in the 1896-7 fighting in Zwimba and these were regarded as
the saints and martyrs of the new church. The Christian solution for
Zwimba was now to be carried out in defiance of the whites rather than in
co-operation with them. Matthew was the first man in Mashonaland to
sound this note and to grasp how effectively Christian imagery and meta-
phor and myth could be allied to tribal pride and the expression of tribal
grievance. His letters to the white representatives of church and state in
1915 bear full quotation.

In August 1915 Matthew wrote to Loveless:

'You better send Manassah Chiota to another Mission Station. For
Zwimba Mission Station was commenced by me to do the missionary
work and I am going to commence the same work on it. As you know that
I went to Kanyemba's kraal in desire of wanting to begin the missionary
work there and the Spirit commanded me that I would not leave my
father's kraal yet. Therefore let there be no quarrel among us two
because I do not this by jealousy, or despising you, but by order, and
honourable to your wish. The time I saw you at Zwimba I had no
chance of explaining you all these things. Remember what I said to the
Native Commissioner that I want not to be under your commanding, in
thinking of troubles those done to me by one of your ministers at
Gatooma, and made me to leave the preaching, and caused me to be in
weakness, and fell into many temptations. I shall be glad to live in com-
fortable with you, and help one to another.'

In the same month he wrote to an official whom he described as the
Temporary Resident, Salisbury. He announced his intention:

'to form the original White Bird Mission which was directed to me by the

B

Spirit of God in the year 1907. O hear me, thou Governor of this country, for all power, honour and favour are with thee. Be merciful and supply thy servant as you do for those missionaries come from over the sea. Let not my Lord and Master be surprised with what thy servant say. For such thing is not in the hand of man but in the hand of Him in the Most High.'

The Rhodesian Government reacted sharply to Zwimba's initiative. Local inquiries produced some disturbing evidence of Matthew's radicalism. He was said to make 'very disparaging remarks about the white men and the white men's laws . . . that the white men did not want the natives to possess cattle and supplied the natives with a poisonous dip after which the cattle licked their bodies and died. The white men did not use the same dip for their own cattle.' He and Mishek 'have repeatedly stated that the white men came to Rhodesia many years ago and that they were driven out by the natives, a positive proof of this was the Zimbabwe ruins. The white men were returning to the country in very large numbers, and were taking over all the land from the natives, they were building large towns all over Rhodesia, but they would not remain much longer as the natives had driven them out once and would do so again and the natives would again rule.' In October the local Native Commissioner served notice on Matthew that he was not 'to preach or teach independently' and sent messengers to every kraal head in Zwimba to warn them not to attend Matthew's services or classes.

On 22 November Matthew responded to this official repression in a long typed letter to Native Commissioner Keigwin:

'Behold, that it is evil thing to send messengers with so bad message to tell these people of darkness, which you know that we have lot troubles of trying them to believe the true God, and to be saved from their sin through faith in Jesus Christ the Saviour. But you blind these people from seeing the salvation of God which he gave all men and shut the gate of paradise for them, and open the gate of hell for them. For you know that when the heathen people hear such sayings from we Christians, they would think there is no God, for why we Christians should not fear him and speak heathenishly to our friends: even now some of them are saying so.

'Even myself, I was not expecting that you Mr Keigwin, Christian, could say so, you were liked these people to learn and receive the word of God. Probably you envy me because I want to be a master for myself in so great work, but don't think so, for he that ordained me to do this work is greater than the European supervision that you want me to be under him. God's spirit can direct me well than a personal direct; even though you despise me, yet he does not, he cares for me, as he cares for some other creatures. He has chosen me out of darkness to be his servant, and a leader of his people in the way of his salvation, truth and to fulfil his ordination, but you want me to please men than God.

'Who had been with me then when God sent me with his word to preach these people day and night, from kraal to kraal? You Governors and rulers were not knew what God was doing with me until now. You could only see the whole Reserve is full of lot churches, for sons and girls of men had heard the word of God that I preached to them; but they had not done so by my own power but of God, for his son says without me you can do nothing.

'Mark now the greater servant than the other, one servant was sent by God, and another by the man, who is the greater servant than the other? The world exalts hers, even the heaven exalts his. I know that you have stopped this people from coming in to my church, or school, you have made them to obey you more than God, and they did so, but where is your obedience to God? When I tell you that God had sent me to preach, and teaching these people his word for myself, and to make them understanding his salvation, but you controvert. I ask you that how long shall this thing be? and what shall be the end of it? For the thing you have done is very offensive to me, and to some other people also, even though you think you did it to this place alone, but for myself I say that you did this thing for all people who shall hear of it. . . .

'Before I left this place for Kanyemba to look for another new mission station there, I was commanded by the Spirit to remain here, and to start the work again. But this seemed very difficult for me to do so, because the inhabitants of the place have lost their first good state; therefore I had compelled myself to go there in thought that it would be better for me to find some people for preaching and teaching the word of God, than those that have heard and received it already. But when I got there after I have done many exertions of trying to live there, the Spirit commanded me these words, "You shall not be at this place, but someone will be here; for you are wanted to be at home and teaching there." At first I did not notice these words, but the second time I did notice when the Spirit commanded me again by these words: "Why do you like to be at this place, and leave your father's kraal alone?"

'Is it not because of this thing why I am requiring to you who are rulers of this country to arrange it, and to allow me to do what the Almighty wants me to do? But now you have prevented these people from attending my church, or school, what has the Spirit brought me back to do here? Are you controverting by what I say that it is not true? When I say to you that the Spirit commands me to stay at this place, and do the church service, could the Lord give a man the Spirit that tells what is not true? . . .

'When I left Gatooma I was dispirited by the confusion that was done in the church by the Minister who was in charge thereof, and some other offences. And when I was at home I saw that the work of God had lost its good state, and the people are not in good order, even in the whole Reserve, for being misconducted by the teachers that have no love of Christ in them but the lovers of work only, zeal to carnal things and to be praised by the people only that they are doers of God's work, but not seeing the errors which destroy God's work. By these many offences my way of light was made obscure darkness and the life became lesser than death, but this could not be done for the Sustainer was near me, but the stumbling block took place instead of death, and by this cause the Lord was very angry with me and smote me by a sore punishments which I shall never forget in all my life. Nevertheless the Lord did not forget his promise that he had done with me; he renewed my heart that I might fulfil his promise; for I had kept not myself far from him. I was cried day and night as a son that has done wrong against his father.'

Matthew believed that he must now redeem himself by doing God's will and restoring Christianity in Zwimba to 'its proper state'. 'Do you think God has done mistake to send me among my own relations to minister his word?' Finally Matthew dealt with his enemies. Loveless had 'spoken blasphemous words against me when he was visiting this circuit'. Matthew himself had no 'jealousy in my heart, or despising or separating. He may do so but such gift is not mine. Let him thank the Lord for the great work he had done through me in this District that he finds some teachers and churches among so hard people.' Then there were the European informants against him – 'white men who brought there some false reports against me time after time'.

'This is the way of evil-doers to prove guiltless themselves, while they have guilty. Never keep in your mind such sayings, you men of truth. The wicked man rages when he is rebuked for his evil deeds but the righteous man obeys. Therefore be careful for the world you who are governors, supreme authorities and superintendents for it includes good men and bad men of every kind; for the good men hate bad men because of their iniquity, and bad men hate good men because of their goodness. Think of this, and see, that you are trusting upon your white men only, and despise us we natives of this country, how bad are we all?'[1]

This was not the manner in which Native Commissioners were accustomed to be addressed in 1915. It remained to be seen whether Matthew Zwimba was a unique eccentric or a portent of things to come.[2]

---

[1] Matthew Zwimba's letters are all in file A 3/6/9.

[2] Matthew Zwimba continued with his church of the White Bird despite official prohibitions and despite further imprisonments. His local prestige was great enough for him to be unanimously entrusted in 1925 to speak on behalf of the chiefs and people of Zwimba Reserve to the Morris Carter Land Commission. His evidence is cited in a later chapter. His reputation survived among the young nationalists of the 1950s as the embodiment of 'independence' and many stories, most no doubt mythical, circulated about him. In one such story Matthew was said to have sent a declaration of war in formal style to the Governor, provoking a full police patrol into the Zwimba Reserve which found Matthew sitting peacefully outside his church.

TWO

Matabeleland
after the Rebellions

1898–1918

The great uprising of 1896 ended rather differently in Matabeleland than in Mashonaland. When it became clear that defeat was inevitable the senior indunas of the Ndebele nation decided to seek for peace and negotiated a conditional surrender with Cecil Rhodes. While the Shona leaders of the rising were prosecuted and in many cases hanged the senior indunas not only saved themselves from prosecution but were offered salaried positions as officially recognized chiefs in the reformed system of Native administration. They and their people were allowed to come out of the hills and settle on the lands round Bulawayo which had belonged to the Ndebele nation before the 1893 war.

The Government was anxious to conciliate the formidable Ndebele but the condition of Matabeleland after the rising was still not very different from the condition of Mashonaland. Destruction of crops and seizure of stock had been carried out even more thoroughly in Matabeleland and for months after the risings there was widespread famine and disease. Some of the more intransigent leaders of the rising, who had refused to negotiate with the whites, were hunted down, tried and hanged. The recognized indunas soon realized the limitations on their authority under the new system. Above all it soon became clear that resettlement of the Ndebele in their old homelands was merely temporary. Title to the land remained with the Europeans who had acquired it in 1894; the Ndebele were allowed to 'squat' on the land in return for labour and a tithe of their produce. For a period of two years they could not be evicted by the European owners but when that period of grace was up they could be turned off the land even if they had fulfilled their rental and other obligations. And if they were turned off the heart lands of the old Ndebele empire there was nowhere else they would willingly go. The areas set aside as Reserves were remote and waterless, the Ndebele had not lived there in the past and were stubborn in their reluctance to move to the Reserves now.

The Ndebele Tradition of Resistance and Umlugulu

There was, then, much the same combination of realization of defeat and resentment at its consequences that we have seen in Mashonaland. And there was the same flood of reports about plans or dreams to resort once again to armed rising. After all, the Ndebele tradition of resistance to the whites, if shorter than the Shona, was still very much a living memory. The Zulu rebellion of 1905 showed that Nguni resistance in arms was far from a thing of the past. And the surviving rebel leaders might hope to use their influence within the new system to rally the Ndebele for a further uprising.

Just as in Mashonaland the ex-rebel Kunzwi-Nyandoro was the focus of hopes and reports of planned insurrection, so in Matabeleland the old high priest of the Ndebele nation, Umlugulu, was singled out for suspicion.

Umlugulu had been entrusted by Lobengula before his death with the responsibility of restoring the monarchy. He had hoped to inaugurate the risings of 1896, of which he was a chief director, with a coronation ceremony. Factions among the Ndebele had made this impossible and Umlugulu had later taken the lead in negotiations with the whites. As a reward he was made a salaried induna. But he had no intention of abandoning his attempt to revive the Ndebele monarchy. In March 1900, while most of the Ndebele indunas were 'vying with each other to get into the good graces of the Government', it was reported by spies that Umlugulu and other ex-rebel indunas were conspiring with the Mwari priest at the Matonjeni shrine 'for the purpose of stirring up a rebellion as soon as the approaching harvest was reaped'. 'That there is a little unrest amongst a certain section of the natives cannot be denied', admitted the Chief Native Commissioner. 'The natives referred to are those living in the immediate vicinity of M'lugulu's kraal; the only reason I can give for this apparent unrest is that their induna has always been an unsubmissive subject of the Government; his constant appealing for a king and his dislike of the whites are only too palpable; and should there be the slightest opportunity to take advantage of the present position of affairs in South Africa, he would, in my opinion be the first person to do so.'

The Native Department believed that division amongst the Ndebele was so great that 'a general combination on the part of the natives to rise is out of the question'. But they took these reports very seriously. 'The utmost precautions are being taken by means of patrols and native spies.' The Chief Native Commissioner thought it very important that patrols should continue 'to show that we still have armed men in this country' since Africans were 'fully aware of the reverses we have met during the present war.'[1]

Reports of this kind continued right into the 1914–18 war. Yet it seems plain that the Ndebele imagination was not possessed in the same way as the Shona with the old idiom of resistance. It is striking that in many of the reports of conspiracy from Matabeleland the conspiratorial groups are identified as Shona rather than as Ndebele. Often, indeed, the Native Department in Matabeleland drew a distinction between the excitement and unrest of the Shona of that province and the calm acceptance of the Ndebele. Thus in 1899 excitement about the Boer War and the movement of Mwari messengers was reported from the Shona area of Belingwe; in 1900 it was said that a Mwari emissary there had ordered the people to rise and kill the whites; in 1904 there were further rumours of an intended uprising in protest against the tax increase and white families in Belingwe were evacuated. The Chief Native Commissioner noted in that year that even if the Belingwe Shona rose their example would not be followed by the Ndebele. Elsewhere in Matabeleland in 1904 the only reported discontent about increased taxation came from scattered Shona groups in Insiza district who were putting up 'passive resistance'. 'The great bulk of the people of Insiza, who are Matabele, have accepted the increase with good grace.' This pattern persists right up into the First World War with reported commands by the Mwari priests to Shona in Belingwe and western Mashonaland to boycott all European stores and goods.[2]

How is this difference to be explained? One reason, perhaps, is that the Shona of Belingwe continued to pay much more respect to the Mwari priesthood than did the Ndebele. But there were a number of other significant differences between the situation of the Shona and the Ndebele.

For one thing many of the Ndebele aristocracy had come to have a vested interest in the system more effectively than any of the Shona paramounts. After the negotiations with the Ndebele leaders in 1896 the authority of the leading indunas over their people had been recognized and for a time every effort was made to conciliate them. 'Loyalists' among them were well rewarded with cattle; even ex-rebels of the royal family were able to build up large herds. The existence in this period of a ready market for cattle meant that owners of large herds could realize quite considerable sums of money if they needed to do so. 'A great number of cattle' were sold to whites in Matabeleland throughout the decade leading to the first world

---

[1] For the 1900 'conspiracy' see, LO 5/7/2; LO 5/7/3; Colonial Office, Confidential Prints, African (South), No. 656.

[2] See LO 5/7/1; LO 5/5/3; A 11/2/12/11.

war and prices rose steadily. Before 1908 the price for African cattle had been between £1 and £2 a head; by 1918 it had risen to £9 a head. The senior indunas and royals of the Ndebele were considerable property holders.

But if this helps to explain why influential leaders urged loyalty upon the Ndebele, there were other factors at work likely to produce grievances which required political expression and likely also to enable these grievances to find new forms of articulation. The Ndebele as a whole – aristocrats, commoners, loyalists and ex-rebels alike – faced an over-riding land problem. Groups of people in Mashonaland were already experiencing great land shortage – the Melsetter district is a case in point. But there was no general Shona crisis over land and no possibility of a general statement of grievance over land on behalf of the whole Shona people. In Matabeleland the case was different. The old Ndebele homelands had been compact; their alienation to whites and the consequent uncertainty of Ndebele 'squatters' upon them affected the great majority of the Ndebele nation. It affected particularly sharply those who owned large herds of cattle and needed large areas of grazing land, so that the land problem precipitated into political protests men who had otherwise good reasons for loyalty to the régime.

The Ndebele had this over-riding grievance. But attempts to remedy it did not need to be conceived only in terms of armed revolt. In particular they possessed in the idea of the monarchy a natural focus for 'modern' political activity and expression. The notion of Ndebele land and Ndebele kingship were inseparable. But the attempt to restore the monarchy need not be pursued, as Umlugulu was suspected of pursuing it, by renewed conspiracy and armed rebellion. The heirs of Lobengula were themselves 'modern' men and the restoration of the monarchy could be sought in 'modern' terms.

Finally, the Ndebele were more drawn into the modern urban and industrial economy during this period than were the Shona. Dr Arrighi has suggested that the pre-colonial Ndebele economy was characterized by a much greater division of labour than among the Shona. Men were not involved in cultivation but in war and cattle keeping. Moreover the impact of the colonial system in Matabeleland involving the dismantling of the Ndebele military state was much more destructive of the Ndebele economy. 'The very foundation of the Matabele economic system was irremediably subverted . . . disguised unemployment was forthwith introduced among males in general and higher caste men in particular. Given the social organization of production Matabele men found themselves partially un-employed once raiding parties became an impossibility and a large proportion of their herds were appropriated by the Europeans. Their contribution to production became insignificant until changes in social organization altered their role in the productive process. . . . The Matabele, among whom disguised unemployment was significantly greater, were readier to take up wage employment.'[1]

There was a flow of Ndebele migration to the towns and mines of South Africa. Bulawayo became the industrial capital and railway centre of Rhodesia. By no means all African workers in Bulawayo were Ndebele or drawn from Matabeleland. But there developed a group of educated would-be permanent town dwellers who were either high caste Ndebele or who associated themselves with Ndebele national values and aspirations. These men came into contact with a variety of new ways of expressing such aspirations.

These factors help to explain why Ndebele politics seem more 'modern' than Shona in this period; why the sons of Ndebele chiefs were usually sent to be educated; why urban welfare associations developed early on in Bulawayo; why young Ndebele were noted for an interest in individual land purchase; and why all this came together after the war to produce an important movement of 'modern' political pressure.

Attempts to Restore the Ndebele Kingship
When Lobengula died three sons born while he was king, and thus eligible in Ndebele custom to succeed him, survived him. These three boys, Mpeseni, Njube and Nguboyena, were taken to South Africa by Cecil Rhodes and put to school there. Mpeseni died in 1898 but Njube and Nguboyena maintained close contacts with their relatives in Matabeleland. During the 1896 rising there were plans to revive the monarchy but in the absence of the legitimate heirs no acceptable candidate could be found. The Rhodesian administration planned at that time to bring Njube up to Bulawayo in an attempt to rally the Ndebele around a loyalist figure-head but this scheme was abandoned when it was pointed out that the return of the king's son would give increased prestige to the leaders of the revolt.

Certainly Njube was never seen by the ex-rebel faction as a loyalist tool of the administration. Almost as soon as the rising was over old Umlugulu and other ex-rebels began to build up a party in his interest. They sent messages to him, urging him to come to Matabeleland on any pretext that he could invent. A number of Njube's artless schoolboy letters to Rhodes, written at this time, have survived. In October 1898 Njube wrote:

[1] G. Arrighi 'Labour supplies in historical perspective'.

'My dearest Master. Please Sir will you let me go Home just fore Holiday only. I will not ask you any more when I have been Home. Will you please have mercy on me. Please Sir I tell you do not think that I will rebell against you. How can I do wicked things against you because you are so kind to me, and you have to be so careful to me, and giving me what I want. You can tell me how many days or weeks I may stay at Home ... Please Sir have mercy on me that I may go and see my friends at Home and I will come back as soon as you want me to come back. And I want to seek for some business and if I see that I can't have anything to do there I will come back again as soon as you want me to come.'[1]

The Rhodesian administration were very much averse to allowing this humble schoolboy back into Matabeleland. There had already been reports of the faction forming in his name – one of Rhodes' correspondents urged him to get rid of Njube quietly since there would always be trouble so long as he was alive. A close watch was kept on the ex-rebel party and their communications with Njube. In April 1899 the young induna Somazheg-wana came to Cape Town to visit Njube; on his return to Matabeleland Somazhegwana became 'intimate with the notorious Karl Kumalo (Loben-gula's Secretary) and among other things had created some unrest among the people by building a kraal to be occupied by Lobengula's principal son'. These activities drew a rebuke to Njube from his mother, Mpoiyana.

'Rumours are about,' she wrote to him, 'that you have ordered a kraal to be built for you by Somazhegwana, son of Mzilane, and others. I wish to know at once if you did order the building of this kraal. My heart is very sore to hear these rumours about you. When I visited you in Cape Town I told you that Mr Rhodes is your only father and that you are not to listen to anybody but him. You faithfully promised to do so. Do you believe people misleading you. My son, cling to Mr Rhodes. He is your only father and guardian.'

In August Njube sent back an angry reply:

'I received your letter alright. It is clear you do not wish me to return home. I wish to know what you want from me. Perhaps it is because you don't like me any more ... I was under the impression that you do not care about me any longer since you drove away Mapitsholo, who came to your kraal to erect me a house. Now you intend to drive away Somazheg-wana. What do you wish me to do? I must wish you all good-bye. If you wish to drive Somazhegwana away do so as you did to Mapitsholo, as I will not come home again even if you reply to this letter, you better

[1] Njube Lobengula to Rhodes, 21 October 1898, Rhodes House, Oxford, Rhodes Papers, C. 27.

understand that I shall not reply to it, as well as I shall not return to my home.'[1]

In 1900 the Rhodesian administration relented and Njube was allowed home for what turned out to be his only visit. It caused a great stir. Old Umlugulu hastened in to Bulawayo to see him without bothering to ask permission from the Native Commissioner of his district – 'remarkable conduct', complained the latter; 'Mlugulu knows very well that he has no right to leave the district without informing me, and in my opinion he deserves to be punished.' Other senior indunas applied and were given permission to visit Njube. There was a general 'curiosity to see and hear all possible about Njube, the son of Lobengula, and the natives were inquisitive as to whether he would remain in Matabeleland'.[2]

He did not remain in Matabeleland. The administration were disturbed by the effect of his visit. 'The Matabele nation are divided on the subject', it was minuted; 'those that rebelled being desirous that he should come back, when an effort would probably be made to secure his recognition as "king", while the "loyal" portion of the nation does not desire his return.' Njube was rapidly taken back to the Cape where he set himself up as a progressive farmer. In 1903 the Administrator put an end to 'agitation among the less well disposed' by informing the indunas that 'Njube would not be brought back'. Njube, however, was less submissive now that Rhodes was dead. He continued to send messages to his party in Matabeleland and in 1904 forced the issue by informing the Chief Native Commissioner that he intended to return home despite the Company's prohibition. The administration acted quickly. At their request the High Commissioner issued a warrant authorizing the Bechuanaland Police to arrest Njube if he entered the territory and to deport him back to Cape Province. 'Information has been laid', ran his warrant, 'that the proceedings of Njube, son of Lobengula, of Matabeleland, endanger the peace of the territories.'[3]

It is doubtful how far Njube really did endanger the peace. The Rhodesian administration professed to fear not a revolt against themselves but a faction fight amongst the Ndebele. The 'loyalists' were said to fear that the return of Njube and especially his achievement of the kingship would mean that their cattle and property would become insecure; the ex-rebels, on the other hand, were said to pin their hopes for the overthrow of the 'loyalists' on the restoration of the monarchy. These estimates may well have been soundly based. But what is even more interesting is the appeal

---

[1] The correspondence between Njube and his mother is in file AM 2/1/7.
[2] Correspondence relating to Njube's visit to Matabeleland is in LO 5/7/4.
[3] Colonial Office, Confidential Prints, No. 746.

that Njube and his brother Nguboyena had to the new educated Ndebele, the men of the Christian solution, as well as to the faction of Umlugulu. Njube and Nguboyena were no old-style Ndebele warrior princes. They were in fact, by a long way, the best educated of the Ndebele nation; the most knowledgeable about the white man's world; the most acquainted with 'modern' forms of organization as they had developed in South Africa. They were the natural leaders of the younger educated Ndebele just as much as of the ex-rebel party. Support for them drew together the old 'traditionalist' indunas and Ndebele catechists and teachers. And since it was hardly possible to conceive of Njube and Nguboyena at the head of a traditionalist insurrection, support for them drew people like old Umlugulu towards 'modern' forms of applying pressure and expressing grievance.

All this became clear with Nguboyena's visit to Bulawayo in 1908. Nguboyena was the academically cleverer of the two brothers; his work was allowed to be 'quite up to European standards'; in 1907 he was sent to England by the Company for further training. The Company idea was that he should train as a veterinary surgeon. Nguboyena's idea was that he should read for the Bar. 'Lobengula is essentially a student', his tutor reported, 'and therefore the career of a Veterinary Surgeon or a Farmer does not appeal to him.' 'I thought I had made it quite clear that it was the Law I would be taking up on coming over here,' wrote Nguboyena. The Company was much disturbed at the prospect. 'I told Mr Hibbert that while no doubt a university education might be very desirable,' wrote the Secretary of the Company, 'I thought in the case of Lobengula it was scarcely necessary.' Secretary Inskipp talked with Nguboyena himself. 'He told me that he was very keen on becoming a barrister. . . . I explained to him that in the very distant future it might be possible for members of the coloured races in South Africa to take up the learned professions as they now do in India and other parts of the world, but that at present he must take the word of those wiser and more experienced than himself that it could not be.' Inskipp asked him whether 'he would be willing to practise his profession in West Africa or in any other part of the world other than the Cape but he is quite firm in his desire to return to South Africa.' Nguboyena persisted; there was a danger of his case being taken up by English sympathizers; reluctantly the Company gave way.[1]

The prospect of a son of Lobengula qualifying as a barrister some half century before Herbert Chitepo, who was to be in fact the first African lawyer in Rhodesia, is a tantalizing one. But it did not materialize. The strains of Nguboyena's life, of his separation from his people and of his

[1] Correspondence relating to Nguboyena's education is in file A 11/2/12/8.

essentially false position as an increasingly educated and qualified man for whom no relevant employment would be available, were beginning to tell. On 31 July 1908 he wrote a pathetic letter to Inskipp which presaged his eventual nervous breakdown.

'I am sorry to have to disappoint you and those concerned with my welfare so soon, by asking you whether it would not be possible for you to send me back home as soon as possible. I really cannot stay here any longer. I have tried my very best, in fact I thought a change might improve matters. But as it is I am no happier nor likely to be. . . . This letter is the result of no hasty conclusion and I should be much obliged if you took it as such, for as to whether I could stay here any longer is a question that I have thought over many a day and night. I know this letter coming so soon after giving you my word that I would help your endeavours on my behalf by doing my best to work hard and get through the Law course, will no doubt grieve you. But I do not see how I can pull through in my present state. Every day is more gloomy than that before it.'[1]

The Rhodesian administration was not afraid of Nguboyena while Njube was alive and were actually prepared to consider employing him as an interpreter in Matabeleland. In September 1908 he arrived in Bulawayo. There he came into immediate contact with the political realities in a heavily paternalistic series of injunctions from the Chief Native Commissioner. The interview ran:

CNC: 'You know, Nguboyena, you are a child still and sometimes it is better to have someone to think for you.'

Nguboyena: 'I think I am old enough to think for myself.'

CNC: 'I represent the Government and you must try to please me so that we can get on well together, you understand? All the black people know that I am in charge . . . as long as they do what I tell them they are all right. I attend to their wants and you are in the same position. . . . We must be good friends otherwise there will be trouble. I am good friends with all my chiefs.'[2]

Nguboyena was far from silenced. He asked for land and met the Chief Native Commissioner's professions of difficulty with 'there is any amount of waste land in this country. I don't see how the Government would suffer in the way of money so far as land goes.' Although he was already suffering from the morbid depression which was soon to make him a permanent recluse, Nguboyena showed a striking capacity to attract support.

[1] Nguboyena to Secretary, BSAC, 31 July 1908, A 11/2/12/8.
[2] CNC to Private Secretary, 3 September 1908, A 11/2/12/8.

The ex-rebel party showed him great attention. But so also did the educated elements. Nguboyena stayed while in Matabeleland with one Ntando, a Methodist teacher, at the Wesleyan Mission. He applied his keen intelligence and relative political sophistication to the problems of his countrymen. 'Nguboyena is an extremely intelligent youth,' noted the Chief Native Commissioner. 'He is at present studying the conditions of native life in this country, and has asked for varied information regarding the Native Reserves, the terms on which the natives reside thereon and has applied for a map shewing the Reserves.' 'Nguboyena does undoubtedly receive sympathy from the educated natives (Matabele and others) in Bulawayo,' concluded the CNC, 'and it is from this direction that he is likely to obtain support in the event of his wishing to give trouble.'[1]

Nguboyena now began to find the difficulties of his native land as great as those of life in Britain. Many of the loyalist indunas, like Gambo, were far from enthusiastic in their welcome to him – 'they do not feel secure in regard to their possession of stock'. The Chief Native Commissioner went out of his way to arrange a series of humiliating meetings to define Nguboyena's position. On 16 September 1908 he told the indunas that there 'is a path he has to tread and that is the straight path which means that he has to do all that I tell him . . . if he misbehaves and there is the slightest attempt to kick against the Government in any one direction I shall take no further responsibility and he will not be allowed to remain in the country. He is a native of the country and he must obey all laws appertaining to natives.' It was not surprising that in November Nguboyena withdrew from the impossible situation in which he found himself and asked to be given land and an allowance in the Cape.[2]

Nguboyena now withdrew into silence and solitude and attention was once more focused on Njube. The ex-rebel faction and the educated group did not despair of forcing through a revival of the Ndebele kingship and a triumph over the loyalists. They continued to press for Njube's recall. In November 1909 all the Ndebele indunas met the High Commissioner together with 'town natives'. They asked once more for Njube; the High Commissioner flatly refused. 'They have said to me again and again that there is one thing that they particularly desire, but they must learn to know me. When I say No, I mean No. The son of Lobengula is well and being well looked after in Cape Colony, *but he is not coming back here.*'[3]

[1] CNC to P.S., 17 September and 10 November 1908, A 11/2/12/8.
[2] Minutes of a meeting between the CNC and the indunas, 16 September 1908, A 11/2/12/8.
[3] High Commissioner's speech, 12 November 1909, A 3/18/18/6.

Njube reacted to this prohibition no longer as the schoolboy but as an angry and formidable man. On 25 November 1909 he wrote to the High Commissioner's secretary in Pretoria:

'I observe from reports of His Excellency's speech in Rhodesia that I am not to be allowed to return to my own country. What the cause of this decision may be I know not and can only assume it is a fresh "Colour Bar" on the eve of Union . . . I am a peaceable man who has done no harm to my king or country, yet I am hounded from my own home while Members of Parliament in England like Mr Victor Grayson, and Mr Keir Hardie, Mr Lloyd George and Mr Winston Churchill, all publicly avowed anti-monarchists and consequently, I assume, rebels, are permitted to continue their propaganda unmolested.'[1]

The High Commissioner found this letter one 'that will require to be carefully answered'. But it was Njube's last protest. In June 1910 he died in Cape Province. With Njube dead, his brother Nguboyena a recluse, and his two sons, Albert and Rhodes, still minors, the agitation for the revival of the Ndebele monarchy temporarily fell away. Obviously nothing had been achieved. But the idea of the monarchy had given some sort of focus to Ndebele aspirations. When land pressure grew intolerable not only the ex-rebels and the educated men of the township but many other Ndebele would turn once more to the idea of a restoration as the only way to improve their situation.

The Ndebele Land Issue
From the beginning of the kingship movement, indeed, one of its main driving forces was the connection between the monarchy and Ndebele land. Traditionally all land had been held to belong to the king; the European claim to the land had derived in the first instance from concessions claimed to have been made by Lobengula and in the second instance from the defeat of Lobengula and the conquest of Matabeleland in 1893. Revival of the monarchy was thus thought of as a means of re-opening the land question and endeavouring to reclaim the Ndebele homeland from its new white owners. In this way Ndebele land grievances contributed to the coherent focus of Ndebele political activity.

The Ndebele homelands had passed into formal white control as early as 1894. Rhodes in his indabas with the rebel leaders in 1896 had given them the impression that their lands would be restored to them; 'it was

[1] Njube Lobengula to Secretary, High Commissioner, 25 November 1909, A 3/18/1.

natural for the Matabele to assume that they would be secured in regard to their tribal lands,' admitted a subsequent Chief Native Commissioner. 'On this assumption they surrendered and returned to their homes.' The facts were different. The Company had not bought out the white owners of the land. White landlords were prevailed upon to allow two years of undisturbed tenure but after that the Ndebele became 'squatters' subject to rental increase, dipping and grazing fees, and to eviction. The Ndebele felt a deep bitterness and sense of betrayal.

Ndebele land grievances became even more acute towards the end of the first decade of the century. To begin with few of the white owners of the old Ndebele land had farmed it very actively. But as European agriculture developed and the Company began to place more and more reliance upon it as a source of the colony's wealth, competition between black and white for the actual use of land sharpened. 'A gradual squeezing out process inevitably took place,' writes Dr Palmer, 'especially in Matabeleland where European farms were much larger and the land was much drier, so that competition for grazing areas was more fierce.' The white landlord was given increased powers of eviction; some people, noted the Chief Native Commissioner, predicted a revolt. There was no revolt but there was very great discontent. In November 1909, when the High Commissioner met the indunas he was faced not only with requests for the return of Njube but also with almost unanimous protests against the eviction of Ndebele squatters from farms.

'The natives like to live together,' he answered, 'and the white men separately. That is why a white man, when he comes to his farm sometimes moves you away.... You do not like moving then, and I understand that, but I want you to understand how the matter is. The white man has one plan of living and you have another. Now, part of the land and the country is for the settlement of white men, and part is a reserve for black men, but there is this difference that on the part that is reserved for white men's farms, if you and the white man come to some arrangement you can stay there, but under no circumstances can the white man live on your Reserve.'[1]

Even those Ndebele who did not live on actively farmed land soon began to feel a squeeze. In 1910 the Private Locations Ordinance came into force. This penalized absentee landlords by imposing a fee of five shillings for each agreement made by them with African squatters. In response the

---

[1] High Commissioner's speech, 12 November 1909, A 3/18/18/6. I have relied in this section on R. H. Palmer, *Aspects of Rhodesian Land Policy, 1890–1936*, The Central African Historical Association, Local Series 22, Salisbury, 1968.

investment land-holding companies increased African rents. In 1912 many companies imposed grazing fees on their tenants in addition. High dipping fees were levied. The whole question of land tenure, wrote the Chief Native Commissioner in 1912, was 'the root of the native question. . . . The natives hate the idea of having to give up their old kraals and associations, but the fresh demands made upon them . . . have made them very uneasy in regard to their land tenure on private property.'[1]

The indunas, usually so reluctant to speak out in their regular indabas with the Administration, began to press home their grievances on land. In 1915 the issue was raised at a series of indabas.

'His Honour found before him the representatives of a broken people,' said induna Ndaniso on 15 April 1915, 'full of grievances. They had no land upon which they could permanently live. They occupied farms upon an insecure tenure and so were continually changing their habitations.'

'We live in the grass', said induna Myuwani, 'and cannot erect permament abodes.'

In October induna Maqoma 'complained that the Gwaai Reserve held no tract of land large enough to accommodate his people en bloc. At present they occupied farms and unalienated land in the Umguza river, and his people were leaving him, one by one, for other Districts owing to the land difficulty.'[2]

By the First World War the land problem touched nearly everybody. The 'loyalists', in possession of large herds of cattle and afraid that the return of a son of Lobengula would imperil their title to them, were less enthusiastic in their support of the colonial *status quo* as they found themselves required to pay grazing fees and dipping fees to European owners or denied access to pasturage. Some of the wealthy indunas began to think in terms of land purchase. So, too, did Ndebele town-dwellers who wanted plots of land near the towns where they could cultivate or keep stock. The Company, however, refused to sell or lease land to Africans. In any event purchase held out no promise of relief to poorer men. By the end of the First World War most of Ndebele society was in a state of acute anxiety over land.

The Problems of Ndebele Town-Dwellers and the Loyal Mandabele Patriotic Society

'In considering the disintegrating effect of civilization on tribalism,' noted

[1] *Report of the Chief Native Commissioner, Matabeleland,* 1912.
[2] Records of indabas, N 9/5/3.

the Chief Native Commissioner, Matabeleland, 'Native Commissioners draw attention to two factors which are hastening the process. An appreciable number of young men are attracted by the glamour and social life of the towns and industrial centres, where it becomes necessary for them to work for their living.' In Bulawayo especially, which was at this period the great industrial centre of Southern Rhodesia, numbers of Ndebele gathered and made their home in the Municipal Locations. Among them were a minority of educated men, in pursuit of the Christian solution, who hoped to make a permanent home in the towns and who constituted themselves as spokesmen of the Ndebele urban population.

Such men spoke in the interests of the new educated; the 'modern' men. They spoke in the vocabulary of the first generation African Christian. But contrary to the Chief Native Commissioner's prediction, they did not regard themselves as in any way de-tribalized. They were the strongest supporters of Njube and Nguboyena and the restoration of the Ndebele monarchy. If anything they felt more passionately Ndebele than their fellow tribesmen in the rural areas; they wished to define themselves against the migrant workers from Mashonaland and from outside Southern Rhodesia. They claimed that they had a special right to status and influence in Bulawayo since they were descendants of the Ndebele who had first founded Bulawayo as the capital of the Ndebele state. In fact they were very successful in asserting superior prestige. In Bulawayo even African migrants from South Africa – Zulu or Sotho Christian clerks or craftsmen – would integrate themselves with the Ndebele nationality, the Zulu claiming to fall in the *Zansi* caste, the Sotho claiming to fall into the *Enhla* caste. Some of these 'adoptive Ndebele' became leading figures in the urban associations. This capacity of the Ndebele nationality to retain prestige even after defeat and to assimilate African migrants contrasted sharply with the situation in Mashonaland where migrants from South Africa and the north stood quite outside Shona society and its values.

The Ndebele and adoptive Ndebele of the towns regarded themselves as having a right, indeed an obligation, to speak for the Ndebele nation as a whole as well as for their special interests as town dwellers. They spoke for a restored monarchy; pleaded for African land rights; inveighed against forces undetermining Ndebele codes of conduct. They were exponents of the Christian solution in a specifically Ndebele guise. But as exponents of the Christian solution they spoke, of course, with deference, with many professions of loyalty.

The voice of this sort of town dweller comes out very clearly from the records of the Loyal Mandabele Patriotic Society, which came into existence in 1915. It arose out of a split within an earlier organization, Ilihlo Lo'muzi, and was headed by a Committee of 'nine earnest young men'. In December 1915 the Society issued a manifesto:

'Wake up! Wake up! Wake up! Mandabele!

Your people are in great danger of being wiped out.

The law of the great God within or written in our heart and our ancestors' hearts is being broken.

The Christian law and the law of Mzilikazi is being broken down by prostitution.

Many of our old and young women are living on mines and Town locations as prostitutes. They are selling their bodies

To evil men for money, clothes and Utchwala (beer). They have brought disgrace to our nation. The white people are despising us . . .

Syphilis, the curse of prostitution, is showing itself in the children

That are born. . . .

How are we to break down and kill this evil? The A. P. Society

Will lead you to break it down by the help of the Almighty God . . .

1 Tell the fathers or the guardian of the fallen women to report them to the Native Commissioner or Police.

2 If you know any bad house point it out to the English detectives.

Honour the King and keep his laws.'[1]

The tone of the Society when approaching the white authorities was one of extravagant loyalty.

'We thank the Administrator for the tidings that he had already seen the evil that exists among the black people,' the Secretaries of the Society wrote in March 1916. 'Let him not weary in his care for a child is always soothed in troubles by his father . . . (we thank him) for the great thing he had done for us in receiving the petition of us who are things so far beneath him.'

The Secretaries described Superintendent of Natives, Jackson, as 'our fountain on which we rely for refreshment and rest – in you, our fountain and shade.' In June 1916 they handed in a resolution on the death of Kitchener:

'We mourn on account of this calamity which has descended upon the nation in regard to the warrior of warriors, the fighter who made war with weapons, whose days have been numbered, and whose guidance of our armies will ever be remembered by whites and blacks. We pray that

[1] Manifesto of 15 December 1915, N 3/21/1. Original in Sindebele.

Providence will give us another leader who will direct our forces until the end.'[1]

The Society hoped to gain favourable recognition in exchange for this loyalty. They sought the setting aside of a special area in which settled married men could live. They sought improvements in the sanitation and health services of the location. They asked that loafers and prostitutes be cleared out and some security be given to 'the more respectable class of natives'. They also ventured to censure the whites for frequenting African prostitutes. 'In all this how can a white man boast of his being in a civilized state as he has fallen so low as to cast away his own blood? White men are supposed to be an example to natives in moral living.'[2]

The Christian Solution as Protest: Reverend Magkatho and the African Methodist Episcopal Church

We have seen how Matthew Zwimba stood out from the Christian conformists of Mashonaland. His equivalent in Bulawayo was Reverend M. D. Makgatho. There were great differences between the two men. Matthew Zwimba's church was an exclusively Shona church, his inspiration was drawn from exclusively Shona roots. Makgatho's church was a great missionary church with its base in South Africa and he was himself a Suto, not an Ndebele. But there was this similarity, that both sought to use the Christian message and the skills of education to assert an African leadership independent of white control.

The African Methodist Episcopal Church originated in America. Its founders had broken away from the American Methodist Episcopal Church and had worked with much success to provide an example of Negro self-reliance. By the end of the nineteenth century the church had its own educational system, its own economic enterprises – and its own missionary outreach. Negro missionaries of the AMEC carried its doctrine of self-reliance to South Africa where they made many converts and had a great effect upon the whole South African Ethiopian movement. In 1903 Bishop Coppin, one of these Negro missionaries, applied for permission to come to Southern Rhodesia and to set up a branch of the AMEC there. The application was refused.

'This society would appear to have aroused in the minds of a considerable section of the natives of South Africa,' commented the Anglican Bishop of Mashonaland, 'political and social aspirations . . . It advocates 'higher'

---

[1] Mahlahla and Zembe to S/N/Bulawayo, 4 March 1916; S/N/Byo. to CNC 10 June 1916; N 3/21/1. The originals are in Sindebele.
[2] Petition of the Loyal Amandabele Patriotic Society, 30 August 1916, N 3/21/1.

education, makes comparison between the political and social position of the American Negro and the African native, talks of a great Native Church to arise in Africa, insists on the autonomy of the black race, need for unity and so forth . . . I am pretty well acquainted with the common talk of educated natives in Cape Colony, Basutoland and elsewhere and am not likely to deprecate any legitimate aspirations. But there is a distinct danger, to my mind, that aspirations may be manufactured for political, social or even religious reasons, and a *manufactured* political cry on the part of the NATIVES of this country is bound to become a RACIAL CRY to an even more dangerous extent than the manufactured political cry of the Dutch. We have seen what an "AFRIKANER BOND" can produce in Africa in the way of trouble; a NATIVE "BOND" would produce an Armageddon from Cape Town to anywhere.'[1]

But although Coppin and other Negro supervisors were refused entry the AMEC *did* enter Rhodesia. It was carried there by some of the educated African migrants from South Africa who entered the colony in its first decade. One such man was the Reverend John N'gono of Bembesi. Another was Makgatho. Makgatho was eminently a progressive and modernizing man. By 1904 he had bought an estate at Riverside, some six miles from Bulawayo, paying as much as £436 for its eighty-nine acres. There he built his church and school and maintained his family from the proceeds of his farm. Unlike nearly all the other articulate spokesmen of African Bulawayo he was completely independent of white patronage or control. From his secure base at Riverside he set out to establish a series of AMEC schools which would provide the Ndebele with modernizing education under African control. With the exception of the short-lived AMEC schools in Barotseland these were by a long way the earliest independent African schools in Central Africa. Makgatho's influence extended to the Fort Victoria area where a number of Basutos had settled; he was their natural ally in their struggle with the Dutch Reformed Church for adequate educational facilities.

The administration watched Makgatho carefully. 'A few pseudo native schools are conducted by representatives of the AMEC,' it was noted in 1908. 'This particular sect endeavours to discourage the attendance of natives at schools conducted by Europeans. This body is known as confusing political propaganda with religious teaching.' It was hoped that Makgatho's movement would die away for lack of funds. But it proved remarkably lasting. In 1921 the Chief Native Commissioner commented that there was much evidence 'of the inclination of the natives to break

[1] Bishop of Mashonaland to CNC, 25 February 1903, A 11/2/18/3.

away from denominational schools and churches and to identify themselves with the movements to establish their own churches of the separatist type.' In 1925 the AMEC was said to be 'showing a new vigour' and by 1929 its educational efforts were so successful that it was officially conceded that 'the teachers of the recognized separatist church, the African Methodist Episcopal Church, are most of them better qualified to teach than the average teacher of kraal schools of other missions.'[1]

If the AMEC schools came to fruition only in the early 1920s it is clear that Makgatho exercised an influence on the thinking of some important Ndebele long before that. Nyamanda, the eldest of Lobengula's sons, knew Makgatho and entrusted one of his own sons to him to be sent for higher education in an AMEC school in South Africa. And there is no doubt that both Makgatho and his sons, especially the eldest, Zacharia, were themselves very politically conscious. Between them they were to be involved in most of the significant political developments of the 1920s.[2]

The Ndebele and the 1914–18 War

By far the greater majority of educated Ndebele, however, stood by the Christian solution as it developed under white guidance. Indeed for all their grievances, all their hopes for a restoration of the monarchy, the Ndebele as a whole gave the white administration very little trouble. The profuse expressions of loyalty presented by the Loyal Amandabele Patriotic Society were rivalled by the support given by the Ndebele indunas to recruiting campaigns during the First World War. The Ndebele leadership as a whole was putting into effect a strategy of loyalty and hoping for commensurate returns.

'We wish to say,' so ran a message from the indunas to the High Commissioner in 1918, 'when the King called upon us for help, we sent our young men, who fought and died beside the English, and we claim that our blood and that of the English are one.'

'I introduce to His Honour's notice,' said the induna Ntola at the Umzingwane indaba of 4 April 1919, 'these returned soldiers. I ask regarding them that they may receive a token of recognition of the work they have done, and to urge that we are entitled to a share in their recognition by being accorded a hut in which to rest, a permanent

---

[1] *Southern Rhodesia: Departmental Reports: Native Affairs*, 1900/01–1923; File A 3/18/18/6.

[2] For Magkatho generally see T. O. Ranger, 'The early history of independency in Southern Rhodesia', *Religion in Africa*, ed. W. Montgomery Watt, Edinburgh, 1964. Additional background is given in file ZAH 1/1/2.

resting place in which we can sit down and drink water in peace. They have proved our loyalty and purchased for us a relief from our grievances.'[1]

It remained to be seen whether the Ndebele indunas and their people and the Ndebele town-dwellers and their allies would remain so loyal and patient in the years after the war if the security of land tenure and the improved residential facilities in the towns for which they asked were not in fact forthcoming.

[1] Record of the Umzingwane indaba, N 9/5/3.

THREE

The South African Influence

1898–1918

By the end of the First World War some Ndebele were moving towards, but can hardly be said to have arrived at, modern forms of political organization. Yet from the beginning of the colonial period in Southern Rhodesia there were numbers of Africans aware of modes of political expression quite different from armed rebellion; Africans fully committed to Christianity and to a Western economy; Africans possessed of literacy and a range of technical skills; Africans who were not at all caught up in memories either of Shona traditions of resistance or in hopes for a restoration of Ndebele traditional institutions. In the 1890s and for a long time thereafter the overwhelming majority of such Africans were immigrants from South Africa, black settlers – described in the terminology of the time as 'Colonial Boys' or 'alien natives'. These black settlers were so deeply committed to the opening up and exploitation of Rhodesia by the whites that it seemed very improbable that they should come to play any part in the development of African opposition politics in the colony. But in fact it was the political experience and connections of these men which added the missing element to Ndebele politics after 1918 and helped to produce new forms of political protest and pressure.

Some of the black settlers arrived in Rhodesia with the Pioneer Column of 1890 which was, as Mr Gann tells us, 'a multi-racial enterprise, containing "Colonial natives" who were employed on transport work and as personal servants, receiving relatively high rates of pay.' Africans from the south served the European community of early Mashonaland as drivers and leaders of oxen, as assistants in stores, as interpreters, as catechists. In these capacities they often clashed with the Shona. In 1893 the settler columns which invaded Matabeleland included 'Cape Boys'; in the rebellions of 1896 they were on hand in most of the key episodes. Some 125 of them took part in the defence of Bulawayo in the early weeks of the rising; a force of 'Cape Boys' specially raised for the emergency played a leading part in the storming of the Mwari cult centre and rebel stronghold of Taba Zi Ka Mambo; Africans from the south were among the emissaries sent by Rhodes to make contact with the Ndebele leaders before his famous indaba.[1]

Committed in this way to white advance these black auxiliaries suffered from the Ndebele and Shona resistance to it. During the rising African catechists and store assistants and drivers and messengers were killed by the rebels; as one Ndebele participant put it, he and his friends killed a Zulu servant as well as his white masters because 'he was as good as a European'.[2]

After the risings had been defeated these black allies were rewarded. 'Some of us fought against the Matabele in the first Matabele War of 1893,' a group of Cape Boys recorded later. 'We also took active part in the Matabele rebellion of 1896. We were again in active service in the Mashona rebellion of 1897. After the Matabele rebellion of 1896 we were promised land by the late Hon. Cecil John Rhodes for services rendered during the above mentioned conflicts.'[3]

Indeed Rhodes was so convinced of the usefulness of black settlers from South Africa that he took steps to bring up much larger numbers of them. In 1898 'Matabele' Thompson was sent to the Transkei to put a proposition to the Fingo people. 'Mr Rhodes had from time to time turned over in his mind what was the best means of solving the native and labour difficulties of Rhodesia,' Thompson told the Fingos. 'Schemes of Egyptians, men from other territories . . . and Indians were thought of . . . I went to Mr Rhodes and . . . I said, "Why not take Fingos?".' Thompson suggested that the Fingos should migrate in considerable numbers to Rhodesia; settle on land to be allocated to them in the Bembesi, Matopos and Nyamandhlovu areas, in a great sweep around the Ndebele homeland; and in return for this land assist with 'labour and defence'. The Fingos were promised 'open competition amongst yourselves and the white man'. Hundreds of Fingo men took up the offer. In 1904 the missionary, H. P. Hale, told a correspondent of his visit to the Fingo settlement at Bembesi. 'The Fingos are Cape Kaffirs, brought up as part of a scheme by Rhodes to form a cordon of loyal natives round Bulawayo to counteract any hostile movements of the Matabele. They are mostly Christians and have a small and thatched mud church.'[4]

[1] L. H. Gann, *A History of Southern Rhodesia Early Days to 1934*, London, 1965, pp. 121, 130, 131, 134.

[2] Statement by Ngangonyi Mhlope, recorded by R. F. Windram, 20 November 1938, WI 8/1/3.

[3] Statement by John Hlazo and others, December 1915, Rhodes House, Oxford, mss. British Empire. S 22, Papers of the Aborigines Protection Society, G 173.

[4] 'Matabele' Thompson's speech to the Fingo people, 1898, A 3/18/24; Letter book of H. P. Hale, 1 December 1904, HA 4/1/1.

The Black Settler Association

These were the two main groups of southern African black settlers, but there were many individuals who came later on to swell their numbers. From the beginning these men were active in forming associations to promote their interests. They were, after all, as much pioneers as the whites and as keenly interested in obtaining a share in the developing Rhodesian economy. A number of associations for South African Africans as a whole were set up – most notably the Union of South Africa Natives Association and the Union Natives Vigilance Organization. There were also groupings for the expression of particular interests – a Basuto Association or less formalized but very active Fingo groupings.

As might have been expected these associations were at first mainly concerned to state their special relationship with the whites and to request special treatment from them. They were anxious to stress their loyalty and their progressiveness; to escape from the disabilities of the indigenous African population rather than to try to mitigate them. For example this comes very clearly out of a petition presented by the Fingo settlers to the High Commissioner in December 1909. Expressing their shame that the 'Matebile refused to salute you in good way', the Fingos asserted:

'We are not in the same spirit as them. The Fingos are in very small numbers in this country and also have unfriendly to the people of the country although they have never been in quarrel with us. Our only friend is the British Government who kept our grandfathers and now has still looking upon us, and he serves us with his good hands and his mouth is full of love to his children under his power.'

On this occasion the Fingos were asking for permission to use firearms and exemption from the pass-laws.[1]

The same note was struck on a more sophisticated level by the representations of the Union of South Africa Natives Association which claimed to speak for 'town natives from the Southern Colonies'. Thus in 1911 the Association protested against its exclusion from the Drill Hall grounds on the occasion of the celebrations for the coronation of George V, which had prevented it from showing its loyalty. At the same time it asked for the abolition of the jury system because of the prejudice shown by European juries towards African defendants. In the same sort of way the Union Natives Vigilance Organization asked in 1914 for exemption from travelling passes on the grounds that 'by reason of their having rendered loyal service during the Matabele war of 1893 and the rebellion of 1896, they should be

[1] Fingo petition, 3 December 1909, A 3/18/1.

granted certificates of exemption.' In 1917 the UNVO asked for exemption from the humiliating obligations imposed on all Africans to walk off the pavements in the towns, 'to take off our hats when we are asked for passes', and so on.

'We, the above mentioned Union, hope and trust that our petition shall be considered. We also have a few words to say to you, Sir, with regard to the present war in which our Empire has taken part. England, as far as we have read in the papers how she entered the war, was for the protection of the weak ones, and in this she was right. We therefore hope that she may be victorious in this just war on her part.'[1]

The Disillusionment of the Black Settlers

It might be thought that such associations had nothing much to contribute to African politics in Southern Rhodesia save an example of respectful élitism. But the situation was not so simple. Even as the black settlers stated and re-stated their claims upon white consideration they were faced with evidence after evidence that these claims were not recognized. The honeymoon between white and black modernizers was soon over.

In 1916, for example, one of the Fingo leaders, Chief Garner Sojini, recorded the Fingo impression of the consequences of their response to Rhodes' invitation:

'We said to Mr Thompson we did not know anything about Rhodesia. Mr Thompson then said that the Fingos could send delegates to Rhodesia and those three lands would be shown to the delegates. . . . The delegates returned and said that they were perfectly satisfied with the three lands that was shown to them. Then the first batch of Fingos migrated to Rhodesia. After we had arrived in Rhodesia the Boer War then broke out and the Chief Native Commissioner said to us you better remain here in Bembesi and not go to the other lands at present. You are still few and so we remained according to his word. In 1900 Mr Rhodes came to Rhodesia and called the Fingo chiefs together on 6 July 1900 and we complained to Mr Rhodes that part of our families have not yet come up . . . Mr Rhodes gave us permission to go and fetch our families. We came with them and others still remained behind as the war was still on. They said they would go to Rhodesia after the war. The war ended in 1901 and it was said we must go and fetch the remainder of our people. We then went and after we had arrived and were preparing to go and

[1] Petitions of the Union of South Africa Natives Association, 1911, A 3/18/4; Petititions of the Union Natives Vigilance Organization, 1914 and 1917, N 3/7/2 and N 3/33/12.

some of the people had already sold their stock, Mr Fynn arrived from Rhodesia and said that he had been instructed by the Chief Native Commissioner to stop the emigration of Fingos at present on account of the East Coast Fever. When it had passed away we again asked to go and fetch our people. The Chief Native Commissioner said that we were knocking our heads against a stone and said that even the land we occupy at Bembesi would be made smaller. This was done and given to European farmers. We were six chiefs. After a time the other chiefs were dismissed. One chief was appointed and the only land that was given to him was part of the land which was fenced during the outbreak of the East Coast fever set apart as quarantine and the rest of the land confiscated. All our people were placed under him against our will and against their will. We still want all our lands as we forfeited all our lands at the Cape Colony and Mr Rhodes had told us that these lands would never be taken away from us and that they would be the inheritance of our children.'[1]

The same disillusionment was suffered by groups of Africans who had been engaged in the 1893 and 1896 fighting. In 1915 such a group, under the leadership of John Hlazo, complained of the treatment they had received:

'After the Matabele rebellion of 1896 we were promised land by the late Hon. Cecil John Rhodes for services rendered during the above mentioned conflicts. In 1898 we had a meeting at which we passed a resolution to request the Chartered Company to grant us the land promised. In reply the Government required us to furnish "Character Certificates" signed by the Magistrates of the Districts from which we came in the Cape Colony, Natal and other places. We could not understand why the Government should require us to furnish the said certificates after being employed in its service and some of us having died fighting for its cause. We again communicated with the Government to grant us the land as promised after which we were told to appoint one as our leader or Chief. We appointed John Hlazo. . . . We were located at a place in Government Farm No. 3, that borders on the Battlefield Block at Bembesi. . . . At that time we were six Native Chiefs in the area. . . . When part of the land was confiscated four of the Fingo Chiefs were expelled, and part of our land was also confiscated. . . . We had confidence in the Government, and relied on its word of honour, not being aware that it could be disregarded at the first opportunity to suit circumstances.'[2]

---

[1] Statement of Garner Sojini, 26 April 1916, Rhodes House, Oxford, Aborigines Protection Society papers, G 173.

[2] Statement by John Hlazo and others, 6 December 1915, APS papers, G 173.

Whether or not these statements are in all respects factually correct – and this was denied by the Company administration at the time – there is no doubt that they do reflect on the white side a decision to withdraw from the alliance with black settlers made by Rhodes and Thompson and on the black side the consequent bitterness and sense of betrayal. Fingos were never settled in Nyamandhlovu or the Matopos. As early as 1904 the administration had come to regard them as a danger rather than as an aid to labour and defence.

'The Fingos are as a whole a source of great danger,' wrote the Attorney General in that year. 'They are at the bottom of all sorts of irregular practices, generally egging others on to commit an offence while clever enough to themselves escape the meshes of the law. . . . Their defiance of authority is almost proverbial and as a class they are inveterate liars and quite unreliable . . . whenever possible these Fingos should be removed to the place whence they came.'

'It is a matter of paramount importance,' added the Chief Native Commissioner, 'to prevent these people from contaminating the indigenous population with that spirit of vain-glorious truculence to which some of them are prone, being carried away by the spectacle of their own slight accomplishments in the first acquisition of civilization.'[1]

The whites had discovered that when it came to the point they much preferred their defeated enemy, the Ndebele, to their over-sophisticated allies and potential rivals, the Fingos. 'The Matabele regard the Fingos as their natural inferiors,' noted a white official in 1904, 'and in respect of moral worth they are certainly right.' This attitude extended from the Fingos to other 'Colonial Boys', even to those who had fought in 1893 and 1896.

In such a situation the tactics of the black settler associations were bound to fail. The whites were determined not to make any concessions to 'alien natives' as a group or to individuals amongst them. The Fingo petition of 1909, quoted above, received a dusty answer. 'Nzimende is to be informed that it is not proper for him to assume that the Matabele are not imbued with the same spirit of loyalty as is possessed by the Fingos . . . Nzimende and his counsellors should be advised to use all their influence to promote a better feeling between his people and the Matabele and they should bear in mind that they are but recent arrivals in the country.' The concessions asked for were not granted. As for individual Fingo applicants who wished

[1] Minute by the Attorney General, 12 December 1904; Chief Native Commissioner to Chief Secretary, Salisbury, 26 October 1904, A 3/18/2.

to lease or purchase Company land so that they could escape the shrunken confines of the Fingo Location, they soon realized that the promised 'open competition amongst yourselves and the white man' was not going to be allowed. In 1904 John N'gono, a Fingo pastor of the African Methodist Episcopal Church, applied for Company land. His application was refused and the attendant correspondence gives a clear impression of official attitudes. N'gono was caught between two fires. On the one hand there was a general objection to the idea of encouraging indigenous Africans to think in terms of individual ownership. 'It is after and not before the complete substitution of European control for that of the native Chiefs has been consummated that the Native may begin to rise from his position of inferiority . . . he cannot vault at one bound into a footing of equality with Europeans.' 'I do not see any necessity for the natives to rise in any hurry from their position of inferiority to the European generally. We want now and will want in the future inferior and unskilled labour.' 'By granting land to natives we would be helping to put them in a position to claim the franchise.' For all these reasons, ran the consensus of official opinion, it was wrong 'that natives of any class should at any time be allowed to obtain land beyond the limits of the Reserves,' since this would 'introduce a new principle in Native existence diametrically opposed to the one obtaining in the country.' 'Alien natives' would just have to wait until massive social transformation had taken place amongst indigenous Africans. On the other hand there were specific objections to the idea of 'alien natives' as landlords. 'These prematurely "educated" natives almost invariably abuse their slender attainments in the way of civilization for the purpose of getting the better of their raw fellows.' 'The native can learn to look up to his white masters before he has done with his native chief; though he cannot and will not recognize two black masters.'[1]

It was the same story in the towns. When 'alien natives' asked for exemption from urban by-laws and the whole discriminatory apparatus of urban administration they were always met with the same double argument: that no exemptions could be made until large numbers of indigenous Africans were 'ready' and that in any case the indigenous town-dwellers disliked the aliens and would resent concessions made to them. Polite and loyal as the black settler associations remained, it is not difficult to imagine the bitterness that lay behind their petitions. By the end of the First World War, if not sooner, many of their members were ready to abandon their old position of constant reference back to an alliance with the whites which the whites did not recognize and to move to a new political alliance with the

[1] Minutes on the application of John N'gono, 1904, L 2/1/175.

Ndebele and the Shona, taking with them their relatively sophisticated attitudes and techniques.

The Experience of Garner Sojini and John Hlazo

This process of alienation is well illustrated by two individual cases. Garner Sojini and John Hlazo were prominent leaders of the black settler groups and prominent members of their associations. But after the First World War they both came to play an important role in the new protest politics in alliance with Rhodesian Africans. It is worth while seeing what brought them to this position.

Chief Garner Sojini was the very model of the successfully modernizing African. He was described by various officers of the administration as 'a progressive native', 'a hard-working man of good character'. By the early 1920s he had built up a herd of well over 200 cattle and was producing some thousands of sacks of mealies a year. He was leasing a farm at an annual rent of £70 and was able to offer £500 to purchase land outright. He was one of the very small and select band of African registered voters, and he employed, like a latter-day Lobengula, someone described as 'teacher, catechist and secretary for Chief Garner Sojini'. His migration to Rhodesia had been, therefore, something of a success story. Yet Sojini had a deep sense of grievance both on behalf of himself and of the Fingos generally. It seemed to him that everything he had been able to achieve had been despite of the Company. He believed that the terms of Rhodes' offer to the Fingos had been broken. He resented the Company's refusal to recognize him as a Chief. He found that he could not work the land allocated to him in the Fingo Location because of lack of water. In 1914 he left the Location to take up a lease of land in the Selukwe area, where many of his followers also leased land from a private investment company, Willoughby's Concessions. 'I Chief Garner Sojini am here at Selukwe through scarcity of land which was given to us. I have to hire a farm at Selukwe and I pay £70 rent a year. Some Fingos £50 down, £15 a year rent. We left all our lands and privileges from Cape Colony as it was said we were purchased lands here in Rhodesia by the late Mr Rhodes.'

Sojini's irritation was increased by the failure of his many attempts to establish himself as a Rhodesian farmer with the full freedoms and privileges of his white counterparts. In 1914 his application to purchase the freehold of a Company farm was refused though he was allowed to lease land on one year's notice. In 1914 also he led a deputation of Fingos to the Superintendent of Natives, Gwelo, asking that they be issued licences to shoot game. In June 1917 he petitioned with other Fingos that 'natives possessing the franchise be exempted from legislation affecting natives only' and that they be permitted to purchase land freely, to own fire-arms and to dispense with passes. The petitions were, of course, unsuccessful. Sojini remained a settler in terms of economic achievement; a 'native' in terms of legal status.

Sojini turned to a wide variety of devices and helpers in his attempts to raise his own case and the Fingo case generally. In 1914 he employed European solicitors to make representations to the High Commissioner that the whole question of Fingo land should be referred to the Reserves Commission: this was refused. In 1916 he appealed for help to the Aborigines Protection Society in London. In 1918 he turned from white lawyers and philanthropists to the South African National Congress lawyer, Alfred Mangena, who came up to Rhodesia to press the Fingo case. In 1919 Sojini himself travelled down to Cape Town 'to see the High Commissioner and lay his case against the Rhodesian Government, or the Chartered Company, before him.' Different though his grievances were from those of the majority of Rhodesian Africans, Sojini had clearly ceased to act as an ally of the whites and had become one of their most persistent and resourceful critics. It comes as no surprise to find him active in the Rhodesian Bantu Voters Association and other élite protest movements of the 1920s.[1]

A more bitter opponent of the Company was John Hlazo, elected leader of the 'Colonial Boys' at Bembesi. When the original Fingo policy was abandoned at Bembesi Hlazo and his men lost some of their land and found themselves obliged to submit either to the authority of the one recognized Fingo headman or of the Ndebele chief of the Reserve which bordered the Fingo Location. In 1916 he and his followers were given notice to quit their land altogether on the grounds that their refusal to recognize Ndebele authority was causing dissension in the area. Hlazo was a combative man and he did not take his removal lying down. In 1915 he appealed to the Aborigines Protection Society, who failed to do anything effective to help him. A letter sent to them in January 1917 illustrates Hlazo's character very clearly and also the depth of his disillusionment with the white alliance:

'I am sorry to say I did not understand your last letter, so far as I understand in your last letter the Authorities did not answer a single point in the statement that I send to them. These are the questions I thought would be answered.

1 Did we not fight for the Government in the Matabele rebellion?

[1] This account of Sojini is based on files N 3/10/5; N 3/7/2; A 3/18/2 and Rhodes House, Oxford, Aborigines Protection Society Papers, G 173.

c

2 Did the Government not give us a piece of ground as a reward for faithful services?

3 Did the Government not give us a sketch or plan of the land to us?

4 Did the Government not say in his letter dated 15 November 1905, that the title will be issued to me after I had liquidated my debt?

5 Has the debt not long since been paid?

6 Have I not waited years for the title?

7 Why did they not give the title after I had liquidated my debt?

8 Was it because they wanted to take away again the land they had given me?

9 All these questions remain unanswered.

'On the 17 December 1916 there came a native policeman in my kraal, he told me that he was sent by the Native Commissioner. He said he was sent to come and ask me when shall I remove? I told him to go back and tell the Native Commissioner that I would come and speak to him personally. I went to the Native Commissioner, when I came he asked me where I came from? I told him that a Native Policeman came to my kraal, and he said he was sent to ask me when I am removing? I showed him the sketch and the boundaries of the land that belongs to me, and the land they told me to go to it is also within my boundaries. His answer was this. "What help did you get by writing to the Anti-Slavery and Aborigines Protection Society, for Mr Harris has written to your Solicitors, and your Solicitors have sent us the copy of that letter which says you must remove." When the Native Commissioner said so I showed him the sketch that was given to me by the Government, and I said, "At the beginning God created heaven and earth and created one man. God gave the (man) the sketch (of) the Garden of Eden. He fixed a law that this man should not break. This man broke the law of God. When God came he removed him from the Garden that he gave him. Adam went away for he found that was true that he has broken the law of God. I should like to know which law did I break under the Government? Because when this land was given to me I was told that nothing would trouble me unless I rebel against the Government." The only answer from the Native Commissioner was this. "I have not heard anything and I searched all the records and I did not find a single crime that you did against the Government."'

'I am an old man, over 70 years of age, and I was born under the British Government. The British Government gives land to a man as God did to Adam. In addition to that the day the land was given to me all the Matabeles were called to see my beacons and they know them as I know them. . . . I also said to the Native Commissioner my crime must be very, very great, more than Adam's because the Government does not tell me what it is, all he says I must leave and yet God told Adam his crime.'[1]

Hlazo's crime was essentially to have eaten of the fruit of the tree of white knowledge. Like Sojini he was able to make this knowledge effective. He employed white lawyers but found them unsatisfactory. He described his Bulawayo lawyer, Charles Coghlan, later the first Prime Minister of Rhodesia, as 'an honest man in a difficult position. He would like to do the right thing but fears to offend the other side.' He turned to Alfred Mangena, the Congress lawyer. And it was through Hlazo and his sons that Mangena and the South African National Congress made contact with rising Ndebele grievances. If Sojini was prominent in the new movements of political pressure and protest in the 1920s, Hlazo and his sons were leading figures in the great Matabele National Home movement of the immediate post-war years.[2]

In this way the 'loyalist' petitioning tradition of the 'alien natives' was drawn upon for different purposes by post-war political movements. The South African 'black' settler allies of the colonial régime played an important part in articulating and modernizing indigenous discontent.

The Impact of South African Radicalism
But even before men like Sojini and Hlazo moved into opposition the attitudes and influence of the black settlers was ambivalent. Even while they professed loyalty and appealed to their alliance with the whites they were in touch with and shared many of the radical ideas of black South Africa. They came, after all, out of a South African environment which was already producing a series of disillusioned responses to white failure to allow 'open competition'. By the 1890s the great South African independent church movement was under way as a protest against the limitations of the Christian solution under white control; African voters in the Cape, under the leadership of Jabavu, were making organized use of their franchise; the vernacular press flourished. The black settlers brought with them to Rhodesia their commitment to the Christian, Western way of life and its economic manifestations. But they also brought with them the ideas of black South Africans who were already sharply critical of the sincerity of the white intention to Christianize and modernize.

This interplay between South African black settlers in Rhodesia and the

[1] Hlazo to Harris, 3 January 1917, Rhodes House APS papers, G 173.
[2] Hlazo to Harris, 26 April 1916, Rhodes House, APS papers, G 173.

developing politics of South Africa itself had a number of significant consequences. One was that 'Ethiopianism', or militant Christian independency,
made a very early appearance in Southern Rhodesia, being carried there by
men like Magkatho and N'gono. Another was that the political movements
of South Africa were from the earliest days of the Colony interested in the
Southern Rhodesian situation and sought to establish contacts there. J. T.
Jabavu's Cape movement, Congress and later the Industrial and Commercial Workers Union all looked upon Southern Rhodesia as a natural extension of their field of activity. And all had contacts or members among
the black settlers. Thus when men like Sojini and Hlazo put indigenous
protest into touch with the South African National Congress or with
South African 'Ethiopianism' this new combination operated in an environment which had already been influenced for decades by South African
deas.

Jabavu, Congress and Southern Rhodesia
The Native Department began to worry about the effect of South African
radicalism on Africans in Rhodesia as early as 1904. In February of that
year the Chief Native Commissioner, Matabeleland, forwarded to Salisbury
a copy of Jabavu's *Imvo Zabantsundu*, an Eastern Cape newspaper, in
which the proposed hut tax increase in Rhodesia was attacked. 'The information gathered therefrom,' he wrote, 'is passed along by the educated
native to his less advanced brother and in the course of transmission from
one to another becomes twisted and exaggerated beyond recognition.' As
time passed, as the Congress movement developed in South Africa, and as
the Rhodesian African population became more aware of political realities,
the fears expressed by the Chief Native Commissioner took on more substance. Mediated partly through 'alien natives', knowledge of the South
African political situation became widespread among educated Africans in
Southern Rhodesia. In 1923 the High Commissioner inquired whether
Africans in Southern Rhodesia were 'watching the movement of protest in
the Union with interest' and whether 'some of them may be in touch with
malcontent individuals or associations in the Union'. Rhodesian officials
agreed in their replies that movements of protest in the Union were indeed
watched with interest. 'Certain natives in this territory are keeping in touch
with the affairs of the Union,' replied the Superintendent of Natives,
Gwelo, 'and are interested in the natives (Urban Areas) Bill. All I can learn
is that considerable ill feeling or discontent does exist and that natives of
Southern Rhodesia are informed of this and are watching with interest.'
'The more advanced natives of this territory are in touch with native

opinion in the Union,' answered the Chief Native Commissioner. 'Any legislation affecting natives introduced in the Union is communicated to the natives of this territory through Union natives resident in this territory. We may expect something in the nature of tacit support to any movement engineered by influential natives in the Union.'[1]

The very process of mediating news of the South African political struggle had an influence on the attitudes of the black settlers in Rhodesia. Together with their own disillusionment, their contacts and sympathy with the Congress Movement began to run counter to their earlier political strategies. In 1923 an observant official summed up their position. 'There is no doubt whatever that in the Union there is a feeling of growing race consciousness among the Bantu of all tribes, a feeling of racial solidarity. This feeling finds expression in, and in turn is strengthened by, the South African Native Congress. The Union natives in Rhodesia are in communication with the leaders of native opinion (as represented in the National Congress) in the Union, and it is probable that to some degree (there will be) a reflection in Rhodesia of this feeling of racial solidarity which has originated in the Union.' The observer noted that 'alien natives' still belonged to such bodies as the Union Bantu Vigilance Organization, 'a society founded to guard the interests of Union natives, as such, in Rhodesia', but he predicted that the growing sense of racial unity would overcome 'the particularism which at present makes the Union natives band themselves together in the UBVO'.[2]

If events in South Africa interested Africans in Rhodesia, events in Rhodesia concerned African political leaders in the Union. In 1923 the same observer asserted that it was 'the desire of the National Congress to extend this race consciousness to the natives in other parts of Africa' and particularly to Rhodesia. But from the 1890s African politicians in South Africa had watched the whole process of the opening up of Rhodesia and the defeat of the Ndebele with close and often agonized interest. Thus in 1896, the radical missionary Joseph Booth, endeavouring to set up a self-improvement movement in Zululand, found that the Zulu intellectuals repudiated him as an ally because the treatment of the Ndebele had convinced them that no white man could be trusted. In the same year the great Cape political leader, J. T. Jabavu, visited Matabeleland to see for himself the effects of the rebellion and its suppression. He was horrified by what

[1] CNC Matabeleland to PS/Salisbury, 12 February 1904, A 11/2/12/11; High Commissioner to Resident Commissioner, 15 June 1923; S/N/Bulawayo to CNC, 26 June 1923; CNC to Secretary, Administrator, 13 July 1923; A 3/18/11.
[2] Memorandum on African politics, 1923, S 84/A/260.

he found and returned to South Africa with a clearer vision of what Rhodes and Jameson achieved in practice on the basis of the famous slogan of equal rights for all civilized men.

This early interest was maintained. There was a flow of comment on Rhodesian developments in the vernacular press of South Africa. Jabavu kept up a correspondence with South African Africans in Rhodesia and took a special interest in the Fingo land case. Congress was concerned from early in its career to represent Rhodesian African interests as well as South African. In April 1914, for example, Congress leaders were in London to protest against the South African Native Lands Act of 1913. At that moment the great question of the ownership of the land in Southern Rhodesia was coming up before the Privy Council. Missionaries from Rhodesia were anxious that the African case should be stated; there was no way, in their view, of achieving an expression of the African viewpoint from indigenous Shona or Ndebele. They turned therefore to the South African Congress delegates. As a result a petition was presented on behalf of 'the Reverend John Langalibalele Dube of Orange, Phoenix, Natal, Principal of the South African Native National Congress, Saul M'sane, a nephew of a former Queen of the Matabele and a member of the N'dandwe tribe of Zulus, part of which is settled at South Melsetter, Rhodesia,' of three other Congress leaders, and of four Anglican and Catholic mission-aries. 'The Native Petitioners are members of the Executive of the South African National Congress charged by the Congress to visit England for the purpose of appealing to His Majesty to protect the rights of African Natives over the soil of their native land. The Rhodesian petitioners are residents in Rhodesia, who desire to secure for their parishioners in particular, and for the native tribes of Rhodesia in general, equitable treatment at the hands of the British Government. The Reverend John Langalibalele Dube has now returned home for the purpose of conferring with the various Indunas of Southern Rhodesia and arranging for the preparation and presentation of the natives' case . . . The natives will contend that Ordi-nances have been made which are inconsistent with their rights in regard to land and that they may rely on the promises of the British Government and that their rights should be preserved to them except in so far as they may have been varied by valid concessions granted in accordance with native custom.'[1]

It was a brave try. But the meeting of the Zulu leaders of Congress and the Ndebele indunas did not take place. 'The canvassing of Rhodesia by irresponsible persons with the object of inducing the natives to set up a

[1] Petition of Dube and others, 1914, N 3/16/3.

claim to the land could not fail to have an unsettling effect on the native mind,' thundered the Company. 'The natives of Southern Rhodesia cannot be ignorant of the fact that a general European war is in progress, indeed it must be regarded as within the bounds of probability that the area of hostilities may spread to South Africa . . . The effect of such inquiries would be to convey to the natives the idea that as the white men are fighting among themselves and as certain persons have come to tell them that the white man's land in Southern Rhodesia really belongs to the natives and that they ought to claim it, the present is a favourable opportunity for getting hold of that land, by force if necessary.' The High Commissioner had 'a talk with Dube' and the Congress project was dropped.[1]

Nevertheless contact between Congress and the black settlers of Rhodesia developed during the years of the war. One important link was the blood relationship between Reverend Radasi, the Church of Scotland minister in the Fingo Location, and Reverend Ngcayiya, a leader of the South African Ethiopian movement and Chaplain of Congress. It was through this link that men like Sojini and Hlazo made contact with such lawyer leaders of Congress as Alfred Mangena and Richard Msimang. And through these contacts the independent Church and Congress Movements of South Africa were eventually brought into alliance with the Ndebele royal family in the Matabele National Home Movement.

Other black settlers were linked with the Jabavu tradition of participation in the politics of the Cape. One of the earliest South African Africans to work in colonial Southern Rhodesia was the Zulu catechist, Frank Sixubu, who had served the Anglican mission to Mashonaland before the 1896 risings. By the 1920s Sixubu had become a landowner, possessing six hundred acres of Waterfall Farm, near Salisbury, employing eight full time labourers and drawing upon the rents of fourteen Shona squatter families. From 1915 another Zulu, Abraham Twala, worked as an Anglican teacher on Waterfall farm, bought land there and struck up a close friendship with Sixubu. Twala was a convinced adherent of the Jabavu tradition which he believed was much more productive than that of Congress. He was a correspondent of J. T. Jabavu's son, Professor Jabavu. Through Twala the Cape tradition was made available to the Rhodesian Bantu Voters Association when it was launched in 1923.[2]

---

[1] Assistant Secretary, BSAC., London to Under-Secretary, Colonial Office, 12 August 1914, N 3/16/3.

[2] Evidence of the career of Sixubu and Twala can be found in the evidence given by them to the Morris Carter Commission of 1925, ZAH 1/1/1.

Southern Rhodesian Migrant Labour in South Africa
Another kind of connection between Southern Rhodesia and South Africa
became increasingly important. This was the constant coming and going of
Rhodesian migrant labour. If some hundreds of black settlers had come up
from South Africa to join in the opening up of Rhodesia, thousands of
Rhodesian Africans were drawn southwards to work at a humbler level in
the booming economy of South Africa. These Rhodesian migrants did not
play the prominent part in South African politics assumed by Nyasa
migrants. But many of them came into contact with South African ideas of
independent Christianity, political organization and trade unionism.
Increasingly news of South African political developments was mediated to
Rhodesian Africans by Rhodesian Africans themselves.

Three examples of this process will suffice. The first concerns the
diffusion into Rhodesia of 'Zionist' independency. Zionism, which was later
to become a very large and influential movement in Rhodesia, was introduced by Ndebele and Shona labourers who had joined Zionist churches in
South Africa. Thus in 1917 two Ndebele migrants, Joyi Mabhena and
Petrus Ndebele, joined the Reverend P. M. Mabiletsa's Christian Catholic
Apostolic Church in Zion in Johannesburg. In February 1918 Mabhena
was issued with a licence to preach, baptize and to lay on hands and soon
after he was sent back to his home kraal in the Insiza district of Matabeleland to set up a mission on Mabiletsa's behalf. He was soon joined there by
Petrus Ndebele and by the beginning of 1919 the pair could claim some 500
members in the kraals and mines of the Insiza district. The administration
regarded Zionism, with its emphasis upon possession by the Holy Spirit,
on healing and prophecy, as a source of potential disorder. 'This is not the
Ethiopian Church,' noted the local Native Commissioner, 'but seems a
bit worse if anything. It is possible that under a cloak of religion they
may spread propaganda which would tend to unsettle the natives.'[1]

The second example concerns a very different sort of attempt, no less
than an endeavour to set up a Congress movement for Southern Rhodesia.
The moving spirit here was another Ndebele migrant and independent
church leader, P. S. Ngwenya. Ngwenya learnt his politics in the Zulu
independency movement. He then founded his own church, the African
Mission Home Church, which had ministers at work in Rhodesia in 1914.
He founded also the Matabele Rhodesian Society as an association for
Ndebele migrants in South Africa. Finally in 1919 he founded, or attempted
to found, the Rhodesian Native National Congress.

---

[1] For Zionism in Rhodesia see Ranger, 'The early history of independency in
Southern Rhodesia'.

'Notice is given to all Rhodesians with a view to their assembling in their places, in their towns and homes so that you may arrange to come to the great meeting which will be on 6 July 1919 at 1 p.m. (being the time of the opening of the meeting): do accordingly.

2. You should begin to meet by 29 June 1919 to arrange for the sending of 'your' delegates or your messengers to come to the great meeting which will take place at 1, Park Lane, Fordsburg, Johannesburg.

3. The agenda are as follows:

(a) to elect a President to preside over the Rhodesian Congress, also a Secretary and Vice-President.

(b) We of Johannesburg have arranged to pay 5s before addressing the Chartered Company Government. Send the money without delay. If there is a single Rhodesian who says "I will not contribute" that one is not a Rhodesian.

From 1893 until 1919 the Government has been bad towards the brown man of Rhodesia. Even if I had killed a man, after such a lapse of time I would be forgiven for having done so. If I have not been forgiven what am I to do? It is good that you should contribute money, and ask others to do so, money being a sword and buckler, for without money you can do nothing and you cannot open your mouth.

You chiefs, too, of Rhodesia listen to this word which is spoken, our chiefs. Help us and we will fight for you. Contribute money so that we can speak to the Rhodesian Government as to the rule under which we are ruled. It is right that you should help us, your people, in this thing we want to do; we say, help us with money and we shall speak.'[1]

The third example illustrates the role played by Rhodesian Africans inside South African politics and the lessons which they were able to draw from Rhodesian experience as well as the other way round. During the great controversy over the pass laws in South Africa in 1923 two Rhodesians, J. E. Sinenke and D. Ngwenya, wrote to *Abantu Batho*. Sinenke was a native of the Chilimanzi district of Rhodesia and General Secretary of the East African Benefit Society, an organization 'for natives from North of the Union who are working in the Union'.

'We want to warn the country,' so ran their letter in translation, 'as to these new and very bad Pass Laws. We find them to be very bad when it appears that the people must carry passes, there being no longer any status of manhood in a man of black Africa: passes destroy the nation. We want to make known to the people of the colony this matter of passes

[1] Ngwenya's appeal, 1919, N 3/5/8. There is no evidence to suggest that the meeting ever took place.

because they do not know it well. We come from Rhodesia where there are passes. Our nation was killed with these passes. . . . We implore the black tribe then not to agree to this bad law in its midst causing bruises to Africans. It is not a proper thing that African-born people should carry passes in addition to the other bad things which are unseemingly heaped upon the African. We say when we read the proceedings of the Commission which went all over the Union in regard to this new law that we find words of leading natives who agree to the white man that passes are proper to be carried by natives. By this mis-statement we are actually killed by our own chiefs. And others are bought with money and kill their own nation for money. What then does Congress say? It says all black people should unite without a division. What then can we say about unity when there are those who sell the country and kill the nation? We say Let Africa Return and let all join Congress and let its work increase.'[1]

Of course none of these examples relates to anything that made much of an impact in Southern Rhodesia before 1920. The Zionist movement did not begin its spectacular expansion until the late 1920s. There is no evidence to suggest that Reverend Ngwenya's Congress was ever anything more than a paper organization. And while Sinenke and Ngwenya were able in South Africa to express their radical criticism of the chiefs and sell-outs there was as yet no similar outlet in Rhodesia. Still it was far from unimportant that Rhodesian Africans were thinking and saying and attempting these things. They were attitudes and strategies that would before long become relevant to Southern Rhodesia itself.[2]

Conclusion

The effects of South African influence in these twenty years were various. In the first place a number of black settler associations introduced the methods of petition, branch organization on a territorial basis, and so on into Southern Rhodesia. These methods, together with the idea that an organization should be territory wide rather than regional or tribal, were later inherited by Southern Rhodesian protest associations. In the second place a number of black settlers came to take an important role in the early

---

[1] Translated letter from *Abantu Batho* enclosed in S/N/Bulawayo to CNC 26 June 1923, A 3/18/11.

[2] Sinenke returned to Rhodesia in 1930 and joined the Bulawayo branch of the Industrial and Commercial Workers Union which is described in chapter Seven. 'The ICU was founded by starvation' he told a meeting in March 1930. 'We have no fight with the white man – all we ask of him is money. Money is like a key which opens a door which would otherwise have to be broken down.'

stages of these Rhodesian associations and in the Matabele Home Movement. Through them the indigenous movements were put into touch with South African allies and examples, whether the protestant tradition of Congress, with its appeals to British and world opinion, or the participant tradition of Jabavu. Finally the complex interplay of Rhodesian and South African politics and the experience of very many Southern Rhodesian Africans of life in South Africa had suffused the Rhodesian atmosphere with ideas and tactics which were not effectively taken up before 1920 but which could be drawn upon when indigenous protest found organized form.

FOUR

The Politics of Protest

NYAMANDA AND THE
NATIONAL HOME MOVEMENT

By the end of the First World War a variety of African voices were making themselves heard in Southern Rhodesia. Ndebele and Shona town-dwellers; Ndebele indunas; the Lobengula family; Shona traditionalists; Zwimba with his pioneering Shona independent church; Magkatho and Ethiopianism; Hlazo and Sojini with their grievances over land and status; the patient Ndebele and Shona catechists and teachers committed to the Christian solution; migrant labourers in touch with the Congress movement, with Zionism and with trade unionism in South Africa; all these were speaking. Yet no single one of these voices, nor a number of them in combination was loud enough to command attention or strong enough to be accepted as representative.

At the same time the need for a strong and representative African voice was being keenly felt. The years of the First World War saw a series of decisions of key importance to Southern Rhodesian Africans being taken without their knowledge or participation. These decisions concerned land. In London the judicial committee of the Privy Council was hearing the great case over the ownership of unalienated land in Southern Rhodesia and seeking to determine whether this belonged to the Company by right of the Lippert Concession or to the British crown by right of conquest or to the African peoples of Southern Rhodesia by virtue of rights unimpaired either by concession or conquest. In Rhodesia the Reserves Commission appointed in 1914 to make final recommendations on the provision of land for African communal tenure was working towards its Report. This Report was published in 1917; the Privy Council decision was published in 1919. Between them they defined the terms of all further discussion on Southern Rhodesian land problems.

Both to the South African National Congress and to the Aborigines Protection Society it seemed necessary and desirable to involve Southern Rhodesian Africans in the resolution of these issues. In particular it seemed essential that the African case should be argued before the Privy Council and that representative Africans in Southern Rhodesia should empower lawyers to represent them there. In April 1914 the South African National

Congress delegation in London asserted its right to speak on behalf of Southern Rhodesian Africans and Dube was commissioned to contact Ndebele indunas and other African leaders inside the Colony. The Aborigines Protection Society, working in conjunction with Congress, decided to send their Secretary, John Harris, to make contact with 'representative native residents in Southern Rhodesia'. Harris carried with him a series of 'Points to Bring before Chiefs'. These described the APS as:

'a body of white people who seek only to do good for native races and they are allowed to speak to the King and his counsellors all the words of their hearts on matters which touch the welfare of native tribes.'

The APS had selected 'three wise men' to speak for the Africans before the Privy Council. 'The chief is a very strong man; he is a King's Pleader and a member of the King's Pitso.' This man required 'a paper signed by you or with the mark of your Chiefs under which he can be empowered to speak on your behalf.'

'The Committee in England know that this will cost a good deal of money and they will make a collection from all your friends in England, but they hope and expect that you will very quietly collect from among your own people some money towards the cost, because this is your palaver and is not only for yourselves but for your children.'[1]

These attempts to involve Southern Rhodesian Africans did not succeed. Dube was not allowed to enter the colony. Harris was admitted but was unable to make any significant contact with African leaders. The Company administration was hostile and the British Government backed them in their refusal to allow Harris a free hand. 'The present time is especially dangerous,' the Colonial Office warned the Aborigines Protection Society in August 1914. Nothing should be done 'likely at this moment to excite the natives against the white man'. The High Commissioner had been instructed 'that the proceedings of the enquirers should be carefully watched and immediate steps taken to check any action which the High Commissioner may consider dangerous'. The APS were eventually allowed to brief lawyers to represent African interests before the Privy Council but they obtained no mandate to do so from Africans themselves nor was there any African contribution towards the expense.[2]

Representation of African interests before the Reserves Commission was even less adequate. Dr Palmer has shown that Africans were not encouraged to give evidence, as the Commission felt 'that it might do more

---

[1] 'Points to Bring before Chiefs', Rhodes House, Oxford, APS Papers, G 172.
[2] Correspondence between the APS and the Colonial Office, August 1914, ibid., G 495.

harm than good by questioning the natives upon a matter of which they were likely to misunderstand the real scope'! A few chiefs gave random evidence. Nor did Europeans who could be regarded as spokesmen for African interests make much of a showing. Many Native Commissioners and missionaries were away at the war fronts; most of the missionaries who remained were content with a general optimistic assumption that the African areas would at least not be decreased.

The actual recommendations of the Reserves Commission and to a lesser extent the Privy Council decision of 1919 came as a great shock to missionary and philanthropic defenders of African interests. The Reserves Commission recommended a complicated series of exchanges of land. It proposed that 5,610,595 acres be added to the Reserves and 6,673,055 acres be deducted. This meant an overall reduction of just over a million acres. The recovery of the lost million acres became the battle cry of radical missionaries. But more serious was the fact that most of the land removed from the reserves was rich agricultural land while most of the land added in exchange was of poor quality. Dr Palmer has shown how this operated to the disadvantage of the Shona in particular. Thus Kunzwi Reserve was reduced by two thirds; the land made available for European settlement was described by the Secretary of the Commission as 'ideal farming land'. Msana Reserve was reduced by a half and described as 'ideal farming country'. According to the Land Settlement Department which eagerly awaited the chance to lease and sell this reclaimed rich farm land to Europeans, 'the greater part of the land . . . recommended (for addition to the Reserves) . . . is of inferior quality and therefore more suited for native than for European occupation.' The recommendations of the Commission, accepted by both the Rhodesian and the British governments, were described as a final settlement of the land question.[1]

The Privy Council rejected the African case for ownership of the unalienated land. At the same time it rejected the Company's case and found the Lippert Concession invalid. It declared that the unalienated land belonged to the British crown by right of conquest. This decision in effect meant that the unalienated land would be in the hands of whoever succeeded the Company administration as the government of Southern Rhodesia and was a victory for the settlers.

These decisions had greatly worsened the present land position of Africans, especially in Mashonaland where there was more good land left to take away from the reserves but also in Matabeleland where the

---

[1] R. H. Palmer, *Aspects of Rhodesian Land Policy, 1890–1936*, p. 29.

position was especially unsatisfactory in the Gwanda and Wankie districts. Moreover the future was also compromised, both by the supposedly final character of the settlement and by the fact that all the unalienated land, out of which any future allocation to Africans would have to come, would be in the hands of a settler government. Radical missionaries decided that the settlement must be fought and fought by them, since 'ignorant as these folks are of the methods of political representation we cannot expect them to formulate any plea on their own behalf'.[1] This was the beginning of the alliance between missionaries like Arthur Shearley Cripps and John White with the Aborigines Protection Society and of the attempt to make the Southern Rhodesia Missionary Conference the trustee and spokesman of Africans. Cripps and White fought for the retention of the million acres and pressed at the same time for the setting up of areas for individual purchase by Africans outside the reserves.

This missionary campaign had some success. Cripps was particularly indignant about deductions of land from the Chiduku Reserve, where the only member of the Commission who visited it had made an admitted underestimate of population; in Inyanga where 'owing to a theory which the Commission held that no Reserve should march with the Portuguese border . . . the Reserve was rendered useless by the exclusion from it of a long strip of land where alone water was to be found'; and in Sabi where land flanking the proposed railway was to be removed from the Reserve. In March 1920 the High Commissioner persuaded the Company to agree to the restoration of the deleted land to Chiduku; to include the watered strip in Inyanga North; and to accept that the line of rail in Sabi should 'deviate to avoid kraals and burial places'. At the same time the Company agreed, in the face of Native Department pressure, to set up Reserves in Gwanda and Wankie.

But what of the response of Africans themselves? There was in fact little articulate response in Mashonaland, though the affected tribesmen who had to move out of the areas ceded to European occupation remembered it with bitterness for many years. But in Matabeleland a movement of protest on a wide scale began to develop. It was still the Ndebele who had the greatest grievance over land. Their situation was spelt out in June 1920 by the Superintendent of Natives, Bulawayo, in a letter which, long as it is, provides the essential background to the Matabele National Home movement.

'The report and findings of the Southern Rhodesia Native Reserves Commission have been carefully studied by the large number of people,

[1] White to Cripps, enclosed in Cripps to Colonial Secretary, 12 March 1923, N 3/16/9.

official and otherwise, interested in the very important matter of Native settlement . . . I wish to advance my own opinion that, through no fault (it would seem) of the Reserves Commission, the formerly dominant tribe of this Territory, through whom the first titles to the Territory were secured by whites (first by concession and later through conquest) are, of all tribes, now in the worst position in respect of land.

It is true that they were usurpers displaced by our usurpation but it is nevertheless an unfortunate fact that the premier native race whose organizing power and gift for government enabled them to impose their will on the minor tribes, and whose inherent character must inevitably establish their major influence for good or bad in the future development and happiness of our natives, should now suffer from an ever-increasing sense of dissatisfaction with the provision made for them in this regard. Their misfortune was in the first place their national predilection for the red and black loams which coincided with the so-called shale formation. The quartz reefs occur here and again coincide with the pasturage which their judgement informed them was the best for their cattle. Within a few months of the European occupation practically the whole of their most valued region ceased to be their patrimony and passed into the private estate of individuals and the commercial property of companies. The whole of what the term "nga pakati kew lizwe" (the midst of the land) conveyed became metamorphosed, although they did not early realize it, into alien soil, and passed out of the direct control even of the Government. (Not so the tribes of Mashonaland who were for the most part left in uncoveted possession of the granite soil preferred by them to all other.) In the native concept Government and Ownership of land are indivisible. That land on which people live, and have lived for generations can be purchased for money is a matter hard to be understood. White men of varied origin and race become in a day their landlords, their overlords, with power to dispossess and drive forth. To an aristocratic race the delegation of such power has appeared unseemly in many cases. The word "amaplazi" . . . meaning "farms" stands, it may be said, for almost all that is distasteful in our rule. Almost it stands for helotage and servitude to a chance-made master. "We owe alliegance to the Government, but we do not understand the amaplazi, and we do not like them. We ask that the Government may help us against the amaplazi" has been reiterated whenever and wherever any representative gathering has been asked to give utterance to grievances. I hope it is clear that the matter of land is an ever-present native grievance. It is an ever increasing one, too, which promises to become acute – which is bound to become acute – unless it is met . . .

I believe that of the Rhodesian native population between 400,000 and 500,000 are living on Reserves . . . upwards of 300,000 of the natives in Mashonaland occupy Reserves, irrespective of those on the newly created Reserves. On the Reserves in the Gwelo Division there are 40,000 and on those in the Bulawayo Division less than 40,000, and consequently less than thirty three per cent of the population. It is significant that more than one district in Mashonaland has, in itself, a larger number of Reserve-accommodated natives than the whole of the eight districts of the Bulawayo Division. In the count of acres Bulawayo Division shows well with upward of four million acres of Reserve lands, but the proportion of waste and waterless land is unduly high, and for the full utilization of the Reserves long journeys are involved to unknown parts reputed to be "untamed" and unhealthy. The districts of Umzingwane and Bulawayo have no outlet accepted by the natives as reasonable. The Matobo district has no adequate relief at hand, being similar in this respect to the Insiza district of the Gwelo Division.

I pointed out to the Chairman of the Reserves Commission how hardly the land situation bore on the Matabele by comparison with other tribes. At the time, however, of the Commission's investigations the wants of the people could not have been satisfactorily met, in my opinion, by converting unalienated land into Reserve land. The harm had been done, as I have already stated, within a short while after the occupation. . . . Two forms of relief are necessary. They seem to me to be not impracticable; both involve considerable expenditure as well as presenting difficulties in the way of organization. The one aims at the supply of water to the Gwaai, Nata and Semokwe Reserves. . . . The other lies in the acquisition, through purchase, of land contiguous to other Reserves.'[1]

'It must be granted,' thought the Superintendent, 'that well-founded and growing discontent by an important section of the community cannot safely or justly be ignored. . . . We have already seen attempts by agitators to make the natives discontented with their lot, the latest effort being by a section of the family of the late Chief Lobengula.' It was, indeed, through the activities of Lobengula's eldest son, Nyamanda, that the long accumulated Ndebele grievance over land found an effective expression.

Nyamanda succeeded in bringing together in a loose coalition the heirs of the rebel faction of indunas, the urban Ndebele 'progressives' and the various South African influences which were at work in Matabeleland. His

[1] S/N/Bulawayo to CNC, 1 June 1920, N 3/16/9.

was in some ways the first significant 'modern' political movement in Southern Rhodesia. Nyamanda was perhaps a surprising leader for such a movement. Unlike his younger brothers, Njube and Nguboyena, he had little education in the western sense. While they had been studying in South Africa he had been a prominent leader of the 1896 rising, regarded as the foremost figure amongst the younger and more militant rebel party and included until the peace negotiations with the Ndebele in the administration's list of proscribed ringleaders. But after Njube's death and Nguboyena's illness Nyamanda was the natural focus of Ndebele aspirations for a restoration of the monarchy, at least until such time as Njube's sons were of age. And he turned out to be quite an effective leader of the sort of movement that sprang out of the Matabeleland environment of the immediate post-war years. He was much better able to speak to the indunas than his younger brothers or his nephews would have been. Moreover he felt the general Ndebele grievance over land with acute personal emotion. He had first settled on land in the Insiza area; had moved from there when the European owner began to develop it; had then settled in the Bubi area and once again been told 'to remove by the Company owning the land'. At the same time Nyamanda was in contact with educated Christian Ndebele like the Wesleyan Ntando. He was on friendly terms with the Reverend M. D. Magkatho, the Ethiopian church leader, and sent his son to an Ethiopian school in South Africa recommended by Magkatho. He was also acquainted with some of the Fingo settlers, especially the Hlazo family. Out of all these connections the National Home movement was born.[1]

Nyamanda's first appearance as a protester was in a strictly personal rather than representative capacity. In October 1915 he met the Administrator to demand the return of his father's cattle now held by 'loyalist' indunas.

'I wish to complain of poverty and hunger. I am the son of the late King Lobengula whose indunas I see are living in affluence while I am poor and hungry. I see my father's dogs in enjoyment of his herds of cattle while I have nothing. I want my father's indunas to be told to give me my cattle; among other indunas I have Gambo in my mind, who possesses large herds of my father's cattle.'

To this the Administrator replied that 'by right of conquest' all cattle had passed to the Company who then 'handed a large proportion of those cattle to the actual holders with a full title of ownership in substitution for the terms on which they held them from your father. The younger

[1] For Nyamanda's land see A 3/18/10; A 3/18/18/6.

sons of your father were provided for and educated by the Government, your father's widows receive pensions to this day and so do you. . . . Had your father been victorious in the war that was waged he would not have sought advice from the surviving English as to the disposal of the booty that fell into his hands.'

Nyamanda: 'My father would not have starved the surviving Englishmen . . . I conclude then that my alliegance is not acceptable to the government.'

Administrator: 'That is not so. You have asked me to give what is not in my power to give.'[1]

Nyamanda remained scornful of the loyalist indunas. In 1919 he claimed that 'the Chiefs consulted by the Government were men of no importance; such men as Gambo and Sikombo were merely *abantu bogo konza* who knew nothing about the Matabele national affairs.' But he gradually came to link his own grievances with those of the Ndebele more generally. The recognition that he desired as Lobengula's eldest son could be combined with the general desire for a king; his grievances over land could be combined with a general protest about Ndebele wrongs and perhaps be remedied through a general redress of those wrongs. By 1918 Nyamanda was ready to put himself forward as the leader of a movement for restoration of the Ndebele National Home as well as of the Ndebele monarchy.[2]

The one thing lacking to begin such a movement – expert and modern political advice – was supplied by means of Nyamanda's contacts with the Hlazo family. In 1918 the Hlazos were employing the Congress lawyer, Alfred Mangena, to take up their own grievance over land. Mangena had been the first African barrister to practise in South Africa, thereby falsifying the predictions made by Secretary Inskipp to Nguboyena. He had been one of the conveners of the inaugural meeting of the South African Native National Congress in 1912. Hlazo now suggested that Mangena should make contact with Nyamanda and offer his legal and political services. 'It is true that I have visited the Royal family of Lobengula,' wrote Mangena to one of John Hlazo's sons, Jeremiah, in September 1918, 'but my anticipations have been a fiasco. I saw Nyamanda who received me with open arms and told me to prolong my stay till he returns from his excursions of great importance to him. However it was most unfortunate for me that I came back without seeing him and arranging matters concerning our programme. Be that as it may, I still cherish the hope of seeing him.' Mangena did see Nyamanda again and it was agreed

---

[1] Interview between Nyamanda and Administrator, 11 October 1915, A 3/18/18/6.
[2] Native Commissioner, Inyati, to S/N/Bulawayo, 29 July 1919, N 3/19/3.

that the lawyer should draw up a petition on Nyamanda's behalf. Before this could be done the watchful Administration pounced. 'Some time after Mangena left Salisbury,' noted the Administrator, 'several of the chiefs in the neighbourhood of the Fingo settlement reported that Mangena was endeavouring to stir up trouble among some of the Matabele living in that part of the country, and as the reports regarding Mangena received, on inquiry, from the Union Department of Native Affairs, were not satisfactory, Mangena was deported from the Territory.'[1]

Nyamanda's contact with Congress members was not broken, however. Mangena deputed his responsibility as Nyamanda's legal adviser to his colleague, Richard Msimang. Msimang was the son of the founder of the Independent Methodist Church of South Africa, had qualified as a solicitor in England, and was another of the conveners of the inaugural meeting of Congress. He had acted as chairman of the committee set up to draft the constitution of Congress. Mangena also recruited the Congress chaplain, Reverend Henry Reed Ngcayiya, leader of the Ethiopian Church of South Africa. Ngcayiya was in contact with Ethiopian leaders in Matabeleland, in particular with Nyamanda's friend, Magkatho and with Reverend Radasi of Bembesi, an ally of the Hlazos.[2]

In February 1919 Ngcayiya travelled to Rhodesia for 'family reasons – principally to see his cousin, the Reverend Radasi of Bembesi'. But his real purpose was to see Nyamanda and to help draft a petition. Ngcayiya had been chosen to go to Europe as one of the Congress delegation to Versailles and London and it was his intention to carry with him a petition setting out the grievances of the Ndebele people.

On 10 March 1919 an interesting gathering congregated at 'the house of Malipe' (Wesleyan catechist) in the Bulawayo location. Nyamanda was there, so was Lobengula's nephew Madhloli, so was another of Hlazo's sons, Titus, so was Ngcayiya. Out of this meeting emerged a document which is in some ways a landmark in Rhodesian African political history, a petition to the King of England in the names of 'Nyamanda and members of the family of the late king Lobengula and others of the Mandabele tribe in Matabeleland and Mashonaland jointly with the President, Ministers, Members and Adherences of the Ethiopian Church of South Africa, representing over twenty thousand members and adherences in South

---

[1] Mangena to Hlazo, 12 September 1918, N 3/19/4; Administrator to High Commissioner, 5 April 1919, A 3/18/18/6.
[2] For Mangena, Msimang and Ngcayiya see Mary Benson, *The African Patriots; the Story of the African National Congress in South Africa*, London, 1963, chapters 1 to 3.

Africa.' The Ndebele signatories spoke, it was claimed, 'for themselves and the people of the Mandabele tribe and others in Matabeleland and Mashonaland. . . . And the President, Members and Adherences of the Ethiopian Church of South Africa are the aboriginal inhabitants of South Africa.'[1] The petition ran:

'The Territory of Matabeleland and Mashonaland as it is well known, belonged to the late King Lobengula and the tribe over which he ruled without any dispute or challenge; but under questionable circumstances through British influence it pleased Her Gracious Majesty the late Queen Victoria to allow Great Britain's local representatives in South Africa to parcel out, sell, grant and otherwise dispose of the land in this Territory, treating the rights of the late King Lobengula and his tribe therein as of negligible importance, and without giving any appreciable pledge or safeguard as to the tribe's vested rights, and their future political status under the new circumstances. As a result thereof the children and relatives of the late King Lobengula, as well as the tribe of the Mandabele people, have no piece of land of their own individually or collectively; no place in which to dwell comfortably and freely in the country formerly held by them. The members of the late King's family, your Petitioners, and several members of the tribe, are now scattered about on farms so parcelled out to white settlers, and are practically created a nomadic people living in this scattered condition under a veiled form of slavery, they not being allowed individually to cross from one farm to another, or from place to place except under a system of permit or Pass, and are practically forced to do labour on these private farms as a condition of their occupying land in Matabeleland.

Your Petitioners are aware that Your Majesty's Imperial Government appointed a Commission in 1914 to enquire into and set apart land for Locations and Reserves to be used for the occupation of the Bantu people in Southern Rhodesia. . . . These Reserves, according to the evidence of the Chiefs in that Territory, are situate in unhealthy districts and consist of forests where wild beasts obtain; some places are dry and uninhabitable. And further it would appear that the recommendations of the Commission aim at securing a further reduction of the land that might otherwise be increased for the native inhabitants. . . .

Referring to Native Laws and treatment, Your Petitioners have experienced with great regret that High Commissioners and Governors General, who are the true representatives of your Majesty, have merely acted as disinterested spectators, whilst Responsible Government parties

[1] S/N/Bulawayo to CNC, 1 April 1919, A 3/18/18/6.

of various names and associations are interpreting the Laws in class legislation to suit their purposes. Your Petitioners pray that in case Rhodesia is granted any form of Government the Imperial Government take over the Aministration of Native Affairs in that Country in the same manner as is the case with regard to British Basutoland, British Bechuanaland and Swaziland.

Your Petitioners are further aware that the Judicial Committee of Your Majesty's Privy Council has found that the so-called unalienated land belongs to the Crown by reason of an alleged right of conquest and the de-thronement of the late King Lobengula. The right of jurisdiction of that alleged conquest, Your Petitioners do not seek to discuss here; but in the interest of right and justice, and in pursuance of the fact that the right of conquest (whether justified or not) is now repudiated by the civilized world, Your Petitioners pray that Your Majesty be pleased to hand back the so-called unalienated land to the family of the late King Lobengula in trust for the tribe according to Bantu custom, and the right of Chieftainship therein to be restored and acknowledged.

Having regard to the increasing population, and future purposes, the Reserves as recommended by the Commission of 1914 should be generously supplemented considering the fact of the unsuitability and inadequacy of the land. And that these areas be so developed in the interests and ultimate benefit of the peoples concerned, under their own self-government and self-developed and free from Passes and taxes and other restrictive regulations.'[1]

This petition was at once carried south by Ngcayiya accompanied by one of the Hlazo brothers. On the afternoon of 18 March Ngcayiya called on the Imperial Secretary to inform him that he was leader of 'a deputation from Rhodesian natives and that they would be leaving for England with the native deputation from the Union in the course of the next two days.' On 19 March Ngcayiya and Hlazo presented the High Commissioner with a copy of the petition; he warned them that the King would probably not receive them. Ngcayiya then sailed for Europe.[2]

In England Ngcayiya was given an interview by Amery of the Colonial Office on 5 June 1919. He was able to bring the petition to the attention of Africanist pressure groups in Britain – it was published in full, for example, in the *Africa and Orient Review*. In short, Ngcayiya succeeded in applying to Southern Rhodesian problems the technique of protest to the tribunal

---

[1] Petition to the King, 10 March 1919, A 3/18/18/6.
[2] High Commissioner to Resident Commissioner, 21 March 1919, A 3/18/18/6.

of British and world opinion that Congress had developed with regard to South Africa.

Meanwhile in Southern Rhodesia itself Nyamanda was busy following the petition up. The petition represented Nyamanda's desires expressed in Ngcayiya's polished language. Now Nyamanda himself wrote a series of letters in Sindebele, calling upon the indunas for support, which reveal him as something of a master of his own political idiom.

'At the beginning I greet thee my child,' ran a letter to induna Mafindo on 11 June 1919. 'Help me, Sitole, by passing on those documents on that subject. When your brother Sibindi was still existing, before his death, I send a word to him as the child of a great induna and said that he was to repeat it to all the izinduna of the nation. Well, I have not yet found his reply. Your word which I tell you ye children of the izinduna of my house is this: You know that all tribes were overcome by the white men but they have a place in which to remain happily. It is only here in this country where the people remain unhappy. Well the other tribes paid money and they pay for their country where they sit down in happiness; we pay our money and sit down on farms (of white men). As for me how do I come to speak of the country? I am unhappy. . . . Why is it that the paths that lead to me are overgrown with grass while you continue to pay each other visits over there? I want your reply seeing that you are the heads of the nation. The child that does not complain dies while working. Understand well men, I shall soon speak.'

'Well men, what do you say?' ran a circulated manifesto of the same date. 'We remain in a scattered state all the time. Even if people have been conquered may they not abide in one place? For myself I ask of you, ye owners of the Territory, inasmuch as ye are the nation. I do not say it is war, my compatriots, I only inquire. You also know that all black tribes in great numbers were overcome by the white people, but they have their piece of land to stay on happily. . . . We, forsooth, pay only for staying on white men's farms and for what reason?'

'Manxeba Kumalo, chief of Minyatini,' Nyamanda wrote on 10 August. 'I write this paper of mine to you all Chiefs of the Regiments . . . I say to you all and the Sky Stabbers, I, Nyamanda Lobengula Kumalo, whom you do not know, you Sky Stabbers all and your chiefs I do not see you, Oh People! I say to you all nations that have been conquered by the English, the Government gave them Chiefs to whom they pay their tax. Look at Khama! he has his country, and Lewanika, he has his plot. His country is settled well, and Mosheshe, he has his land. Also the son of Dinizulu has his country. All natives have their bit of ground where they pay their taxes. They pay taxes they know and are not like you who pay for what you know not. You do not know what is done with your money. . . . At the same time you undergo tribulation.'

'Ntola Kumalo,' runs the last of these remarkable letters, 'I say to you Big Chief of the Dynasty tell those other chiefs of yours, Kumalo, I have put in my word to the Big King, "Thunderer as he sits", "Silence let us hear", King George asking him what did father wrong to the Big Queen who never ends. This is where the matter is, with the King; I say tell me, our Sky Stabbers, if this that I am doing is not right you should tell me quickly if you do not agree. If you agree help me with "tickeys", people of my father, because I require money from you so that I can essay the road to cross the Ocean and go to the King over the Water in England and go and talk with the Big King George. I say to you, O People!, a child who does not cry out dies at labour. If you are happy in your present state let me know.'[1]

The Administration had believed that Nyamanda's pretensions were ridiculed by the majority of Ndebele but the response to these letters was widespread. Induna Ntola, for example, recipient of the last letter cited, at first professed opposition to the idea of a subscription. 'Yesterday however,' wrote the Native Commissioner Umzingwani in September, 'he sent two messengers to inform me that the natives of every other district have already given their help to Nyamanda and that there was such a growing feeling against his standing out that he had decided to follow the general lead. My own opinion is that he has all along been in favour of the movement, but was afraid to act secretly.'[2]

If Nyamanda had been as successful in his appeals to British opinion as he was in his appeals to Ndebele grievances, in fact, his movement would have been a formidable one. But even while Nyamanda, in ignorance of the Colonial Office reply to Ngcayiya, was collecting funds to follow up the petition, British policy had been laid down. The answer to Ngcayiya, delivered on 19 June 1919 was a flat rejection of the petition. The Colonial Secretary replied that 'there is no foundation for the statements' contained in the petition. 'As regards the request of the Petitioners that further land in Southern Rhodesia should be handed over for occupation by members of Lobengula's family and other natives . . . Lord Milner is satisfied that the recommendations of the Commission make ample provision for the present and future requirements of the natives.' (This answer was a good

---

[1] Files A 3/18/18/6 and N 3/19/4. I quote the Native Department translation of the original Sindebele.

[2] N. C. Umzingwani to S/N/Bulawayo, 27 September 1919, N 3/19/4.

deal more confident than the Rhodesian administration itself. While the British Government was standing by the 'ample provision' offered by the Reserves the Administrator's office was preparing a memorandum which began with the words: 'It appears certain that some of the Reserves as defined by the Native Reserves Commission will not be large enough to accommodate all the natives who might naturally be expected to live in such Reserves . . . considerable numbers of natives will eventually be unable to remain where they are or to find accommodation in the neighbouring Reserves.')[1]

Nyamanda's attempts to follow up the petition were firmly discouraged. Permission was refused for him to go down to see the High Commissioner. Permission was refused for Msimang to come up to see him. 'The action taken in preventing the entry of Msimang was taken in the best interest of the natives themselves.' In November 1919 Msimang was informed that any further 'representations or requests which Nyamanda may wish to make should be submitted through His Honour the Administrator of Southern Rhodesia.'[2]

For the moment, then, Nyamanda and his party were obliged to see if anything could be gained by approaches to the Administrator though they did not abandon their plans to renew the appeal to Britain. At the same time the Rhodesian authorities were wondering whether they should not buy Nyamanda off. They were worried by the possible extension of Ethiopian influence; they were surprised and disturbed by Ndebele response to Nyamanda. 'As the land difficulty becomes more acute,' wrote the Superintendent of Natives, Bulawayo, 'Nyamanda's policy of constantly harping upon it is certain to augment his following with the effect of consolidating native opinion in an undesirable manner.'[3]

The Native Department, who had not yet discovered the texts of Nyamanda's letters to the indunas, were inclined to believe that he was still motivated exclusively by personal grievance and that the whole complex of wider political references had been imported by Ngcayiya. Thus in March 1920 the Native Commissioner, Inyati, reported that Nyamanda had assured him 'that his association with the Fingos was entirely due to the unsettled state of his affairs owing to his not having any land'. 'Being landless and at the mercy of any purchaser of land was a difficult position and a bitter pill for a man of his standing to swallow, and that he felt that the

[1] Colonial Office to Ngcayiya, 19 June 1919, A 3/18/10; Administrative minute, A 12/1/16.
[2] Assistant Imperial Secretary to Msimang, 26 December 1919, A 3/18/18/6.
[3] S/N/Bulawayo to CNC, 1 June 1920, N 3/16/9.

Government had no sympathy or regard for his difficulties or troubles. That in these circumstances the Fingos had approached him, and told him that they were in a position to make representations which would lead to the country being divided between himself, as representing the Matabele nation, and the white inhabitants of the country. All that was necessary to the success of the scheme was that he should lend his name to it . . . he subscribed and signed the petition.' The Native Commissioner recommended that he be given ample and fertile land to prevent him from becoming a 'convenient focus for malcontents of all sorts'. The Chief Native Commissioner endorsed this view. Nyamanda was potentially dangerous. 'He is already in touch with educated natives in the Union of South Africa, and with their help and that of their sympathizers among the Matabele he may eventually become the leading spirit in a faction which, although not capable of being a menace, may be a nuisance.' He recommended that the Administrator meet Nyamanda and offer him a generous land grant.[1]

But before this meeting took place on 19 April the Administration had discovered that Nyamanda already was 'the leading spirit' in such a faction. They learnt more about his letters and his meetings with Ndebele leaders; they heard that he was calling for money contributions in order to purchase land. The Native Commissioner, Inyati, in a second interview with Nyamanda derived a quite different impression of his intentions.

'His idea is to get a large piece of country set aside for himself and any chiefs and people who will join him. He wishes to be recognized as the Head Chief of Matabeleland . . . He says that he wants this because there is no rest for him or his people as long as the land is being bought up by farmers. He admits that he is endeavouring to raise money with a view to purchasing land if he cannot get it by gift. The land he aspires to is not a matter of a farm or two but a very large area. . . . He says he is encouraged in raising the matter by an offer he alleged Mr Rhodes made to the Matabele Chiefs after the conquest. This offer, according to him, was that the land should be divided between the white people and the Matabele; the Matabele were to have all the rivers that flow into the Zambezi and the whites were to have those that flow to the Crocodile River. In other words the railway was to be roughly the dividing line.'[2] Obviously Nyamanda was not just the tool of Southern agitators.

The meeting with the Administrator now took on a different complexion; it was to be an occasion of threat and reprimand rather than of conciliation. In preparatory notes for the meeting the Superintendent of Natives sug-

---

[1] N. C. Inyati to S/N/Bulawayo, 16 March 1920, A 3/18/18/6.
[2] N. C. Inyati to S/N/Bulawayo, 31 March 1920, A 3/18/18/6.

gested that the Administrator should tell Nyamanda that he must 'give up definitely your hopes of being granted a large tract of country. You are not and never will be entitled to represent yourself as the official head of the Matabele nation . . . I further warn you to discontinue making demands upon my people for subscriptions towards the furtherance of your projects. You have no right to impoverish my people.' 'I think Nyamanda should be given clearly to understand,' wrote the CNC, 'that if he continues with his present course of action steps will have to be taken to restrict his movements, and if his activities assume a political aspect, that he will be removed from the Territory.'[1]

The interview of 19 April 1920 was, then, something of a show-down between the two sides. Nyamanda attended with his uncles Bidi and Makwelambila, brothers of Lobengula, his cousins Madhloli, Joyi and Mbamba, induna Maledanisa and twelve others. Nyamanda acted as spokesman:

Nyamanda : 'My heart tells me that I should live in the country where my father's people were. I have asked my people for money to buy land and it would be decided by Your Honour what land should be given to me. . . . The Shangani Reserve is a wild forest. I cannot live on the Gwaai Reserve. The Gwaai Reserve is waterless. . . . I have authority to get the money from the people; they themselves gave me the authority. I put the matter before the people and they agreed to buy land with their money. I am not exacting money from the people. I simply put the matter before them and it is for our mutual benefit to acquire this land. . . . All we want is for the Government to say 'This is a tract of land for Lobengula's people.' I went and put my case before foreign natives because I was afraid. We had made many complaints and we had expressed to you our grievances and they had not been redressed.'

He asked for land 'from Thabas Induna to Mwala kopjes, thence to Passe Passe, thence to the Magokweni Drift on the Khama River, then down the railway line, including all land watered by the rivers flowing into the Zambezi . . . I know that some of the land within these boundaries is already occupied. It is for Your Honour to decide how I am to acquire it. We will find the money. I do not want a sovereignty over a large tract of country. We wish to continue our alliegance to the Government and to live side by side with the white people. Our griev-

<hr />

[1] Notes by S/N/Bulawayo, April 1920, A 3/18/18/6; CNC to Secretary, Administrator, 9 April 1920. There are two versions of this letter. One which merely says that Nyamanda 'will incur the displeasure of the Government' is in file A 3/18/18/6. The version cited is in file N 3/19/4.

ances come from land congestion and the many white owners where we live who keep on turning us away and prevent our cultivating the land. The native Reserves are in the wilds; they are full of mosquitoes and wild beasts. I suggest that we follow the plan made by Mr Rhodes.'

Joyi: 'We are all contributing to the purchase of land: the whole nation is doing it: it is not Nyamanda only.'

The Administrator said that they could not acquire land already alienated. To this Nyamanda rejoined: 'That means we have to go into a far country to be finished off by disease and wild animals.'

Administrator: 'The question of so large a tract of country is out of the question.'

Nyamanda: 'Then my only course is to go on until I drop.'

Administrator: 'You are to understand that you have no responsibility for the wants of the people. You may speak for yourself and your own personal grievances. When your father was conquered the requirements of his people became my responsibility.'

Nyamanda: 'Must I go and live alone in a forest?'

Administrator: 'You have lived very well for the past twenty years as you are.'

Nyamanda: 'That is true but the present state of affairs was caused by force of circumstance and all the white people coming into the country.'

Administrator: 'You must accept the result of the war.'

Joyi: 'We are your children by right of conquest. Is it good policy for you to drive us away from you and not allow us to see you? Is it wise to drive your children away to the far away parts of the country?'

Haubasa: 'You accept responsibility for the people belonging to the overcome king and you must take care of the orphans.'

Bidi: 'We as earnestly desire this tract of land as our nephew Nyamanda. We don't want to be always troubling the Government: we are chased from farm to farm.'[1]

The meeting ended with the Administrator offering Nyamanda an area in the reserves to meet his personal needs and warning him from taking further his advocacy of the Ndebele grievance as a whole. But Nyamanda's heart was set on obtaining the Ndebele National Home. The very day after the interview with the Administrator the same delegation waited upon the Superintendent of Natives. They said they had been impressed by the Administrator's warning to go through official channels only. 'In this case they had done so and His Honour has told them that he was unable to accede to their request for a tract of land. They now asked for permission to

[1] Notes of interview of 19 April 1920, A 3/18/10.

send two or three delegates to England to present their request to the king.' Defiantly 'Nyamanda and Joyi claimed that their petition was made on behalf of the whole Matabele nation.' On 25 May they repeated this request to the Chief Native Commissioner. 'Nyamanda stated that he did not want land for his personal occupation but for the people of his late father.' The administration was beginning to appreciate Nyamanda's seriousness and persistence. In May also they obtained translations of his letters to the indunas. 'In my judgement,' commented the Superintendent of Natives, 'Nyamanda's motive is ambition – not necessarily a bad ambition *in se*; he may be a patriot – and these documents only confirm my belief that he has found in the land question the one grievance more likely than any other to find widespread support from the Matabele at large and a means of affecting unity.' 'I think he simply feels,' minuted the translator of the letters, 'that all the best land in the country has been taken by the whites and they have none to themselves. Possibly he dreams of segregation of the natives – with local option – or even perhaps Responsible Government!'[1]

At any rate Nyamanda's activities had now become a matter of widespread interest in Matabeleland. The Native Commissioner, Plumtree, reported that 'so many rumours have been flying around the district about Nyamanda, his doings and aspirations, the meetings he has held, the letters he has sent, messengers going to and fro; that he and some chiefs had met the Administrator in Bulawayo, that he had been severely reprimanded, that he had seen you (the Superintendent) and had been told to return in three weeks, and finally, as I heard a few days ago, that certain Chiefs and Headmen were going to him this week, I called in Chiefs and Headmen to meet me today'. The Native Commissioner told them 'that this intriguing with Nyamanda must cease . . . that if any Chief or Headman continued to visit Nyamanda . . . and to carry on further intrigues, that I should report such a one as unfit for the position of Chief or Headman'.[2]

Nyamanda had now become such a marked man, in fact, that it was thought best by his party to put forward Madhloli as an alternative spokesman. Madhloli had considerable land grievances of his own. He kept his considerable herds of cattle on land bought by one Dechow. Madhloli had originally gone to this land on the advice of the Native Department but now found that Dechow had the power to order him from the land and was anxious to do so. Madhloli, 'a man of substance and influence among the

[1] S/N/Bulawayo to CNC, 4 May 1920; W. E. Thomas to CNC, 11 May 1920, A 3/18/18/6.
[2] N. C. Plumtree to S/N/Bulawayo, 11 May 1920, A 3/18/18/6.

natives', then applied to purchase land for his own use but was refused by the Company. At the end of 1918, two months before Madhloli put his signature to the first petition, he had been warned by the Native Commissioner, Nyamandhlovu, that he must cease planting and move off the land as soon as possible. On 23 June Madhloli wrote to the Native Commissioner, Nyamandhlovu:

'As you know we have been . . . to see Mr Tailor and Mr Jackson about matter of Farmas Troubles and Mr Tailor told us about the native resevs to stay their. Know we asking you to give us the road to pass and see the High Commissioner at Pretoria. We been weting and thinkin that the Government will settle this matter. . . . Yesterday I sent rent money to Mr Deachow with my boy and Mr Deachow says I must go away from his farm. I don't see where I can go because you want to sent me to the dry place. If Mr Deachow want to kill me she can kill me.'[1]

The High Commissioner decided to see Madhloli in Cape Town in order to prevent the allegation that Madhloli had been refused access to him, but assured the Administrator that he would give Madhloli no encouragement or sympathy whatever. Nevertheless the opportunity of the Cape Town meeting excited Madhloli and Nyamanda. It was, after all, the first time that they had managed to get their case in person to a British representative. A second elaborate petition was prepared. Madhloli travelled with Titus Hlazo, the Wesleyan teacher Ntando, and a number of others. On 18 August they presented their petition in Cape Town. It opened with a farewell address to Buxton from 'the royal house of Nyamanda'.

'The Matabele tribe of Southern Rhodesia desire the High Commissioner to convey to the King their elastic allegiance to the British throne . . . and that in spite of the disabilities suffered by the King's loyal subjects under the Administration of Rhodesia, nothing, however discouraging, will induce the Matabele tribe to be averse to British protection.'

The petition then traversed much the same ground as its predecessor. It maintained that Colonial Secretary Milner, in his reply to the first petition 'upheld the report of the Commission without obtaining an expression of opinion from the Chiefs who are concerned in the matter'. The petitioners demanded that land be provided 'to appease the existing discontent between the people and the Rhodesian Government'. Madhloli's personal case was set out in detail.[2]

At the actual meeting the teacher Ntando acted as spokesman. He added some of the characteristic grievances of the Christian educated:

[1] Madhloli to N. C. Nyamandhlovu, 23 June 1920, A 3/18/18/6.
[2] Petition of 12 August 1920, A 3/18/18/6.

'The Administration under which we are domiciled is not a satisfactory government. When the Administration took over the government of the native part of the country they took all the chiefs to educate them, and we were very thankful to the Government that the sons of chiefs should be given the blessings of civilization. We should like the High Commissioner to carry on this principle of government. Ever since then we have not had anything and there has been no improvement whatever.' He asked once again for a king; without one 'there will always be discontent and confusion among the people'.

Once again, of course, these pleas met with a firm negative. The monarchy could not be restored. 'I must say to the Chief that the decision of the commission cannot now be altered and that if he declines even to look for land in the Reserves, I am afraid that I am not able to give him any further help.'[1]

It took considerable optimism to imagine after these repeated rebuffs that the tactic of appeal to Britain could ever succeed. But Nyamanda and Madhloli possessed what the Superintendent of Natives called 'a doggedness of purpose that may achieve more than is desirable'. They had failed to move Lord Buxton but Lord Buxton was leaving South Africa. They might fare better with the new High Commissioner, Prince Arthur of Connaught. Nyamanda collected more money, held more meetings and on 15 December 1920 signed, together with Joyi and Madhloli, an address of welcome to the new High Commissioner. The address, which had been drawn up by Msimang in Pretoria, asked that Nyamanda should go in person to present to the Prince the loyal greetings of the Ndebele nation.

'This appointment is an omen of good things and is hailed by the whole of the Matabele tribe with great satisfaction and rejoicings because her late Majesty Queen Victoria was not only a Protector and Friend of subject races like ourselves but was the symbol of Justice and Right for all peoples. As a descendant of that High and Noble ruler, the Mandabele tribe regard Your Royal Highness appointment as a signal proof that His Majesty's Imperial Government intends to live up to the ideals, traditions and policy of Your Royal Highness' Grandmother.'[2]

Events were now moving towards the confrontation of Nyamanda and a representative of the Imperial Government which he had so long desired. Connaught planned to visit Southern Rhodesia in 1921 and expressed his readiness not only to speak at a general indaba of indunas but also to meet Nyamanda. Nyamanda's interview with Connaught on 13 August 1921

[1] Notes of meeting of 18 August 1920, A 3/18/18/6.
[2] Petition of 15 December 1920, A 3/18/10.

was the final effort of the National Home movement. Nyamanda submitted another petition signed by himself and thirty-five others. In the name of 'the headmen and councillors of the people of the Amandabele and the Mashona and the other tribes in this Territory' it made the following pertinent demands:

'That the Native areas as a whole instead of being small patches here and there . . . be one large composite Reserve or Native territory of the size adequate enough to meet the needs of the present and future population of the peoples concerned under the chieftainship of the acknowledged son of the late Lobengula.

That the Government and Control of the said Reserve or Native territory be under the Imperial Government.

We learn that a welcome change of Government in this Territory of Southern Rhodesia is about to take place and in regard thereto we would most respectfully request Your Royal Highness as High Commissioner to make representations on our behalf to His Majesty's Government that the Natives of this country be given an opportunity to express their wishes in the Rights and the form of Government they would prefer and on the safeguards that might be made in their welfare and protection.'[1]

For a brief period after this interview there were euphoric hopes among Nyamanda's supporters. It was rumoured that the High Commissioner had been receptive; that he had given Nyamanda consent to make further collections of money; that he had encouraged Nyamanda to hope that his requests might be granted. Then on 23 October Connaught put his reply on paper with a request that it be published widely in order to scotch such hopes once and for all.

'I will be patient and tell you once again that you cannot now have another ruler besides the Government under which you live, to divide the rule of that land with the Government. Neither will the King take land from that Government, which has governed you wisely, to place it under a ruler of your own choosing. You are prosperous and you and your families and your increasing herds are not molested, and the King does not wish you to go back from this pleasant state of things, even though you are foolish and ask it.' The reserves 'are wide and fertile and are sufficient for the needs of the people for whom they are intended for very many years'. Africans who remained on European farms had 'chosen for themselves to experience conditions of life which must be different from what they would experience among their own people.' As for African anxiety over the change of government, 'I may tell you that

[1] Petition of 13 August 1921, A 3/18/10.

native interests are always watched over carefully by the King's Government.' It was 'wholly untrue' that he had permitted Nyamanda to collect money; the collection 'has caused me grave displeasure' and the money must be returned.[1]

The publication of this reply marked the end of Nyamanda's movement. Eccentric Europeans, like J. V. Walston, might still see him as a menace but the administration did so no longer. In October 1921 Walston wrote to say that 'Nyamanda and Madhloli . . . are raising and obtaining money among the natives for the purposes of establishing a black king and presumably a blacker kingdom. . . . Nothing would be easier than for Madhloli to start off from here with five hundred natives, join his cousin Nyamanda at sawmills or Ngusi with the Umguza natives and be outside of Bulawayo in forty-eight hours from a thousand to fifteen hundred strong. The easiest way to nip these various schemes in the bud is to send a patrol to gather in their fire-arms, put Nyamanda and Madhloli in a quiet place until the general tenor of the world becomes a bit more peaceful and sternly impress upon the others the necessity of not interfering with white people or their property.' But the Native Department – 'weak-minded, well-meaning willy-nillies' to Walston's mind – advised against any prosecution of Nyamanda. The publication of the answer of Queen Victoria's grandson combined with the rapid move towards settler control of the Rhodesian government would be enough to end any hopes of success for Nyamanda's politics of protest.[2]

The ambiguities and weakness of Nyamanda's movement are obvious enough. Nyamanda had not the slightest right to claim to speak in the interests of the Shona; his movement was obviously one of Ndebele nationality feeling. The Native Department were also right to say that he did not speak for all the Ndebele; for every man attracted to him by his position on land another was alarmed at the thought of the use he might make of his power if the kingship were revived. There seemed to be obvious ambiguities in the support given by Christian Ndebele teachers and Congress lawyers for what appeared in general a 'reactionary' policy. The detailed solutions offered by Nyamanda were also impossible or if possible undesirable. There was no doubt that the Ndebele needed more land and that land should have been bought back from white owners, particularly from the large investment companies who were not developing their land in any case. But the idea of the one coherent Native Territory would have run into great African opposition had it ever been attempted. Yet with all

---

[1] Connaught to Nyamanda, 23 October 1921, A 3/18/10.
[2] J. V. Walston to Administrator, 15 October 1921, A 3/18/11.

D

these reservations Nyamanda's movement was by no means absurd. It did give expression to essential African demands for land, for consultation of their interests. In its ambiguities it was characteristic of many African political movements of the same period rather than unique or eccentric. At the same time, for example, the Lozi paramount, Yeta III, was contesting the Company's claims to land ownership in Northern Rhodesia, demanding direct British protection of Barotseland and asserting the African right to be heard over the change of government. Yeta had the support of educated and progressive Lozi migrants throughout Southern Africa, including those in the towns of Southern Rhodesia. He had the advice of South African politicians. He was backed by the Aborigines Protection Society. Yet Yeta had no right to speak in the name of all the people even of North-Western Rhodesia. His legal position, at any rate on the land issue, was almost as weak in view of Lewanika's concessions as was Nyamanda's in view of Lobengula's defeat. Yeta was a determined enforcer of royal privilege and power inside Barotseland, an autocrat as well as a 'progressive'. The same sort of pattern emerges from the alliances made in South Africa between the lawyers and politicians of Congress and the paramounts of Zululand and Swaziland.

Movements of this sort appear to have constituted throughout southern Africa a necessary phase in the development of African politics. I have argued elsewhere that Yeta's movement was a significant stage in the African political history of Northern Rhodesia. In the same way it will not do simply to label Nyamanda's movement as 'reactionary'. Nyamanda's failure was so complete not so much because of the flaws of his movement but because in Southern Rhodesia the tactic of appeal to the British Government could not be fruitful. Nyamanda could never under the most favourable colonial circumstances have achieved everything he wanted; but in different colonial circumstances he might well have achieved significant concessions on land and representation. Many of Yeta's demands were realized – though by no means all – because of one simple contrast between Northern and Southern Rhodesia. When Nyamanda began his movement both territories were under Company administration. But as his movement came to an end the political situation in the two Rhodesias was a sharply contrasting one. As the Company prepared to withdraw from its governmental responsibilities, the British Government prepared to take over the administration of Northern Rhodesia. Yeta was speaking to the power directly responsible for the government of his people. In Southern Rhodesia, however, it had been effectively determined very many years before that when the Company went the political future of the Colony would be determined by the vote of the white settlers. The only choice was between settler control of a separate so-called 'Responsible Government' in Southern Rhodesia; or settler control of Rhodesia within the Union of South Africa. Nyamanda was appealing to Britain just at the time when responsibility for land and law was being handed over to the settlers.

FIVE

The Politics of Participation

THE RHODESIAN BANTU VOTERS' ASSOCIATION

In the early 1920s the issue which dwarfed all others in Southern Rhodesian politics was the future of the Colony when Company administration came to an end in 1923. Rhodesian whites were divided into two active political groupings, one campaigning for Responsible Government, the other for Union. Africans reacted to this situation in a variety of ways. At one level Nyamanda, advised by the South African National Congress, petitioned for direct British control of the African areas and against either Responsible Government or Union. At another level the Mwari priests of Matonjeni cave sent orders to Africans in western Mashonaland to store grain and prepare themselves for another struggle between the British and the Boers. At yet another level a Watch Tower preacher in Bulawayo told his audience in 1923 that the millennial crisis, in which the white world would tear itself apart, was coming 'some time between next September and November of this year', the months in which the Responsible Government administration was to take office. 'The time is at hand,' he proclaimed. 'The end of the world is near.'[1]

Other Africans, very different indeed in their experience and attitudes from the Watch Tower preacher, also believed in 1923 that one political world was coming to an end and another beginning. Watching developments, a group of the best educated and most articulate Africans in Southern Rhodesia concluded that it no longer made sense to petition the High Commissioner or the King. Power was to be firmly in the hands of local whites. In 1922 they inaugurated a move away from the politics of protest and towards the politics of participation.

It is difficult to achieve a sympathetic understanding of the assumptions and tactics of these men without looking briefly at the over-all situation. Most Africans and most of the missionaries who assumed the responsibility for speaking for Africans knew what they would have *liked* to succeed Company rule – direct British colonial administration. That was what

[1] CID reports on the preaching of Kunga, N 3/5/3.

Nyamanda had been asking for; it was what radical missionaries like Arthur Shearley Cripps kept coming back to in the early 1920s; it was what most of the leaders of participant politics would themselves have wished. But it was just not a practical possibility. For decades the British Government had been committed to allowing the white settlers to decide the fate of Southern Rhodesia. The only real choice, as Cripps' friend and ally in Britain John Harris, of the Aborigines Protection Society, kept on telling him was that between Union and Responsible Government.

Both for white missionaries and for African politicians this was a very difficult choice to make. On the one hand they disliked the native policies of the Union. On the other hand they suspected the motives of the Responsible Government party and believed that settler rule in Rhodesia would be harsher and more discriminatory than Company rule. The dilemma of Africans in such a situation is given point by the agonies of decision experienced by the better informed and more influential missionaries.

Men like Cripps and John White found themselves presented by their philanthropic ally, Harris, with an argument of remorseless political realism. To Harris there was only one choice. The Union would make no change in its native policies if Southern Rhodesia joined; nor would Britain so much as try to persuade it to do so. But settler Responsible Government could only be obtained on British terms as set out in the 1921 Buxton Commission report. If the settlers voted for Responsible Government they would have to accept British power to veto discriminatory legislation, British control of appointments to the Native Department, the entrenchment in the new Constitution of the Reserves and of the right to buy land anywhere outside them, and the continuance of a theoretically colour-blind franchise. These preserved whatever was desirable from the old system; in Harris' eyes they also represented a considerable advance over the old system because African land rights had never before been constitutionally entrenched. Responsible Government was clearly the choice that had to be made. And once it was made, Harris argued, more might be gained. The struggle between those who desired Responsible Government and those who wished to join the Union was a fierce one. In Britain at any rate most people expected the Unionists to win. The formidable propaganda machine of the Company was at work on the Unionist side. Responsible Government men needed allies. Harris was prepared to offer them his alliance; to throw the weight of the Aborigines Protection Society on to the Responsible Government side; and to bargain for concessions in return.

Harris carried this strategy through, and managed to win the very reluctant assent of Cripps and White, who had a much clearer and more accurate notion of what Responsible Government would really be like. He discussed possible reforms with the Responsible Government leader, Charles Coghlan, and was encouraged by Coghlan's readiness to re-open the land question. In 1923, indeed, Harris was very optimistic that large concessions would be made by a Responsible Government administration which he believed would wish to seek for social stability and long-term economic solutions rather than to pursue an exclusively short-term financial interest as Harris believed the Company had done. But Harris emphasized to Cripps and White that it was not possible to demand too much from the Responsible Government party before the voting took place. After all they had to sell their solution to the white electorate against the advantages of Union.[1]

Abraham Twala and the Founding of the Rhodesian Bantu Voters Association

Among the Africans of Southern Rhodesia there were some who saw the situation in much the same way as Harris. Union was at all costs to be avoided. On the other hand something might be gained by offering support to the Responsible Government party in return for significant concessions to African opinion. The philosopher of this strategy of participation was the Zulu Anglican teacher, Abraham Twala. Twala was an admirer of the John Tengo Jabavu tradition of Cape politics. This tradition had just been eloquently re-stated by John Tengo's son, Professor D. D. T. Jabavu, in a biography of his father. Jabavu, wrote his son, had taught Cape Africans:

'What the word vote meant;

what its importance was;

how it should be used;

how its strength lay in combined action;

how the vote built up a parliamentary party;

how it thus constituted a powerful weapon in their hands to determine the policy of the Ministry with regard to legislation affecting Native interests; how the Native vote frequently held the balance of scales in Government majorities;

[1] I base this account on the very full correspondence between Harris and Cripps and White in the files of the Aborigines Protection Society, Rhodes House, Oxford. Mrs Rachel Whitehead is working on this and other APS material and her dissertation will throw very important light on many aspects of Rhodesian political history.

how it was thus a modern substitute for the antiquated assegai and warfare.'[1]

These were lessons that Twala aspired to teach Rhodesian Africans. He urged that resistance by force was out of the question. He argued that indigenous protest and appeals to Britain had never had any effect. The example of the South African National Congress was thus not a helpful one for Rhodesian Africans and its influence should be resisted. But the Jabavu strategy should at least be tried. With a theoretically colour-blind franchise Southern Rhodesia seemed to offer at least the potentials of the Cape situation. In March 1922 Twala set out his diagnosis of the situation in a letter to the *Rhodesia Herald*.

'It is unfortunate that the important Closer Union delegation entrusted with the destiny of Southern Rhodesia did not see the wisdom of including in their personnel any one from the Native Affairs Department to represent the interests of His Majesty's loyal subject races, whose future very much hangs in the balance. I sincerely believe that Southern Rhodesia has one of the finest Native Administrations south of the Zambezi, if not the finest. It is no longer necessary to think about this since the Mission has gone.

I wish, however, to make a few observations. Presumably the natives are brooding over the so-called 'Imperial Reservations of Native Affairs' as per the recommendations of Viscount Buxton's Committee, and the Responsible Government Draft Constitution. I am afraid that they are living in a paradise of fools. History repeats itself. As the result of the obnoxious Natives Land Act (of South Africa) 1913 a very influential delegation was sent to England to ask His Majesty the King to veto the Act. . . . The deputation was distinctly and emphatically told to return to the Union of South Africa and have matters adjusted and that "the Imperial Government cannot interfere in internal matters after the granting of Responsible Government"! All other subsequent deputations met at Downing Street with the same fate – "a wild goose chase".

Therefore, whatever constitution will be acceptable to the inhabitants of Southern Rhodesia (R. G. or Union) will mean vesting powers with the colonists. We want a platform, not of planks. We want a constructive policy agreeable to all sections of the community. Experience has taught us that our salvation does not lie at Downing Street. I strongly advise our native fledglings in Southern Rhodesia indulging in politics to find out and

---

[1] D. D. T. Jabavu, *The Life of John Tengo Jabavu editor of 'Imvo Zabantsundu'*, *1884–1921*, Lovedale Institution Press, 1922, pp. 63–64.

make their friends in Southern Rhodesia. When this has been done we shall see what the harvest shall be.'[1]

Twala then proceeded to plan a new organization which would bring together those Africans who already had the vote, encourage others to obtain it, and offer the organized support of the African electorate to those white politicians or parties prepared to give guarantees of a liberal native policy. He was able to recruit as organizers of the inaugural meeting two prominent figures in Ndebele urban society. One was an Ndebele schoolteacher from Gwelo, Ernest Dube, admitted by the Native Department to be 'an exceptionally intelligent man'. Dube was prepared to act as Secretary of the new organization. The other was Thomas Maziyani, a Basuto migrant to Rhodesia who had completely identified himself with the Ndebele and was accepted by them as a member of the Enhla caste. Maziyani had acted as Secretary of the Amandabele Patriotic Society in 1915; later he supported the Nyamanda movement. He was a man of substance. In 1922 he was working as Chief Messenger on the Beira and Mashonaland and Rhodesian Railways. He owned a nine-acre farm outside Bulawayo which he had bought in 1914 for £150. He had put up a £200 house there and employed a man full time to work the farm. He was ready to act as Chairman of the Bulawayo branch of the new association.[2]

Dube and Maziyani linked the new movement with previous Ndebele political movements. Twala's other important recruits were all 'alien' Africans. The Fingos had been the dominant group in Cape participant politics and it was not difficult for Twala to obtain the support of Fingo leaders in Southern Rhodesia. 'Chief' Garner Sojini, the very model of the successful African farmer, agreed to become national Chairman of the new body. In this way Sojini, whose increasing discontent with the white alliance was described in Chapter Three, moved from Fingo politics to territorial politics, bringing with him his able sons and many of his Fingo followers. Another important Fingo recruit was the Apostolic Faith Mission teacher, Martha Ngano, who was to become the moving spirit of the whole enterprise. Martha had come to Rhodesia in 1897. She and her husband lived in the Brickfields area of Bulawayo where they owned a house. Martha was widely known in Matabeleland mission and administrative circles as the most forceful and 'advanced' African woman in the colony. Finally Twala was able to recruit Zacharia Makgatho, son of the

[1] *Rhodesia Herald* 3 March 1922. The African National Congress delegation of 1913 referred to by Twala had also endeavoured to take up the question of Southern Rhodesian land.

[2] S/N/Bulawayo to CNC, 23 May 1924, S 84/A/260; evidence of Maziyani, Morris Carter Commission, ZAH 1/1/2, pp. 683 to 693.

Basuto Ethiopian church leader, Reverend Makgatho. Zacharia, who lived on his father's farm at Riverside, Bulawayo, agreed to act as Treasurer.

Through these recruits Twala's new organization could tap many of Southern Rhodesia's African political traditions, the tradition of the Union Bantu Vigilance Association and of Fingo politics, the tradition of Bulawayo township politics and of the Matabele Home movement, the tradition of Ethiopianism. Although its strategy was quite differently conceived Twala's movement was not planned as in any sense a rival to the Nyamanda grouping. It was rather seen as a successor and Nyamanda himself soon became a supporter. But while he was able to link up with the politics of Matabeleland Twala was either unable or unwilling to bring 'progressive' Shona into his movement. He lived in Mashonaland and taught among the Shona but he did not regard them as the stuff of modern politics. In 1925, for instance, he went on record as believing that there was a clear distinction between modernizing Ndebele and conservative Shona, at least in terms of land purchase and progressive farming. 'One thing I am sure of is that the Matabeles would buy the farms, but the indigenous natives would not understand. The indigenous natives are simply looking forward to being given a Reserve and staying under communal tenure. They just want to be together.'[1]

Despite this Twala intended his new association to be in the fullest sense territorial. It was to speak to the political centre on behalf of all Africans. He tried hard to make its inaugural meeting an impressive success. He invited to it a representative of the Asian community, M. S. Pillay of the Rhodesia British India Association, a representative of liberal European opinion, Reverend J. F. Niebuhr, and the Superintendent of Natives, Gwelo, to represent the Native Department. He also invited two members of the Legislative Council, and of the Responsible Government Party, Major Boggie and Douglas Jones, to meet and answer questions from black voters in the way that had become familiar in the Cape but had never before happened in Southern Rhodesia. His letter of invitation to these white politicians spelt out very interestingly his intentions for the meeting.

'The meeting to be non-political but to get as much enlightenment on our legitimate rights as loyal citizens of the British Empire.

To cooperate as much as necessary with the present MLCs who carried out RG propaganda and get their views on different unwritten laws of Southern Rhodesia now operating on natives irrespective of status (specific cases to be adduced).

[1] Evidence of Abraham Twala, Morris Carter Commission, ZAH 1/1/1, pp. 427–438.

Grant in aid to schools for natives – Govt. Notice No. 265, 27 May 1921 – Order D, Schools for Natives by Abraham Z. Twala, critical analysis of the order with a view of bringing same to notice of MLCs.

Enrolment of new eligible Native voters in order to be ready for next election.

To bring to the notice of the Natives at large the necessity of Rhodesia carrying out the Responsible Government as the RG has promised to carry out British justice as heretofore.

Other matters and the formation of the 'Constitutions'. 'I wish the Natives to understand', he concluded, 'that we don't want a political organization but a meeting that will bring about the co-operation of the Europeans with us in all matters affecting our people. I am especially interested in the education of the Natives, first and foremost on industrial lines.'[1]

Twala, in short, was attempting the Harris strategy and offering his support to the Responsible Government Party. Despite his protestations the concept was the most explicitly and consistently political that had yet been voiced by Africans in Southern Rhodesia. Twala's new organization was to be no mere welfare association but a co-ordinator of African voters. But when the inaugural meeting of the Rhodesian Bantu Voters' Association, as the new body was to be called, took place in Gwelo on 20 January 1923, Twala was not in fact there. He was seriously ill but he had sent Ernest Dube notes of 'how I think the meeting should be formed'. Maziyani was not there either. He had spent all his money in support for Lobengula's grandson, Rhodes, on his recent visit to Bulawayo and could not afford to travel. Garner Sojini was present, however, and took the chair. Dube acted as Secretary and Martha Ngano came from Bulawayo. These three, together with Garner Sojini's son, Stuart, were the only voters present but the meeting was attended by numbers of African non-voters.

The meeting began with the reading of messages of support. Then a list of grievances was presented to the two MLCs who were called upon to comment. 'An assurance was asked that under the change of government there should be no restrictions on the purchase of land by natives in any area. It was stated that in the past natives had not been allowed to purchase land by the British South Africa Company.' The meeting requested 'the reduction in the number of passes to be carried by registered voters', 'better education facilities, particularly higher education', and 'modification in the franchise qualifications' so that the literacy test might be taken

[1] Twala to Boggie and Jones, 15 January 1923, S 84/A/260.

in the vernacular rather than in English. The most detailed criticism came in Twala's memorandum on schools which charged that grants for African education were grossly inadequate, that teachers were ill-qualified and standards low, that there should be regular official inspection as in white schools, and asserted that 'natives should be granted the same facilities as coloured people for higher education'.[1]

Jones and Boggie then spoke in answer to these requests, all of which were clearly conceived very much in the interests of the progressive élite. They gave no assurances and treated some of the requests cavalierly – Boggie for example meeting objections to passes by pointing out that 'passports were still necessary for Europeans in many countries'. But the mere fact of their exposure to African questioning was felt to be important. The meeting then concluded with a resolution to form an association; a committee was appointed to draw up a Constitution which was to be submitted to a general meeting in July 1923. And on the instructions of the organizing committee Ernest Dube wrote to *Abantu Batho* to announce the formation of the Rhodesian Bantu Voters' Association.

'Perhaps our brothers in South Africa', wrote Dube, 'would like to hear that in Rhodesia the year 1923 will be a year of events beyond past events, for on 20 January 1923 the brown voters of Rhodesia formed a Union known as the Rhodesian Bantu Voters' Association to aim and strive for the betterment of the brown race in school and in government. Today Rhodesia expects to be visited by Professor Jabavu (B.A. London). All this gives hope that he will go to Rhodesia on 11 and 12 July and on Founders Day the Rhodesian Bantu Voters Association will hold its first meeting after its institution on 20 January. . . . The brown people of this country are very backward, but we hope that with the help we will get from our brothers in the South of Africa things will right themselves.'[2]

The birth of the RBVA received a good deal of attention from the outgoing Company administration. They took Twala's comments on education surprisingly seriously. Indeed his memorandum triggered off a full-scale debate on the adequacy or otherwise of financial support for African schools. The Director of Education completely endorsed Twala's view that a grant of three shillings per pupil was quite inadequate. 'When it is considered that in European schools the expenditure per head on school requisites alone in the junior classes of the schools (corresponding to the classes in which the natives are usually found) average about fifteen shillings a head, it will be seen how inadequate the grant is. It is utterly

[1] S/N/Gwelo to CNC, 24 January 1923, S 84/A/260.
[2] Dube's letter is in file A 3/18/11.

impossible to expect any substantial progress in native third class schools so long as the grant averages only three shillings per pupil enrolled in them. I do not think that a very high standard of education can be looked for in native teachers until the grants allowed are sufficient to provide them with a wage at least equal to that of the native artisan working in or around the towns.' The Secretary to the Treasury pointed out that grants had in fact been rising. £15,000 had been paid in 1921–2, £18,000 was budgeted for 1923–4. 'I do not think we can go any faster than this.' Finally the Administrator himself concluded the discussion. 'An out-going Government should not be asked to pledge its successors to an increase of expenditure.' Ironically the only outcome of the discussion was an instruction from the Chief Native Commissioner to Native Department officers that although the Education Department could not afford inspection of African schools the Native Department should visit them as regularly as possible since 'left to themselves' they might 'disseminate doctrine of a subversive nature'. As so often the interests of security took precedence over those of development. But although Twala had not achieved anything concrete he had at least received a good deal of attention from the outgoing Company administration. It remained to be seen whether the MLCs of the Responsible Government Party for whom his memorandum had been intended had paid as much attention to it and whether the RBVA would be taken as seriously by the Company's successors.[1]

Professor D. D. T. Jabavu did not come to Rhodesia to preside over the July meeting of the RBVA. But the meeting was attended by 'a good number of natives' and under Sojini's chairmanship the draft Constitution was adopted and resolutions passed. The motto of the new Association was: '*Not by might, nor by power, but by my spirit saith the Lord of Hosts.*' The Association was to be:

'a constructive and co-operative society, formed by persons desiring to work for the general uplift of the Bantus irrespective of tribe and status. We pledge ourselves to conserve the rights of our people and do all in our power to develop their dormant potentialities by means of practical education and industry . . . We believe that justice must be done to our people and their legitimate rights respected; we believe that only by means of industrial education, a test of Christianity, our people will rise gradually in the scale of civilization and that religion must be fostered to grow as the true foundation of a man's character.'

The objects of the Association were:

'To safeguard the interest of the Bantu people domiciled in Rhodesia.'

[1] Correspondence on grants, 1923, S/84/A/260.

'To be the medium of expression of representative opinion and to formulate a standard policy on Native Affairs for the guidance of the Parliament.'

'To endeavour to secure co-operation with the "Powers that be" and all
others interested in the advancement of the Bantu peoples without
laying an embargo in their way.'

'To establish confraternity among Bantu people and co-operation and
understanding with the ruling race.'

These objects were to be achieved by 'means of constitutional resolutions', 'peaceful propaganda', and 'by appealing to the highest tribunal
constitutionally and distributing literature and holding lectures educating
the public as well as the Bantus'. Similar work on behalf of the special
interests of African women was to be undertaken by a Native Women's
League which would strive for 'the native women's uplift morally, socially
and educationally and advise on all matters affecting the sex'.[1]

Nathan Shamuyarira has described this as 'a mild constitution, written
by an obedient group of educated men'. Yet in the Southern Rhodesian
context the whole concept of the RBVA was a startling innovation. It was
all very well for Twala to say that he did not intend 'a political organization'
but the essential point of the RBVA was African participation in politics.
The general meeting of July 1924 certainly did not in effect pin all its hopes
on resolutions and propaganda but also aspired to affect policy through the
use of the vote. They did not only declare their intention to consult 'the
Native Affairs Department, MPs and Missionaries' but also called upon
MLCs to make a 'Circuit . . . for the purpose of explaining to Natives laws
that will govern the country under RG in so far as the Natives are concerned.' And they called again for simplification of the registration procedure so that more Africans might have the vote in the forthcoming elections
for Rhodesia's new government. Richard Gray's comment would seem
valid. 'Taken by themselves,' he writes of the resolutions of the January
and July meetings, 'these requests could hardly be described as extremist
or revolutionary, but the movement as a whole seemed to strike at the very
basis of European policy. For the first time Africans in Southern Rhodesia
were asking for a greater share of the white man's world; their organization
was founded on the political system of the Europeans, through which they
sought to exercise their rights effectively; they were turning their backs
on the shattered traditional basis of society and the life of the Reserves,
and they faced the challenge of an 'open society'. In all this they were

[1] S/N/Bulawayo to CNC, 23 May 1924; Ernest Dube to S/N/Gwelo, 14 July
1923, S 84/A/260.

strengthened by a new spirit of racial solidarity, a consciousness of potential African unity spreading in from South Africa and indeed possibly even from the United States.'[1]

The Bulawayo branch and the leadership of Martha Ngano

The challenge implicit in the RBVA became sharper in 1924. In that year Twala, whose influence on the Constitution was paramount even though he did not take office, returned for a period to South Africa. So also did his close friend, Ernest Dube, who went south for further education. Effective initiative in the RBVA was exercised from early 1924 onwards by the two main figures of the movement in Bulawayo, Thomas Maziyani and Martha Ngano. Martha succeeded Dube as Secretary. At the annual general meeting in 1924, which was held in Bulawayo, Maziyani presided as Acting President. The main reason for this shift of power was that the Bulawayo branch of the Association was the only strong and active one. No branch had been formed in Salisbury or anywhere else in Mashonaland. The Gwelo and Selukwe branches under Garner and Stuart Sojini were numerically weak. The Bulawayo branch, however, claimed one hundred members in May 1924, sixteen of them being voters. Moreover it proved possible to carry the RBVA into the Matabeleland countryside partly because of Martha Ngano's personality and energy and partly because of the links between the new movement's leadership and the earlier Nyamanda movement. By July 1924 there were RBVA branches at Plumtree, Mzing-wane, Umguza, Nyamandhlovu and other places within the sphere of activity of the Bulawayo branch. Nyamanda attended some of Martha's country meetings and expressed support for the RBVA; later both he and Madhloli joined the Association. At one point the Chairmanship of the RBVA was offered to Rhodes Lobengula, educated grandson of the last Ndebele king, but he was prohibited from accepting the position by the Rhodesian government.

As initiative shifted to Bulawayo so the tone of the RBVA altered. This was partly because of the increasing disillusionment of Martha Ngano and Thomas Maziyani with the effects of Twala's strategy. That strategy was hampered by two main flaws. One was that the RBVA had come into existence too late for it to be able to exercise any effective influence on the choice between Responsible Government or Union with South Africa. By the time the Association was formed the voters of Southern Rhodesia had already expressed their preference for Responsible Government in the

[1] N. Shamuyarira, *Crisis in Rhodesia*, London 1965, p. 31; Richard Gray, *The Two Nations, Aspects of the Development of Race Relations in the Rhodesias and Nyasaland*, London, 1960, p. 161.

referendum of October 1922 and there was no doubt in anybody's minds that the Responsible Government party would win the coming elections. If the RBVA had emerged earlier and been able to impress British liberal opinion that it was representative its requests might have been taken more seriously. The Aborigines Protection Society complained in the early 1920s that its task of safeguarding African interests in Rhodesia was hampered by the lack of any African political body with which to work. But Twala had foresworn the idea of being able to affect Rhodesia by means of communication with England and he made no effort to contact the APS. Within the context of purely Rhodesian politics and in 1923 the RBVA did not have much to offer in return for concessions. In particular, and this was the second and fatal flaw, it had very few votes to offer. In the year that Twala developed his strategy there were less than thirty African voters on the Southern Rhodesian rolls. Nor was there any possibility of increasing the number very quickly. In the hey-day of participant politics in the Cape the rivalry between Boer and Briton had resulted in the enfranchisement of large numbers of Africans as a balance against the Boer. At this period Cape Africans were able to register for the vote on the basis of their share in communally held tribal property and with no very stringent education test. The RBVA kept on asking for similar registration regulations in Southern Rhodesia but there was no chance of getting them. The RBVA found that many people whom it brought forward to register for the vote failed either because of the property or the education qualification. Martha Ngano's husband was one of these. He qualified in every other respect but failed because he could not write fifty words in English, though literate in the vernacular. The Native Administration thought that Martha had become 'the live wire' of the RBVA partly because 'her husband failed to secure registration'.[1]

Certainly Martha decided that if the RBVA were to get anywhere it must be able to show that it had at least the potentialities of power. She pressed harder – though perhaps without much hope – for a simplification of voting requirements. In April 1924 she sought an interview with the Governor 'to discuss franchise questions'. When this was refused she wrote on 7 May to the Governor:

'The question of the franchise is very hard and most difficult to us natives. (1) We must have the wages of £100 a year whereas very few who get the wages of £50 a year. (2) We must write 50 words in English whereas all the outside natives' schools had been teaching the aboriginal language, such schools as Inyati, Hope Fountain, Shiloh and others.

[1] S/N/Bulawayo to CNC, 23 May 1924, S 84/A/260.

(3) Why can't we vote our live stock? We humbly ask the Government to take away these (above) bars.'[1]

At the same time Martha campaigned 'in the surrounding districts' to recruit large numbers of people who were not at all qualified for the vote but whose adherence might justify the RBVA's claim to be representative. Martha's message in these rural meetings was an impeccably 'progressive' one. She was the last person to make concessions to conservative or traditional feeling. She denounced 'the drunkenness of so many of the older chiefs'; she told the tribesmen that 'the education of their children was the only way of saving their race from sinking into sloth and brutishness'. At the same time, however, she preached a political gospel. Official reports record her as saying that Africans 'should combine with a view to securing the franchise . . . Natives should combine in an attempt to become as clever as the white man . . . to prosper there must be combination and only by combination could they bring forward their grievances.'

And in these rural meetings Martha heard perhaps for the first time the spokesmen of rural grievances. The sort of people who took the lead in these rural branches of the RBVA were men like the Chairman of the Gwanda branch, Mawagelana, a builders' labourer, or its Secretary, John Dokoti, a cattle buyer. These men introduced a new note into RBVA discussions. A CID report of the meetings of the RBVA in Gwanda, where it was called 'IVOTE', remarked that the need for education was the main subject of discussion and after that compulsory dipping, 'a certain winner for the educated native agitator who wishes to claim the interest of the kraal native', low cattle prices and land shortage. These subjects in fact were not brought to Gwanda by Martha as an 'educated native agitator' but carried back from Gwanda by her when she returned to Bulawayo. In this way the RBVA programme became less élitist and more popular.[2]

These developments were clearly reflected in the tone of the 1924 general meeting which was held in July in Bulawayo. In an opening address which was far removed from the humility of his Amandabele Patriotic Society days, Maziyani told the delegates that 'they are there to show the Europeans that they are not ashamed of being black and that they were created by the same Almighty God', calling on them to show pride in

[1] Martha Ngano to Governor, 7 May 1924, S 84/A/260.
[2] District Superintendent, BSAP to N.C. Gwanda, 23 October 1929, N. C. Gwanda to S/N/Bulawayo, 9 December 1929, S 84/A/300. According to official reports there was some confusion about the RBVA in the rural areas. Its members were known as 'Ghandi's men' and its purpose described as 'doing away with all European laws and the substitution of laws framed by the natives themselves'.

'their black skins'. Some of the resolutions mirrored this incipient negritude. One requested recognition of 'our professions, native Doctors, Ministers, teachers, etc. Our native Doctors know much of our native disease.' Others displayed the resentment of the RBVA at the character of the attacks being made by Europeans upon the morals of the African population. Maziyani himself particularly resented the fuss being raised about the so-called Black Peril, alleged assaults by African men on European women. As a counter to this the meeting raised the issue of miscegenation. 'The country of or the Colony of Southern Rhodesia, it is true, is a wonderful Colony for creating laws as well as creating a new nation, known as half-castes, without a father. Is it then justice to have one-sided laws? As the Government knows that the natives are not getting more than one pound a month as their wages, can they support these fatherless children without demanding more money so as to educate these children? We would not mind the Europeans marrying our native sisters so that they become our legal brother-in-law. It is a painful sight to see that our poor sisters are being kept as temporal wives, without a claim. Good example is expected from long, long civilized Nation, especially the Great Britons, the lovers of justice and liberty to all her inferior and hopeless subjects. In some cases we know our grievances have been misrepresented to the Government or to some Commission of Inquiry.'

Demands which had been made before were now more sharply worded. 'The third class schools in Southern Rhodesia is absolutely meant to keep the black man down.' 'We feel there is a great colour bar in this country although we have often heard that in Rhodesia there is no colour bar. We demand the issue of our franchise as in the full meaning of the word.' 'We desire the Government to sell or operate the sale of unalienated lands adjoining native Reserves to natives. The Government should give ample time to purchasers.'

Instead of the humbly expressed intention to consult members of the Native Department, expressed in 1923, or Twala's praise of it in 1922 as the finest south of the Zambezi, the meeting declared that 'all our rights and interests are being kept down by (the Native Commissioners) and thus we are unable to develop as a Bantu nation'. Instead of the polite request to members of the Responsible Government Party to explain their native policy there was now an open expression of disillusionment. 'During the elections the questions were put to the candidates of the Rhodesian party as follows. "Why are natives forbidden to walk on the foot-paths?"' Yet nothing had been done and the 'great grievance' remained.

Finally, as the minutes record, 'the outside delegates brought a discussion about dipping fees'. To many of the urban dwelling members of the RBVA this was their first encounter with the new element that Martha Ngano had brought into the movement. They were not experts on dipping fees: 'the right position is unknown to all the delegates'. And the minutes go on to record vividly the exchange between the educated leaders, attempting to soothe the new members, and then the spokesmen of rural discontent. 'The delegates were assured that if they lived in the Reserves it is where King George the Fifth in person rules. Some said the Reserves are insufficient for the masses and they are unsuitable for human inhabitation to inherit them.'[1]

On 25 July Garner Sojini forwarded a copy of the minutes and resolution to the Governor, Sir John Chancellor, with a return to the bland manner of 1923. 'I have a confidence that during your rule in this Colony our minor grievances now existing will be met with fairness, and I have no doubt that Your Excellency's sympathy accorded . . . to the natives of Mauritius and Trinidad will . . . be extended to the natives of this country. I am told Your Excellency's sympathy and tactfulness in dealing with the Native Problems in those islands left nothing that could be desired.'[2]

Government Hostility to the RBVA

In this instance, however, the minutes were first commented upon by the Native Department without much tact or sympathy. The Department was angry at the direct criticism of Native Commissioners and alarmed at the recruitment of rural members. It fastened upon the meeting's call that Africans should report all their grievances to the RBVA since the Association stood 'for protection to all those that are loyal to the British throne'. The RBVA was making a bid for power. 'I think that possibly a few registered voters resent Native Commissioners not taking active measures to increase the membership of the Association and to secure better franchise conditions,' wrote the Superintendent of Natives, Bulawayo. 'Also, it is probable that they resent our support of tribal control and consider that they, being registered voters, should be recognized as Leaders of the masses.' Many of the resolutions of the July meeting, such as the resolutions on African doctors and on dipping fees, were thought to be aimed at gaining 'support from the masses'. Others, such as the call for native purchase areas, were regarded as attempts to anticipate forthcoming government action so that the RBVA could 'later claim the credit

[1] Minutes and Resolutions, 14 July 1924, S 84/A/260.
[2] Sojini to Chancellor, 25 July 1924, S 84/A/260.

of having obtained concessions for the masses'. The RBVA was seeking to become a mass nationalist party, 'to break down tribal barriers and thus to create a common sense of nationality amongst all Bantu peoples'.[1]

Reacting somewhat too vigorously in this way to the challenge of the new model RBVA the Department was not much disposed to deal with or to answer the complaints as complaints but much more concerned to dispute the representative character of the Association. 'The majority of the leaders in this association are from other Colonies. A determined effort is being made to interest uneducated indigenous natives.' It defended the Native Commissioners. 'The Native Commissioners with their intimate knowledge of the natives and their customs keep a watchful eye on the rights and interests of all natives.' The only positive recommendations made by the Department were that official representations should be made to private landowners that their dipping fees were too high. 'It is very necessary,' minuted the Chief Native Commissioner, 'for this Department to keep in close touch with the movement.'

The attitude of the Responsible Government politicians themselves towards the RBVA was defined in February 1925 as the result of Martha Ngano's continued campaigning in the rural areas of Matabeleland. Sir Charles Coghlan himself sounded what was in effect the death-knell of Twala's hopes for an amicable working relationship between organized African voters and white politicians. 'It is difficult to see what else we can do but tolerate the movement,' wrote Coghlan. 'On general principles, however, I do not approve of sectional political associations whether based on creed, colour, race or particular interest. They are in my opinion unsound as tending to create and promote a policy of particularist aggrandizement. . . . Where the Association is founded . . . on race and colour itself its potentiality for mischief is undoubtedly increased, in fact I detect the germs of such mischief in the present action of Martha Ngano, whoever she may be.' Martha appeared 'anxious to get natives to act through her Association in regard to matters affecting their general welfare, instead of laying these directly before their official supervisors. Natives should be tactfully informed that the Government's desire is that they should make their representations direct to their officials and not to trust themselves to political agitators.

It is easy enough to dismiss the strategy of the RBVA as absurdly unreal

---

[1] CNC to Secretary, Premier, 22 September 1924; S/N/Bulawayo to CNC, 2 September 1924, S 84/A/260.

and their hopes of gaining concessions as absurd. Once again it is as well to remember the parallel dilemma and parallel failure of European liberals. By 1925 John Harris of the Aborigines Protection Society was as disillusioned as the leaders of the RBVA. There were few signs that any return was going to be made for the support he had given the Responsible Government party or that he enjoyed any influence with them. The APS was moving into a position of deep suspicion, soon to become open hostility, towards the settler régime. It had been useful for the Responsible Government leaders to be able to claim the goodwill of the philanthropic lobby and of some sections of articulate African opinion. But after 1923 this goodwill did not count for very much; certainly not enough to earn any significant concessions in return.

Other African Associations in the 1920s
Any association of educated Africans would have been politically weak in the 1920s in Southern Rhodesia, even if it had achieved a genuine territorial reality. But the RBVA failed to achieve so much. Its intention was a fully territorial one: it claimed to speak in the name of all Africans in Rhodesia to 'the highest tribunal' of the colony. This central focus was very significant. African politicians were not thinking in these terms in Northern Rhodesia, or in Kenya or in Uganda at this time. In Nyasaland and in Tanganyika the idea of the representative appeal to the centre existed only in a much more diffused and less articulated way. In Southern Rhodesia the tradition of territorial politics ran unbroken from the RBVA through the Bantu Congress of the 1930s to the revived Congress of the 1950s and its successors. But until the 1950s practice did not come up to theory. In practice the RBVA was effective only in Matabeleland and in the Bulawayo district.

This was not because modern style associations were impossible elsewhere. The leaders of the RBVA had not made effective contact with 'progressive' Shona, but this did not mean that there were none to contact. There were teachers and preachers like Enoch Mapondera; there were farmers like Kawadza of Manicaland, who paid as much as £750 for part of the Buffalo farm in the Makoni district and produced rich crops through the use of European ploughs; there were government servants like John Kapuya or like Walter Chipwaya, who was educated at Waddilove, served in the army and as a messenger-interpreter and who was characterized by the Chief Native Commissioner as 'an intelligent, educated and industrious man'. There were also in Mashonaland a number of 'alien natives' who had made more contact with these Shona 'progressives' than had Twala. It was these two groups in combination that formed the RBVA's great rival, the Rhodesian Native Association.[1]

The character of the Rhodesian Native Association was rather different from the RBVA. It was less concerned with specifically political action; it was more acceptable to the administration which tended to play off the 'moderate' Rhodesian Native Association against the incipiently 'radical' RBVA. The stand of the RNA leadership comes out of an article written by the President of the Association, J. S. Mokwile, in 1924. Mokwile's background was in fact very similar to that of the leaders of the RBVA. He was the son of a Suto evangelist who had worked in the service of the Dutch Reformed Church from the earliest days of white settlement in Rhodesia and had later joined with other Sutos to buy the farm of Niekerk's Rust in the Fort Victoria district. Mokwile himself had been sent for education to the Tiger Kloof Institution in South Africa for industrial training and acknowledged in his article that without this South African experience he would have found it difficult to give leadership in Southern Rhodesia. He saw himself as following very much in the footsteps of his father and was proud 'to carry on the work of my father amongst the younger generation in Rhodesia'. But Mokwile explicitly repudiated the Jabavu tradition and all frankly political activities. Jabavu's paper had claimed, wrote Mokwile, that Africans were now sufficiently grown up to detect the injustices done to them. 'I am afraid that if I do live long I may become an old man before I am able to witness any improvement in native administration being brought about by extravagant talk of men who make leadership their only profession. It will not be those who seek higher education that natives will listen to. Their real leaders will be men of the soil; men who have learned how to use the soil, and who are not ashamed to be seen with their coats off; because education is not a garment which a man puts on to secure material advancement and to secure the applause of a crowd. To ape civilization costs nothing; its genuine acquisition must be governed by internal principles. These imply moral force, and the driving power of that force is Christianity.' Mokwile was a man of the Christian solution. He was also very much a moderate, believing that 'any opportunity for improvement . . . we must thankfully admit is possible only by the presence of the white man in our country.'[2]

[1] For Chipwaya and the Rhodesian Native Association generally see: J. R. Hooker, 'Welfare Associations and other Instruments of Accommodation in the Rhodesias between the World Wars', *Comparative Studies in Society and History*, vol. 9, no. 1, 1965, October 1966.

[2] J. S. Mokwile, 'Native Ideals', *The Southern Rhodesian Native Affairs Department Annual*, No. 1, December 1924.

The Rhodesian Native Association was the movement of the 'men of the soil', the 'progressive' farmers of Mashonaland. It did not have the same links with a tradition of urban politics as the RBVA with its vigorous Bulawayo membership. Nor did it have the possibility of drawing upon previous traditions of tribal or nationality politics. In Matabeleland the RBVA was able to draw not only on the urban tradition but also the existing traditions of the Ndebele kingship movement with its combination of traditional and modern, and thus reach the discontent of the Ndebele rural areas. The Rhodesian Native Association had no previous example of how to combine élite and mass grievances. And there was possibly one further difference. Fingo landowners like Sojini seem to have been confident of their own ability to compete with whites if allowed to do so on equal terms. The 'men of the soil' in Mashonaland were much less self confident and much more inclined to seek the favour and protection of the Native Department.

As a result there was a chorus of Native Department praise for the RNA through the 1920s. Soon after its foundation it was described as 'a non-political body compared to the Union Vigilance Association consisting of the more advanced natives of purely Rhodesian origin . . . a reputable organization not associated with those organizations of South Africa, wanting Africa for the Africans.' Even when its Presidency was taken over by the Xhosa mission teacher, Matabese, and he began a vigorous campaign to extend its activities, the Department's comment was very different from that accorded to Martha Ngano. 'The past history of the Association has been free from blame. Their future programme is more ambitious but is not necessarily harmful.' In 1928 the Department commented that the RNA 'continues to flourish on stable lines and has furnished sound indications of advanced native sentiment. Its representations have been of help in many instances.' In the next year it noted that RNA 'continues to have the most intelligent and intelligible aims. Other societies of indigenous origin show want of continuity of purpose except, perhaps, for the Native Self Constructing Society of Melsetter district and several farmers' associations.'[1]

The leaders of the RNA were ready to make capital out of the contrast between themselves and the RBVA, especially after 1924. For one thing there was a good deal of anti-Ndebele or anti-Matabeleland feeling in the RNA and this was sometimes appealed to. In 1925 the Manyika farmer Kawadza, who was characteristic of one strand of RNA support, told the

---

[1] Memorandum, Acting CNC, 1 September 1926, S 84/A/260; *Departmental Reports: Native Affairs*, 1928 and 1929.

Carter Commission that he had come 'to express my gratitude for the white man's occupation of the country. We formerly lived in holes like baboons but at the present time we are able to live under much better conditions. . . . The white people advise us to save our money and to keep our money . . . I have followed out what I was advised to do. I kept my money, and I have now bought a farm.' 'What made you live in the hills like baboons?' asked the gratified Commission. 'The Matabeles,' replied Kawadza. 'I am a farmer now. I am an agriculturalist, I plough the land and cultivate a good many mealies, which I sell.' In 1930 J. S. Mokwile was bitterly attacked by African opponents for saying that the British conquest of Southern Rhodesia had saved the Shona from the Ndebele.[1]

Yet it would be unjust to regard the RNA merely as a stooge organization favoured by government in order to play off Shona against Ndebele and to undercut the RBVA. The claim that Nyamanda spoke for all the African people of Southern Rhodesia was at least as far away from a genuine territorial nationalism as Mokwile's reminders of Ndebele raids. Moreover the RNA, despite its moderation, was genuinely expressive of significant African feeling. As Richard Gray comments the RNA demonstrated in a less coherent and assertive form 'the same blend of ideas' as the RBVA; 'a desire to be recognized by the European's world, to escape from the criterion of colour, and at the same time, a racial reaction, a dawning consciousness of African unity.' Gray cites as convincing evidence President J. S. Mokwile's article 'Native Ideals', in the 1924 issue of the Native Department journal. Here Mokwile noted that whites ignored all differences of education and ability among Africans and lumped them together as 'natives'. Very interestingly this leader of an élite association went on to accept the common identity of 'high, low, rich, poor, Christian, non-Christian, uncivilized, educated and un-educated . . . we are just plain natives of Africa, sons of the soil. But we must not be too proud just because we own the title of being the sons of the soil'.[2]

The RNA pressed for representation of African interests in the discussions of Union or Responsible Government though, like Twala, they were thinking in terms of Native Department representation. In 1924 the organization presented the Department with seven 'points which the Rhodesian Native Association wishes to press upon the new Government'. It was certainly done in a different manner from the RBVA's attempt to expose the Responsible Government politicians to the electors. The seven

---

[1] Evidence of Kawadza, Morris Carter Commission, ZAH 1/1/3 pp. 995–8; Hooker, 'Welfare Associations'.

[2] Gray, The Two Nations, p. 162.

point programme was described as 'rather a notice of Association policy than a presentation of grievances'. Three of the seven points were obsessed with the old issue of African prostitution. But the remaining four reiterated the essential demands of the RBVA: increased educational facilities; 'the allocation of plots of land for purchase by individual natives'; 'facilities for representing the points of view directly to the Government in order to ensure better treatment of the native'; and a demand for the reduction of the voting qualification.

Moreover, even if they often spoke as a Shona organization, the RNA also stressed the importance of a single territorial association and aspired to become one. Its announced aim was to 'express the cries of the Native people before the government'. Its attacks on the RBVA were motivated by the desire to eliminate competition at least as much as by suspicion or dislike of Matabeleland. Thus in 1925 the President of the RNA asked Sir Charles Coghlan to 'put the Rhodesian Native Association in a special relationship to Government so that the other two groups, the Rhodesian Bantu Voters Association and the Union Bantu Vigilance Association no longer could confuse progressive Africans who wished to join a legitimate association.'[1]

In fact the failure of any one body to become a national organization in reality was not due to any irreconcilable Ndebele-Shona hostility. The *effective* unit of organization was in fact much smaller than a province. This comes out very clearly in the story of the third association of the early 1920s, the Gwelo Native Welfare Association. The GNWA began quite explicitly as an organization for the Gwelo locality. There was no anti-Ndebele feeling among its leaders; nor was there any hostility against the RBVA, which had held its first meeting at Gwelo and which possessed Gwelo and Selukwe branches. Indeed when the GNWA began to develop and to attract local rural support on quite a large scale leading members of the RBVA came into the association and exercised a powerful influence on its policy. The GNWA arose merely because the interests of Gwelo Africans seemed to require local representation. Its inspirer was the Reverend T. O. Beattie, who suggested the name of the Association and several other points in its Constitution. The twelve founder members were all Christians. The Constitution allowed for the admission of missionaries as honorary members. The moving spirit was A. Maliwa Figode, a member of Beattie's congregation, and in the employment of the town clerk. He was the product of a marriage between a Fingo father and a Shona mother, and was described by the Native Department as 'very outspoken and

[1] Hooker, 'Welfare Associations'.

intelligent'. The Association was described by its founders as 'a Society organized to forward the social and moral welfare of natives in Gwelo and outside district and to act as a channel between them and the Government and municipal authorities'. The movement was inspired, thought the Native Commissioner, by 'a quasi-Christian and quite a constitutional attitude of mind'.[1]

Yet the story of the Gwelo Native Welfare Association was not one merely of polite localism, undermining attempts at a genuinely representative territorial body. As powerful as the tendency towards localism was the tendency towards centralism; as powerful as the tendency towards politeness was the tendency towards alliance with rural grievance. It was not long before the Gwelo Native Welfare Association was calling itself the Southern Rhodesian Native Welfare Association and founding a branch in Bulawayo. It was not long after that that the name was changed once again to the African Welfare Association. And at the same time as these bids for wider leadership the local character of the movement did enable it to sink deeper roots than the Gwelo and Selukwe branches of the RBVA. The Association soon ceased to be a 'good-boys' organization and, playing on the land issue, began to draw in a good deal of rural support. By the mid 1920s, in fact, Southern Rhodesia possessed three modern style African political associations, all claiming territorial existence and all in reality representing a region – Bulawayo, the Midlands, Mashonaland – and two at least of the three beginning to establish links between the educated élite and the rural mass.

[1] Constitution of the Gwelo Native Welfare Association, enclosed in N. C. Gwelo to S/N/Matabeleland, 9 September 1924, S 84/A/261.

SIX

The Morris Carter Commission and Land Apportionment

By 1924 men like John Harris or the leaders of the RBVA were disillusioned with the fruits of Responsible Government. But they still retained enough optimism to welcome the news of another Commission of inquiry into the land problem. Harris hoped that the recommendations of this Commission and the subsequent legislation would realize the verbal promises made to him by Responsible Government leaders that they would strive for a just and final land settlement. The leaders of the RBVA were also hopeful of considerable gains. When Garner Sojini was told of the Commission in September 1924 'he expressed his appreciation of the interest the Government was taking'. Martha Ngano was sufficiently confident that the outcome of the Commission would be favourable to Africans to claim in Gwanda 'that her association had been instrumental in securing (its) appointment'.[1]

Not only the RBVA but the other associations regarded the Morris Carter Commission as the great opportunity for the employment of their essential strategy. The issue could hardly have been better chosen. Many of the leaders of the associations were themselves landowners or leasers and were keenly interested in acquiring more land. And the land issue as a whole, though not land purchase as such, was the issue upon which it was easiest to gain mass support. Finally the Commission intended to seek as much African evidence as possible and would provide an ideal forum for the kind of informed representation that the RBVA and the other associations existed to provide. Now, if ever, was the opportunity for them to have an effect on policy.

Partly because of the existence of the associations and of the attitudes which had brought them into existence there was an impressive amount of coherent African testimony to the Carter Commission. Evidence does not seem to have been submitted by the associations themselves, but the leading

[1] N. C. Gwanda to S/N/Bulawayo, 26 January 1925 and S/N/Bulawayo to CNC, January 1925, S 84/A/300.

figures of all three bodies gave evidence as individuals. A good deal of this chapter will be devoted to an examination of their evidence. But the interest of the African evidence to the Carter Commission is not restricted to the light it throws upon the thinking of the association leaders. In addition to them scores of other Africans gave evidence. There were mission teachers and independent church leaders, Ndebele indunas and Shona chiefs, the leaders of the old Matabele Home movement, clerks and messengers and agricultural demonstrators, even peasant farmers. In all their evidence constitutes the most important single source for the African voice, or for African voices, in Southern Rhodesia in the 1920s. But the full significance of what they were saying cannot be appreciated without a brief account of the situation in which the Commission came to be appointed and the dilemmas faced by those who wanted a just land settlement.

The essence of the land situation and of African land grievances has been brought out in previous chapters. We have seen the acute grievance of the Ndebele over their loss of ownership of their central homelands, their unrest as the new white owners began to evict tenants, their dissatisfaction with the reserves offered as alternative homes, the high rents and dipping fees faced by those who remained on European land, the efforts made to regain a National Home. In Mashonaland, too, there were many groups which were barred from their original territory. In many Shona Reserves population pressure was already being felt. Much good land had been removed as a result of the recommendations of the Reserves Commission. Shona 'squatters' on farms felt the weight of rents and dipping fees, while those Shona who lived on unalienated land resisted bitterly the attempt to collect a government rent.

All these grievances were accentuated in the mid 1920s by the sharply declining prosperity of African agriculture. Before the First World War, as we have seen, African peasant farmers had enjoyed a great advantage over other producers for the agricultural market. As Dr Arrighi writes, 'African peasants were overwhelmingly subsistence producers . . . They had no – or insignificant – monetary costs and therefore they, or the traders on their behalf, could undersell capitalist producers who . . . had to recover outlays fairly quickly, given their weak financial position.' It was, in fact, 'more profitable for Europeans to engage in trading African produce rather than become producers themselves'. For many years African produce supplied the greater part of the Rhodesian demand and Africans were able to obtain necessary cash from its sale.

Gradually, however, a European capitalist agriculture began to develop. The British South Africa Company, disillusioned with the prospects of mining, came to base most of its hopes of economic development upon European farming. For their part 'European producers, just as they did with their labour problems, resorted to political action to strengthen their competitive position. This action manifested itself mainly in the appropriation of land . . . the best land resources were appropriated by the European farmers.' The recommendations of the Reserves Commission were an important part of this process. At the same time the Company administration implemented a number of schemes 'in order to foster the growth of European farming. Experimental stations, free expert advice, credit facilities, provision of fertilizers, seeds and stock at subsidized cost, irrigation works, road construction etc, were all directed to the advantage of the European farmers, assisting them to get on their feet.'[1]

After the advent of Responsible Government in 1923 the way was open for still further government support for European agriculture, and discriminatory price and support structures were built up to favour the European as against the African farmer. All this combined with the pressure of human and animal population in many of the reserves meant that the efficiency and profitability of European farming rapidly outpaced African. In the Gwaii and Shangani Reserves, for example, very large areas of land were potentially arable land. But in fact, as the Department of Native Development later admitted, 'much of the arable land . . . cannot be tilled and must remain unoccupied until artificial water supplies are provided. In spite of the fact that the chart on the agricultural status of Reserve Natives reveals that there are 160 acres of arable land per person on the Gwaii Reserve, the Native Commissioner reports that the arable land along the river and in the vicinity of windmills is fully occupied and well stocked with cattle, and that other land in the Reserve, no matter how good it might be, cannot even be regarded as grazing land for cattle until further development is made in the erection of windmills.' In the Shangani Reserve the land along the river was densely populated and intensively farmed, while the extensive areas away from the river remained unusable. For the first African farmers the arable lands along the Gwaii and Shangani rivers had been rich and profitable. Now the pressure upon them meant that a high proportion of this land could already be classified as 'worn out'.[2]

The 1920s saw the triumph of European agriculture over African. By 1930 official reports could record that 'commercial agricultural production consists of about seventy-five per cent European to twenty-five per cent Native'. Prices for African agricultural produce had fallen. The sale of

---

[1] G. Arrighi, 'Labour Supplies in Historical Perspective'.
[2] E. D. Alvord, *Agricultural Demonstration Work on Native Reserves*.

African cattle, which had been a steady source of income, particularly in Matabeleland, was now falling away as European herds became established. By 1930 the Department of Native Development was even expressing its anxiety over the inadequacy of African subsistence agriculture and anticipating its failure to provide the food needed by the African population itself.[1]

This decline in the profitability of African agriculture was a very important, if largely concealed, factor in the discussions over land apportionment. It made talk of land purchase unrealistic for most Africans since they had no means of raising the purchase money. It also made the question of access to roads and railways and the closeness of farms to towns acutely important for those Africans who still wanted to compete with Europeans and who could produce an agricultural surplus for sale.

Most Africans hoped to deal with these difficulties through an enlargement of the reserves, and especially through the allocation to the reserves of more good arable land. Then at least more Africans would be able to escape from the demand for rents or fees or labour and the subsistence economy would be secure, even if the African share of the commercial agricultural market continued to decline. Many witnesses came before the Commission specifically to request this. There was, however, no question of an extension being made. In 1923, as the Commission repeatedly told witnesses, the Government's position was that enough land was already available for communal occupation. The Reserves, after long uncertainties, were now entrenched in the 1923 Constitution. The job of the Carter Commission was to recommend what should be done *outside* the reserves, and especially in the unalienated areas where land had not been taken up by white farmers. The task of the Commission was to explore the possibilities of individual tenure and of land purchase.

Here, too, there was a clear African interest. Although the overwhelming majority of Rhodesian Africans were interested only in an extension of the reserves, there were many Africans who wanted to buy land. Some of these were indunas or chiefs who wanted to buy land for their own people which would then be communally farmed, as Nyamanda had wished to do. Others were wealthy Ndebele cattle owners who could not find sufficient grazing land either on European owned farms or in the arid reserves and wanted to buy large areas of ranchland.

There were also an increasing number of Africans who wanted to set up as progressive farmers or to build up market gardening businesses near the

[1] *Production and Trade of Southern Rhodesia*, Empire Marketing Board, London, February 1931.

towns or to buy land in the towns on which to build secure homes. Some Africans had already succeeded in doing this. But the British South Africa Company had consistently refused to accept African applications to purchase or lease government land and most European landowners would not sell to Africans. Consequently African land purchase had been negligible up to 1925. According to the Commissioners in that year, 'at the present time 31,000,000 acres of land have been bought by the white people and 40,000 have been purchased by the natives in the country'.[1]

This small group of African land purchasers was, however, heavily over-represented in the leadership of the associations. Men like Sojini and Twala and Makgatho were keenly interested in the findings of the Commission on land purchase. They wanted to buy more land themselves. They wanted the restraints imposed by the Company on African purchase to be broken down. They were anxious that land should be available to Africans near the towns and the communications systems. They accepted more generally that individual tenure and improved farming were the key to desirable modernization. Moreover, some sort of land purchase scheme seemed to be the only way of effectively adding to overall African land holdings. Because of all this the associations had passed before 1925 a whole series of resolutions on land purchase. Sometimes these merely demanded that Africans be enabled to buy land anywhere, as was their right in law but not in practice. Sometimes they asked that special areas be set aside where smaller plots could be bought on easier conditions. But it is important to realize that this request did not necessarily involve any acceptance of the idea of segregation. It is plain that before 1925 most of the members of the associations saw no reason why the right to purchase land anywhere should not co-exist with the setting aside of special areas for African purchase. When the associations welcomed the appointment of the Carter Commission, therefore, they were welcoming the idea of land purchase not the idea of segregation.

But just as the Rhodesian Government was not prepared to contemplate an extension of the reserves, so it was not prepared to meet the demands of those Africans who were interested in land purchase. As the Commission repeatedly made clear to African witnesses who argued for the idea, the Government would not allow communal purchase of land. It was interested only in individual tenure. Nor was the Commission itself ready to recommend that Africans should be allowed to purchase areas of land large enough to provide grazing for large herds of cattle. Finally, the Government was certainly not prepared to implement in practice the legal right of

[1] Evidence of Solomon Mazwi, ZAH/1/2, p. 608.

purchase anywhere irrespective of race. All that it was prepared to consider was a final settlement which set aside areas outside the reserves for African purchase in exchange for exclusive white rights of occupation in the rest of the territory. And the pressure of the European farming interest upon Government would almost certainly ensure that any Native Purchase Areas would be remote from lines of communication and that they would constitute no threat to European dominance of commercial agriculture.

These facts were not plain to most Africans before the meetings of the Commission. Numbers of witnesses still argued for extensions to the reserves, for communal purchase, for unrestricted purchase rights, or for a situation in which there could be open and free competition between progressive African farmers and Europeans. But as it became clear to African witnesses that nothing would be acceptable to Government save a segregation bargain they were faced with a remarkably difficult choice. They responded in many different ways. Some repudiated such a bargain entirely. Others accepted it for want of any other alternative provided it was a fair bargain. To such men the practical details of how much land was allocated to whom and where were the key things, rather than the principle of possessory segregation. Others spoke in favour of that principle, but it would be quite untrue to say that the majority of the African witnesses to the Commission were committed to it and still more untrue to say that they were prepared to accept the sort of bargain that came out of the Commission's recommendations. The many things that Africans wanted and could not get come very clearly out of the Commission evidence; so does the provisional character of the acceptance of segregation on the part of most of those articulate witnesses who did accept it. Anything which fell much short of an equal partition of the unalienated land between black and white was going to cause these men profound disillusionment.

It will be seen that I am seeking to dispute the established interpretation of African evidence to the Commission – namely, that the important thing was African acceptance of the principle of segregation. This point will come out more clearly with the citation of some of the detailed evidence given to the Commission. But I think it would be useful to conclude this general discussion by once again comparing the position of the African leaders with the position of missionary and philanthropic spokesmen for Africans on this issue.

It is often said that missionary radicals like Arthur Cripps and John White were the strongest advocates of segregation. It is certainly true that they came to accept its necessity and argued for such acceptance by the rest of their missionary colleagues. But it is also true that they came to the

idea of possessory segregation only after trying every other method of en-
larging African land holdings and that when they did accept it they did so
only with the same important proviso – that the final division be fair. Men
like John White, indeed, bore a heavy and terrifying responsibility in this
matter. As long as philanthropic opinion rejected the idea of segregation the
British Government would not agree to the appointment of a Commission
to investigate Land Apportionment. For years White held out for the free
right of purchase. He argued for extensions of land to the Reserves. He
argued for special areas set aside for individual purchase on easy financial
terms without the corollary of segregation. He tried to get these things
written into the Responsible Government bargain with Britain. At the time
of the accession to office of the first Responsible Government administration White felt an overpowering sense of failure and despair that all these
attempts had failed. 'Here we are in Southern Rhodesia trying to get a bit
of land set apart for individual purchase by Natives but so far as one can
see we are not a step nearer the goal . . . The new Government is not a
kind that will brook a moment's disfavour to gain any reform for the
natives . . . It is called Responsible Government but it represents only one
section of the community. The voice of the Native people will never be
heard'.[1]

It was only as a result of the failure of all his previous efforts and as a
result of realizing that the Colonial Office could certainly not now persuade
or compel the new Rhodesian Government to make fair land provision
that White at last reluctantly accepted that the segregation bargain must be
tried. In December 1923 he wrote to Harris of the Aborigines Protection
Society to tell him of discussions with Coghlan. Coghlan had told White
that 'the corollary of setting aside land for exclusive use by natives is the
setting apart of areas for Europeans only. In other words it carried with it
segregation. Against such racial division in the past I have protested in
principle. I could not see the justice of it. My views have undergone a
change. The right of natives to purchase land anywhere means that they
purchase nowhere. The practical difficulties seem insurmountable. If the
Government would set aside a fair proportion of land suitable for native
cultivation and cede it to them on reasonable terms, I for one would be
prepared to agree to the condition they wish to impose, viz. that the natives
be excluded from the white areas. I have written rather fully on this
question because you will notice that Sir Charles suggests that until the
Colonial Office cede this point nothing can be done by the local legislature.
If you could get in touch with the Colonial Office and have this matter out

[1] White to Harris, 6 September 1923, Rhodes House, Oxford, APS papers, G 166.

with them and see where they stand and perhaps express the opinions of some of us on the spot some forward step might be taken.'[1]

Harris himself had long ago come to the same conclusion and was quick to represent White's support for a segregation bargain to the Colonial Office. In June 1924 White, again noting that he and Cripps had 'assented to a modified form of segregation', emphasized that what was offered must be 'a good bargain'. 'Their recommendations must be carefully scrutinized . . . and the friends of the natives must fight against the surrender of clause 43 (which entrenched the right to purchase land anywhere) unless the bargain is a fair one.' Thus White had moved along the path that some of the leaders of the associations were to travel, arriving with reluctance and even agony of mind, at the acceptance of 'a fair bargain'.[2]

Against this background we can look at the evidence of African spokesmen in 1925 with greater understanding and sympathy. The leaders of the associations had a less terrible responsibility than John White, whose assent to the idea of segregation had done much to set the whole Land Apportionment process in motion, but they had a very real responsibility nevertheless. In particular they had a responsibility to rise to the occasion by speaking for more than their own interests. This they did with varying success.

African Evidence to the Carter Commission: the Leaders of the Rhodesian Bantu Voters' Union
Most of the top leaders of the RBVA gave evidence to the Carter Commission. Twala, Sojini, Zacharia Magkatho, Thomas Maziyani, Martha Ngano – all appeared before it. The differences between their evidence illustrates well both the division between the moderate and radical leadership of the RBVA and also the way in which witnesses had to respond to the situation revealed to them by the questions of the Commissioners.

Twala and Sojini spoke for the moderates of the RBVA, Maziyani and Martha Ngano for the radicals. Twala and Sojini restricted themselves to the interests of the progressive élite and went a long way to accept the segregation principle. Twala, who had returned from South Africa where he had passed the examination qualifying him for the ministry, explicitly accepted 'partial segregation'.

Twala: 'Personally, I would support what I read some time back by the Chief Native Commissioner, that it would be advisable if the natives should have land in close proximity to the Reserves. I believe in

[1] White to Harris, 3 December 1923, APS papers, G 166.
[2] White to Harris, 28 June 1924, APS papers, G 166.

E

partial segregation, but I do not believe in complete segregation for the natives.'

Commission: 'Why do you believe in partial segregation?'

Twala: 'Because I cannot see what is going to become of the native people if they are absorbed by the Europeans.'

Commission: 'If areas are set aside for natives, in which they can buy land, what acreage do you think that each native should be permitted to purchase? Do you think that there should be any limitation as to the size of the farm they could buy?'

Twala: 'No, I do not think so. I think that they should be allowed to buy as much land as they are able to. I understand that the Christian natives would form up syndicates, as we have done in Natal, and they would get a large area of land together. They would be those natives who have got a little money, and they would feel that they would like to live their lives there, and therefore it would be hard to say that there should be a limitation.'

This question of the size of the new purchase area farms was Sojini's main concern.

'In regard to the farms which the Government has already stated will be sold to the natives,' he told the Commission, 'we are desirous of buying farms adjoining our Native Reserves . . . I may say that we would not like these farms to be on the same principle as the Glen Grey Act, as that system is at present carried out in the Transkei. The Glen Grey system provides that we cannot purchase the farms outright and we cannot buy as much land as we would like to buy. You can only buy a small portion of land and even then it does not belong to you.'[1]

As might have been expected, Thomas Maziyani's evidence was very different in tone. He also believed that African purchasers should be able to buy as much land as they liked. After all there was no limitation on the size of European farms and Maziyani believed that if they were able to do so Africans should compete with Europeans on equal terms. He admired Sojini for showing that this was possible.

Maziyani: 'I would not like to put a limitation on the acreage of land that a man could buy. It should be according to a person's purse. . . . I have been to Selukwe and have seen a native there who can get one thousand bags off his land.'

Commission: 'A native?'

Maziyani: 'Yes.'

[1] Evidence of Twala, ZAH 1/1/1, pp. 429–30; evidence of Sojini, ZAH 1/1/3, p. 927.

Commission: 'What is his name?'

Maziyani: 'Sojini. He has a lot of land.

But Maziyani differed from Twala and Sojini in two important respects. In the first place he was more logical than they in following through his desire for the development of a 'progressive' African landowning class. If such a class were to emerge they must enjoy every possible economic advantage and in particular they must be able to buy good land where they could find it and have access to towns and to communications. For this and other reasons Maziyani totally rejected the segregation bargain.

Maziyani: 'I understand that this Commission is inquiring into the question of land for natives. My opinion is that a native should be allowed to buy land anywhere he likes. I think that the natives should be allowed to buy small plots of land near to the townships so that they can live there with their wives and families . . . I do not see why the Subjects of any one King should be separated. Seeing that all the natives are ruled by the British Government there should be no distinction in regard to their being able to purchase land. If a native is a neighbour to a white man he should look to the white man as his guardian and adviser and not as an enemy. The same thing should happen as regards the white man to the native. He should look to the native as his adopted child, and he should act as a true guardian. In regard to the reserves, it is said that they are dry and sandy and sickly, and they are not fit for anybody to live in them. I understand that the aim of the Commission is to try and get the natives to buy land by themselves, and that certain areas should be set aside for the white people and certain areas for the natives. In referring to Clause 43 of the Draft Letters Patent, it says that "a native may acquire, hold, encumber and dispose of land on the same conditions as a person who is not a native". How is that going to stand, Sir?'

Maziyani refused to be shaken from these views by a persistent cross-examination. The Commissioners told him that if free competition were allowed 'the natives will not be able to purchase any land as the Europeans by that time will have purchased, at any rate, all the best land in the country'. It was suggested to him that 'instead of letting everyone buy land anywhere, it might be better, in the interests of the natives themselves, to have certain areas set aside, because some Europeans do not like to have natives as their neighbours'. To these points Maziyani merely replied by placing the desire and the initiative for segregation firmly with the whites.

Maziyani: 'You mentioned a little while ago that the Europeans object to having a native neighbour. I would ask what is the hatred of the

European against the native? Is it his colour or his doings? If a native commits any crime the police always find out who is the guilty party. When anything is missing it is always said that it is a native.'

In the second place Maziyani spoke up vigorously for the interests of the Ndebele masses. Most of his evidence was concerned with the desirability of developing progressive African farming and with the desire of African residents of Bulawayo for plots of land outside the Municipal Location. But suddenly Maziyani took up the Ndebele case.

Maziyani: 'The Matabeles are a little puzzled. There are some other tribes round about Bulawayo, and they ask why it is that the Europeans are trying to scatter the Matabele natives, and they consider that it is the desire to get them mixed up with other tribes. They cannot understand how the white people do things. The Matabele think that the white people are trying to finish them altogether, and that is the reason why they do not wish to go to the Reserves. If you shift them to Selukwe the Mashonas are there, and if you move them to Plumtree you get another tribe. They do not want to be shifted. They also say that the Europeans think that they are not loyal subjects of His Majesty the King.'[1]

Perhaps the most interesting evidence given by any of the RBVA leaders was that of Martha Ngano. Like her ally Maziyani she began with the statement that 'the law should continue as it exists at the present time, that the natives should be allowed to buy land just where they like, and that the white people should do the same.' But where Maziyani had made no attempt to argue with the Commission, Martha tried to meet their objections. Thus the Commissioners at once followed her opening statement by pointing out the practical effects of the existing situation.

'But at the present time white people are coming into the country and they are buying up large areas of land. The natives have not got much money at the present time. That state of affairs may continue for the next fifty years, and when the time arrives that the natives have the necessary money to purchase land it might be found that all the best land has already been taken up by the white people. That is what might happen if things are left as at present.'

To this objection Martha answered that 'certain land might be set apart as native land'. By this she meant that in addition to the Reserves and to the right of purchase anywhere there should be areas reserved for purchase by Africans.

'I know that (particular areas have already been set aside for native reserves), but it is not altogether good land, and I think that it would be

[1] Evidence of Maziyani, ZAH 1/1/2, pp. 683–93.

better if separate areas were now set aside for the natives. Some of the natives have not got the necessary money at present with which to purchase land, and other natives are quite ignorant in regard to the purchase of land. I think that it would be a very good thing if land is set aside for the natives to purchase.'

Martha had moved some way from her opening proposition – that there should be no restriction of either white or black purchasing rights outside the reserves. She was now proposing restriction of white purchasing right in order to protect African interests. As the discussion continued she moved further. The Commissioners impressed upon her that there was no chance of any restriction being placed upon white purchasing rights without curtailment of African rights to hold land. There had to be a segregation bargain. In response to this, Martha came up with a very interesting proposal, which was later to be adopted by the Aborigines Protection Society in England as their land policy for Rhodesia. She suggested that the land as yet unalienated should be divided into two equal areas, one for exclusive white occupation, the other for exclusive black occupation. The reserves should remain for African communal occupation. And the land already alienated, which included, of course, all the urban areas and the land flanking the main communications networks, and most of the best agricultural land, should remain open to free purchase by anyone of any race. 'I think that the natives ought to have some areas of land near to the towns.'

Martha appeared to have deserted her original position in contrast to Maziyani's stout defence of it. But she was showing a much greater sensitivity to the needs of those Africans who could not compete in the open land market. Maziyani had been reduced to answering the Commissioners' reminder of the unequal rate of purchase by Africans and Europeans under the free purchase system by saying that:

'there are the reserves set aside for any natives who desire to live in them. The natives can continue to live in these reserves. But those natives who wish to buy land can do so. They should continue to have that right and those who are not in a position to purchase land, then it is their own fault.'

Martha was proposing to allow enterprising Africans the chance of competition in the developed land market while at the same time offering land purchase on special terms and in special areas for those unable to compete. She went on to make the very important point that the area of land to be reserved for African purchase could not be judged on the basis of the numbers of Africans who were able and ready in 1925 to buy land.

'Most of the natives in this country do not understand about the buying of land. They want to have the land which belonged to the King. They are merely like children and they do not know anything about it. In the course of time they will understand that the buying of land is a very good thing for them. But today they simply want land which belonged to the King, as they consider that is native land, and it is free. That is the land for which they only pay their tax. I think, however, that there should be land surveyed for them to purchase, and then later on it will be appreciated by them. Even now the younger natives do not like to live amongst old people. They would like to become farmers. . . . Most of the natives do not like the reserves. That is what they tell me, and the reason they give is that such land is too far away from their father's land. I think several of them would buy land.'

Finally she turned to the problem of the towns.

Martha: 'The natives complain a good deal about the location, and the natives who are working in the town would like to have a little piece of land, a little farther out than the location on which they can build a house and cultivate a little garden and live there with their wives and families.'

Commissioners: 'Can you tell us why the natives do not like to live in the location?'

Martha: 'Yes, they say that they are not well treated there by the Superintendent of the location. He does not want them to build houses. He is having some houses built and they are rather small. He wants them to pay a lot of money, as they cannot do as they did before. They used to get a stand and they would build rooms on them which they used to let to other natives, and now they are not allowed to do that. It is very hard on them as the men cannot get sufficient money to support their wives.'

Obviously Martha had her own limitations of vision. In particular she could not conceive that communal agricultural production could possibly provide an answer to economic or social development. Nevertheless, if the Commission had taken up her suggestions something very close to a just bargain might have emerged.[1]

Evidence given by Leaders of other Associations

Leaders of the RBVA were particularly prominent in their eagerness to testify before the Commission. But leading figures of the other associations also appeared. One example in each case will suffice. The most interesting evidence given by a member of the Rhodesian Native Association was that

[1] Evidence of Martha Ngano, ZAH 1/1/2, pp. 603–7.

of Matabese, shortly to become President of that organization. Matabese appeared with a fellow teacher from Waddilove, a Rozwi named Gatzi. They argued that the right to purchase land anywhere should remain but that land should be added to the reserves and that other land should be set aside for African purchase.

'At the present time,' said Matabese, 'we can buy land wherever we like, and I think it would be best if the Government allowed us to retain that right to purchase land wherever we chose, but the first thing I wish to put forward is that I would urge that the land in the reserves should be enlarged.'

Matabese was not prepared to accept that the segregation bargain was necessary. 'But if these specific areas were to be set aside,' urged the Commissioners, 'the natives would cease to have the right to purchase land in other parts.' 'I do not think,' replied Matabese, 'that a native should be deprived of the right to purchase land anywhere.' He argued that the African population of Southern Rhodesia was growing rapidly. In thirty years' time it would have doubled in size. Land provision for Africans must be made on this assumption. The Commissioners objected that in many parts of the world, including Britain, population increase had resulted in loss of land rights: 'a lot of the people must go out and work; they cannot go on the land.' But in reply Matabese proclaimed the status of Africans as 'sons of the soil'.

'The natives of Africa being natives of the land, they would find it very difficult, because they do not have the advantages of the British people of going elsewhere to other parts of the world. If this provision is not made for the natives to continue to have the right to purchase land anywhere, in addition to having land set aside for them, then it will be a serious matter for the natives thirty years hence, and the natives will not then know what to do.'

The Rozwi, Gatzi added to Matabese's arguments a statement of the plight of those Africans living on European farms:

'I have nothing to say about the enlargement of the reserves because I understand that it is not within the province of this Commission. I would like to mention that there are many natives living on farms, and it is very difficult for them; they are unable to move on to the reserves owing to the inadequacy of the latter. . . . In the Gwelo district there is one Chief living on private land near to Lalapanzi and there is no reserve at all where he and his people can go. There are numerous natives who live on private land who have to pay dipping fees and rent and all their money goes in these charges. The dipping fees amount up to 2s 6d per head. I would ask whether the Government could not provide land for such natives as these, owing to the reserves being inadequate.

'On the question of separate areas being set aside for the natives and for the white people, in my opinion there is mutual assistance rendered by the one race to the other. The white man gets assistance from the natives, and vice versa, and if separate areas are set aside, there is always the danger of that mutual assistance ceasing. The natives have not the means of purchasing land on the same scale as the Europeans. On account of the inability on the part of the natives to purchase land in the same ways as the Europeans at the present time, I think it advisable that areas should be set aside.'[1]

Finally, we may turn to the evidence of Moses Mfazi, a Fingo from Selukwe, who was soon to become an executive member of the Southern Rhodesian Native Welfare Association of Gwelo. Mfazi appeared before the Commission with John Ngono, the Ethiopian minister whose applications to purchase land had been so consistently refused by the Company. These two men were much more favourable to segregation than the other association witnesses. At the same time, however, they emphasized that any scheme of segregation must be based upon an equal division. Conditions of land holding in the African and the European areas should be the same. There should not be, as the Commissioners suggested, a Native Land Settlement Board to investigate 'the capacity of the applicant to make a success of the purchase', but a 'Board for the Europeans and the natives'. Africans and Europeans were to be separate but equal. 'We do not wish any distinction made. We do not want any conditions attached to land for the natives which do not apply to the land for the Europeans.' As for the amount and quality of the land to be allocated to Africans, Mfazi and Ngono had this to say:

Mfazi: 'If you set aside separate areas for natives and for Europeans, then I suggest that you should allow the natives to acquire some good lands. If you cannot do that, then give us the right to purchase land together with the Europeans, so that we can select suitable land for ourselves.'

Commissioners: 'Have you got anything else to say?'

Mfazi: 'Under the present conditions the land set aside for the natives amounts to 21 million acres and the white people have got 31 million acres. The white people are far less in numbers than we are, and yet they have 10 million more acres of land. Our population is a very large one indeed.'

[1] Evidence of Matabese and Gatzi, ZAH 1/1/3, pp. 1136-9.

Ngono: 'We consider that we should be allocated five-eighths of the remaining land which at present is unalienated, and the balance of three-eighths should be set aside for the Europeans.'

Mfazi: 'The three-eighths for the Europeans would be in addition to the 31 million which they hold at the present. We would like to have adequate room for expansion, and a place for our children.'[1]

It will be seen from these examples that it is difficult to summarize the evidence given by the leaders of the associations. A very wide range of suggestions were made and views were expressed. But two points do stand out particularly importantly. One is that a number of witnesses, and among them some of the most impressive, rejected the whole idea of total possessory segregation. The other is that witnesses who did accept the idea, like Mfazi and Ngono, accepted it only as a bargain, 'if you cannot do that then give us the right to purchase land together with the Europeans,' and a bargain which must give at least an equal share of Rhodesian land to Africans. The evidence of the association leaders does little to support the idea that Africans were at all ready to accept the sort of Land Apportionment arrangements which did in fact emerge from the Commission's report.

The Evidence of other 'Modernizers'

In addition to the evidence of leading figures in the associations a number of other 'progressives' gave evidence to the Commission and brought out some interesting points. One of these was Johnny Mfogazana, an Ndebele messenger in Salisbury. Mfogazana was in favour of segregation on the grounds that 'we are black people and we know that some European or white people dislike us because we are black.' (James Situmbu, a Fingo farmer who appeared at the same time as Mfogazana, accepted segregation because 'in the Colony where I come from the natives have farms there amongst the Europeans and there is no trouble at all, but in this country it is very different. The white people in this country are not so kind to the natives as the white people in the Cape Colony.') But Mfogazana strongly objected to the idea that land for African purchase should be sold at the same rate as land for European purchase.

Mfogazana: 'We natives do not earn the same amount of money as a white man.'

Commissioners: 'But a native would purchase a smaller piece of land. The natives obtain money just the same way as Europeans earn it, that is, by working and earning.'

[1] Evidence of Mfazi and Ngono, ZAH 1/1/3, pp. 862–866.

Mfogazana: 'Yes, but the wages earned by a European per month are very much higher than those of a native. The work of the native is much harder than that of the white man. Outside natives have to work very hard.[1]'

Another Salisbury messenger Chidzungu, a Kore-Kore from Lomagundi, also emphasized what was indeed the essential point for many African witnesses – that they would like to buy land and would accept segregation in order to get it, but that they could not afford it. Chidzungu added two further points of inequality – that Europeans could afford to pay labour to work land while they lived in town and that superior European education assisted them to work land successfully.

'I have come here to say that we have not got a government College where the natives can learn furniture making and building and also cultivation. We have a desire to buy land, but the difficulty is that we shall not have anyone who knows how to work it for us. We are not like the white people, who can engage labourers to work on the land. In the case of a native employed in the town, he has got a piece of land outside, and he requires a boy to work it for him. When I want to hire a native to work for me he wants twenty-five shilling a month and my salary is only one pound a month. It is desirable that a man should be educated before he buys land. He would then know what he is doing. An uneducated native who buys land might work it and possibly would only get one bag yield because he does not know what he is doing. A white man who buys a farm has been taught and he knows how to work it. In towns we natives are only taught the native language. We are not taught English. Education is not on the proper lines. In the Lomagundi district where I came from all the white people have bought up all the land, and the natives have been driven farther afield, and we have to settle in the mountains now as there is no more land available. We want to buy land but the trouble is that we have not got the money to buy land.'[2]

By no means all the indigenous 'progressives', however, accepted the premise of segregation or were satisfied with pointing out that in Southern Rhodesia separate could not be equal. One of the most articulate and interesting witnesses was Ndawana Ka Sinyanga, an Ndebele who had been educated at Dombashawa, had acted as an agricultural demonstrator, and was in 1925 working as a tennis court maker in the Salisbury neighbourhood and earning as much as three pounds a week. His objections to segregation were acute:

[1] Evidence of Mfogazana, ZAH 1/1/1, pp. 396–7.
[2] Evidence of Chidzungu, ZAH 1/1/1, pp. 478–9.

'I am opposed to the idea of the separate areas. I should like to see them together. Furthermore, it would raise the idea in the minds of some of them that certain areas that were set aside for the natives contained inferior land . . . My point of view is let every man select land where he likes, whether it is in any area. If a man wants to buy a farm, a white man, let him do so if the land suits him. As far as the reserves are concerned, they are a matter of disappointment to us in so far as the soil is poor and some of them have no water, and I feel that if separate areas were set aside for purely native purchase the same thing may happen in regard to those areas as has happened to the reserves . . . No doubt there would be trouble arising from the fact that the natives bought land indiscriminately from white people. I think there might be greater dissatisfaction if separate areas were set aside for native purchase purely and simply. The natives will consider it inferior land and they will say, "Why will the white men not buy this land?" and they will think that it is not good soil.'

Equally acute and to the point were his proposals for reducing the inequalities of free land purchase. 'No doubt the white people would purchase most of the land. But what I regard as a necessary thing is that the Government should pass a law to restrict the white people as regards the holdings of land. There are many white people with huge tracts of land at the present time, but if they were restricted in future from purchasing such large areas there will not be much chance of all the land being taken up by them.' He added that he thought African purchasers should also be restricted in the amount of land that they could buy.

Completing what was perhaps the most incisive African evidence before the Commission, Sinyanga emphasized the importance of Africans having a fair share of the opportunities provided by the towns.

'I think it would be a good thing to have farms near to the towns on account of the mutual assistance that can be rendered to each other by the farmers and by the town people . . . I hope that the Government will make provision for the natives outside in the shape of farms.

'Secondly, provision should be made for them in the towns where they can own lands, and they can have sufficient gardens and so forth, and a house where their friends can come and see them, and the third point is the question of plots in the vicinity of towns. The point that I wish to particularly emphasize is that there should be actually sufficient provision for natives in the towns where they can live. . . . I do not mean like the location, but a place where they can open their own business, where the people from outside can come into the towns and dispose of their produce, and visit their friends . . . Take the laundry work here, it is all done by the Indians; there are Indian stores and Chinamen have eating houses and they cook food for the natives which they will not eat themselves. I think that the natives themselves should have facilities for opening up their business places. I think that stands in town should be provided for the natives for business purposes. There are a number of natives who would desire to open up a business . . . I made an endeavour to open up a business here, an eating house, but I was refused.'[1]

This point – that it was as important *where* land was allocated to Africans as how much – was stressed by other 'progressive' witnesses. 'I should like to see the natives have the opportunity of buying land anywhere in the country,' said Jacob Mwela, a Nyasa teacher. 'If they can only get land a long way from white people the natives would have some difficulty in disposing of their produce.' 'Take the case of the Gwaii reserve and the Shangani reserve,' said William Chiminya, a Northern Rhodesian preacher; 'if a man is energetic and he cultivates his lands there, how is he going to sell his produce? We are nowhere near the railways there, and it would not do.'[2]

It is impossible of course to cite all the evidence given by educated Africans which rejected segregation, or demanded large concessions in return for it, or raised real difficulties which were only too often swept aside and ignored by the Commission. The evidence already cited is enough to make the point. But it must be admitted that there was also 'progressive' evidence which accepted the essential arguments of the Commissioners, which accepted that segregation was not only inescapable but also inherently desirable, and that Government could be trusted to allocate land. Thus six evangelists and teachers from Charter told the Commission that 'our one great hope is to have areas entirely away from the Europeans'. A court interpreter at Mazoe believed that 'black and white cannot live alongside each other peaceably'. There were many other such statements.

Some of them were ambiguous support at best for the official policy of possessory segregation. What the government wanted was to establish the idea that individual property-owning farmers would be better off in segregated African areas. What many even of the 'progressive' witnesses were concerned with was rather to use segregation to preserve communal, tribal identity. Thus the six Charter teachers were spokesmen not for those who

[1] Evidence of Sinyanga, ZAH 1/1/1, pp. 480–91.
[2] Evidence of Mwela, ZAH 1/1/1, p. 472; evidence of Chiminya, ZAH 1/1/2, pp. 620–3.

wanted to break away from tribal economic and social institutions but for the Bahera tribe as a whole.

'I live on private land,' said one; 'it is unsatisfactory as there are numerous obligations which may be increased and no security of tenure; the land adjoins the Mangeni reserve; I was born near and now I am to be turned off and have to go away to other tribes. I hope that something can be done in providing land of the kind we are accustomed to. We Bahera have had our land taken from us and are moved from pillar to post, other tribes are not so badly treated, we are attached to our land, as farms become more occupied we have to leave it, the Europeans did not tell us when they came that our country was being taken away.'

'The Bahera have been so badly treated in the past,' said another, 'they would like a separate area entirely for their own tribe and not to be mixed with others.'

'We desire most that we should get some of our country back,' said a third, 'rather than that we should go to distant parts.'[1]

The Commissioners certainly had not the least intention that Native Purchase should be used in this way to restore to tribal communities land lost to them. Much closer to the Commission's way of thinking were the eight Native Department messengers who gave evidence at the Range in favour of the idea of special areas for individual African farmers. These men saw the idea of Native Purchase as a means to avoid returning to the tribe rather than as a means of rejoining it.

'They were very pleased to hear yesterday's discussions. As Government servants they would like a special area set apart for them where they can live together, as during their service they must run foul of many people and when their authority is at an end they would find trouble awaiting them if they had to live among other people.'[2]

But it must be admitted that there was evidence in favour of the official concept of possessory segregation which did not suffer from these various ambiguities. To close this section we may quote one example of this sort of evidence. It was given by the Reverend Matthew Rusiki, a Shona Methodist minister, who was later to be active in the political movements of the 1930s.

'I would like to tell the Commission,' said Rusiki, 'that it would be a very good thing to allow the natives to purchase some land between the reserves and the farms, but I do not think that the natives should be mixed up with the white people, because if you mix the natives up with white farmers in years to come the natives will have to have their own

---

[1] Evidence of Assavera and others, ZAH 1/1/4, p. 1335.
[2] Evidence of Mjuru and others, ZAH 1/1/4, p. 1345.

schools, and it would not do to have them among the white people. I therefore think it is very good indeed to have the natives separated from the white people. . . . Those natives who can afford it should be allowed to buy land on terms. It should not be necessary for them to put all the cash down at once. They should be permitted to pay so much per year until they have completed the payment of the purchase price. Then the land should belong to them for all time, and it should descend to their children, and so on. The cattle belonging to such natives who purchase that land should be allowed to graze on the Reserves.'[1]

Evidence given by Tribesmen: the Ndebele
In addition to the evidence given by educated Africans and townsmen scores of witnesses from the rural areas were heard by the Commission. This rural evidence was characterized by the imperfect understanding of the issues involved displayed by nearly all the witnesses. Very many had no idea until they were told by the Commissioners that Africans *had* an existing right to buy land anywhere. Such witnesses often began to thank the Commission for telling them of this right only to be informed that it did not amount to much in practice and that instead of it Government proposed to set aside special African areas. This news was commonly also greeted with enthusiasm because witnesses wrongly imagined that it meant some sort of extension to the Reserves. Expressions of agreement with government policy under these circumstances did not signify a very great deal. But the rural evidence is very interesting nevertheless.

In Matabeleland the evidence revealed the existence of a group of senior indunas or members of the royal family who had already moved to land purchase. Most of these had been members of the Nyamanda party. Nyamanda had attempted to raise funds in order to buy land for the Ndebele people as a whole. When this attempt failed a number of individual indunas sold cattle and bought land with the proceeds. But they were very reluctant 'progressives'. They had bought land because they could get no peace otherwise. This comes out clearly enough from the evidence of Nyamanda's close ally, Madhloli, who had bought a farm in 1922. 'I was compelled to buy the farm,' said Madhloli, 'owing to the trouble that I was having with the farmers. I was compelled by the circumstances to buy the farm. I had been constantly moved about.' He had paid 500 head of cattle for the farm and used it mostly to graze his remaining herd but he also used ploughs on the arable land and for a time sold timber to the sawmills, making £70 a month. Madhloli seemed an excellent

[3] Evidence of Rusiki, ZAH 1/1/3, p. 962.

example of the model which the Commissioners held up to more conservative Ndebele cattleowners. But he hardly approached the business of land ownership in a commercial or business-like way. He regarded his farm as home for his cattle and his 'people'; there were five other kraals on the land to whom he charged no rent, either in cash or labour. 'When I want them to work I go and make beer for them and then they work.' And for all his ploughing and timber carrying and cattle raising he found it hard to make his farm pay. His real desire, as he made plain to the Commissioners, was to be given suitable land either in a new reserve or at very low rents. In short Madhloli believed that only the government's failure to do him justice had led to his emergence as an individual landowning farmer; he was not prepared to agree that it was a more rational or desirable state of affairs.

Commissioners: 'Are you pleased now that you bought that piece of land, or are you sorry that you did so?'

Madhloli: 'If I had a chance to sell it and the Government set apart definite areas for natives I would sell my land because I find that it is a burden and I cannot pay it off. If I could sell it, and could get on to ground which is cheaper, I should certainly do so.'

Commissioners: 'Have you any general views that you wish to express to us?'

Madhloli: 'The general principle of setting aside the land is a good one, but whether the natives have the money to pay for the land is another matter.'

Commissioners: 'It is not the idea of the Government to set aside areas for natives who do not pay for it.'[1]

Most Ndebele indunas were considerably less prepared than Madhloli to contemplate selling cattle or to take the risks of buying land, nor did they like the idea of individual rather than communal purchase. This came out vividly, for example, in a meeting of the Commission with a large number of chiefs from the Insiza, Bubi and Matabo districts. Mdala, induna of the Insiza district, began the meeting with a flat repudiation of the utility of so much as discussing land purchase.

'There is no question of our being able to buy the land, because we have not the necessary money, in fact some of us even owe tax and we are prosecuted because we have no money to pay for it.'

There followed a long discussion of the Commission's suggestion that cattle might be sold to buy land and that in future there should be a balance maintained between cattle and cultivation so that each cattle owner would

[1] Evidence of Madhloli, ZAH 1/1/2, pp. 529–31.

require less grazing land. The idea was totally unacceptable to the indunas. Despite the very considerable trade in cattle which had taken place in previous years they refused to equate ownership of cattle with possession of the means to buy land. Government should make provision for a man and for his cattle. 'We have certainly got the cattle but . . . we have not got the means.' 'There is no doubt at all that the cattle have increased, but on the other hand there is no value attached to them at the present time.' 'How can I possibly go in for the cultivation of more land? At my kraal, if we plough any more land for cultivation where are we going to get the land for the cattle to graze on?'

The indunas went on to point out with cogency that the small plots of land envisaged under the Native Purchase scheme were little use to cattle herders. 'If we bought a small piece of land there would be the question of our stock. Where would we be able to graze our stock?' There was no other solution, they all agreed, but for more good land to be added to the reserves. 'We would much rather that the Government should provide additional areas and then the people could be told that they could go and live there.'

As it became clear, however, that there was no chance of the Commission recommending this, some of the indunas turned to another possibility – communal purchase of land for communal farming. The possibility was raised by induna Maledanisa, who had been a member of Nyamanda's party.

Maledanisa : 'The question I should like to ask is in regard to a chief purchasing a piece of land for his people.'

Commission : 'The Government considers that it has made all the necessary provision for the Chiefs and their people in the Reserves.'

Sihlango, son of chief Ndaniso : 'The position is this: take the case of my father. He lives on private land and there is always the question of various obligations. If Chief Ndaniso would combine with his following and purchase the land, it could be done collectively for our benefit and use.'

Commissioners : 'That would be a wasteful way of doing it, whereas if you had your own piece of land the best possible use is made of the land. Besides the Government considers that you have enough land which is occupied in that manner at the present time, and if any more land is granted for the natives it can only be on condition that it is properly used, and that it is taken up, either purchased or leased, under individual ownership.'

Mvumi, representing chief Ndaniso, Matobo : 'In that case the authority of the chief would be affected. A man who owned a piece of land would then cease to obey the Chief.'

Maledanisa: 'Would it not be best if the Government allowed us to buy land collectively so that we would be able to settle on such land and then we could graze our cattle communally?'

Commissioners: 'No, because the Government considers that the natives are increasing rapidly, the white people are increasing in the country, and the number of cattle which there are in the country is also increasing, and the probability is that soon it will be found that there is not sufficient land to go round. If any further land is going to be set aside for the natives in the future, the Government intends to see that it will be properly used in individual ownership.'

Sinti, induna of Matobo: 'Wherever you may be, the lazy relatives of the native will always come along and they will want to be provided for.'

Finally, the indunas returned to the problem of raising money for any sort of purchase. 'We live right in the heart of the farms. Can we not be relieved of paying rent and dipping fees until we find we are in a position to buy? We could accumulate money in that way . . . The money that we could save in that way we could utilize for the purpose of purchasing farms and land generally. It would be a matter for the Government to arrange.' 'I am afraid,' returned Sir Morris Carter, 'that does not come within our province.'[1]

During the whole course of this long interview the chief of the Fingo location, Nzimende, acted as a one-man party of dissent. He attacked the idea of further communal tenure; but welcomed the possibility of land purchase. But it was he rather than the Ndebele indunas who repudiated a notion which was being floated by the Commissioners of individual purchase and ownership of land *within* the area of the reserves.

'How can any man buy land in a reserve? I am opposed to buying land in a reserve . . . Take the case of the Shangani reserve; supposing that a man bought land in that reserve he would be crowding the others out . . . The land in the reserves is not a skin that you can stretch. What would the other natives say if I were to purchase land in that reserve? If I were a wealthy man, and I had a lot of stock, and I were in a position to buy land in the reserves I should buy all my neighbours' ground, and then where would they be? The reserve contains many people who are poor, those who have practically no stock, or very little stock indeed, and the

[1] Evidence of Indunas of the Insiza, Matobo and Bubi districts, ZAH 1/1/2, pp. 565–75.

Government has found a sort of place or refuge for them . . . If a man lives in the reserve and he is a poor man, he must have an opportunity of cultivating his land because he pays his tax the same as any other man.' It is worth remembering that there was hardly an African witness before the Commission no matter how committed to the idea of unrestrained individual purchase outside the Reserves, who would not have agreed with Nzimende's propositions.

Evidence given by Tribesmen: the Shona

It is clear that the Ndebele indunas got very little encouragement out of their interviews with the Commission or out of the Commission's subsequent recommendations. The sort of small scale individually owned Native Purchase farm envisaged by the Commission had nothing to offer the Ndebele cattle herders with their collective economic and social assumptions. The pattern of evidence given by Shona chiefs differed in some ways.

For one thing no Shona chief had been able to buy a farm through the sale of cattle, nor were Shona herds generally so considerable that this way of raising money for land purchase could sensibly be recommended to them. Shona cereals and vegetables, which at one time had commanded good prices, had largely been replaced in the urban markets and at the mining compounds by the products of European farmers. Prices were very low. Thus Shona statements of the irrelevance of the idea of land purchase were even more vigorous than Ndebele ones. Headman Msodza at the Mtoko sessions spoke for many:

'I have been quite happy but most of our country has been taken away from us and where are we going to get money to buy land? Our people have to cultivate among the mountains where they are continually worried by the baboons. None of my people have the money to buy the land. What has been troubling me is the question of money . . . Why I rejoiced at the Commission coming was that I hoped that my reserve would be added to. It is becoming congested as most of our country has been taken away.'

Later at the same session another Budja tribesman cut into the evidence of a local teacher, who was agreeing that separate Native Purchase areas were a good idea, with the cry: 'All our talking is dreaming, there is no man who can act. I agree with Msodza that there is no-one who can buy land.'[1]

There was franker expression of Shona discontents, perhaps because the Shona had had no Nyamanda movement and the Commission provided the first opportunity to voice them at all widely. 'When the white man came we

---

[1] Evidence of Msodza and Chingwena, ZAH 1/1/4, p. 1453.

thought we were going to be looked after, but it is not so, they have taken land as farms, and our sons work for five shillings and then only get a small piece of cloth. We see no prospect of improvement.' 'We were a people who had many cattle, they have all gone. We complained to a people who did not listen.'[1]

Nearly always when there was acceptance of the idea of land purchase and of consequent segregation the proviso was made that the land made available must be adequate and good. A characteristic discussion took place at Melsetter between the Commissioners, Ngani and Maremba, representing the local chiefs, and Maswiswa, a Dutch Reformed Church evangelist.

Ngani: 'If separate areas of suitable land were set aside that would be very acceptable to us, but when we look round in this district we find that all the suitable land has been taken up. As long as the area is in the midst of the white people it would be all right, but we do not wish to be pushed on one side.'

Maremba: 'It is hard for me to say that separate areas should be set aside for the native because when I look around I see all the best areas have been taken up and what is left is bad. If there were any land available for the natives amongst the farms where they could buy that would be very acceptable to us.'

Maswiswa: 'My house is also among the stones. My father, the last witness, used to live on the mountains here, where now is one of Mr Longden's farms, which is good land. The farms we speak of we used to live upon before the Europeans came.'

Maremba: 'I should prefer to buy among the Europeans because I know the land is good.'

Ngani: 'What perplexes us about the question is that it is only now for the first time that we have heard that natives have a right to buy land. Now I know the facts and I would like the Government to provide areas where we could buy land, although we should lose the right to buy or lease the white man's farms.'[2]

On quantity the key answer was that given at the Hartley sessions. There a group of Zezuru and Ndebele accepted the idea of separate areas in 'suitable' places, 'land with black vleis and red soil because the sand areas on which we are living have been disastrous to us . . . areas of good rich soil'. The gathering allowed itself to dream, although all present said that they had not the means to buy land. 'I know of a part of the country between the Gwelo and the Shangani rivers in the Gwelo district. It is very

---

[1] Evidence of Chief Zwimba, ZAH 1/1/4, p. 1440.
[2] Evidence of Ngani, Maremba and Maswiswa, ZAH 1/1/4, pp. 1533-5.

good country with black vleis, red soil and strips of sand, not like this country here. The two rivers are permanent, little rivers flow into them, some with permanent water, and some not; people could live alongside them.' Then John Kapuya, Zezuru clerk at the Native Commissioner's office, Hartley, and Bernard Mizeki's first convert in the 1890s, answered the key question:

> *Commissioners:* 'If the land available is to be divided into white and black areas what should be given to the whites and what should be given to the native?'
>
> *Kapuya:* 'The loaf should be cut in half.'[1]

The best prepared and most coherent Shona rural evidence was that given for the Zwimba Reserve. Here the chiefs, headmen and people had elected Matthew Zwimba, founder and leader of the Church of the White Bird, to act as their spokesman. Matthew spoke on this occasion, as he had always aspired to do, as the interpreter between two worlds.

> 'With regard to the new statement just now made, that the Government proposes to set aside special areas for the natives we would be satisfied if a very large area were to be set aside for us. No white man should be permitted to acquire land in that area. The land which is set aside for the natives should be held solely for them, only for those who might wish to purchase land in the future. If we are to be in a position to buy that land and to pay for it we should also expect to be paid higher wages. Our wages should be increased to such a rate that would place us in a position to pay for the land. When we sell our cattle we should like to get more money for them. We should also like to get more money for the produce of our lands. As far as our work is concerned we seem to be going backwards, and we do not seem to acquire anything from our work. If we are to live with the white people let the treatment be the same; let us get the same pay as the white people. Then we should be in a position to acquire land when there is any to be obtained.'[2]

This, indeed, was what the bulk of the Shona rural evidence amounted to. Give us more land for communal cultivation; give us back our old tribal lands. Or if you will not do that and wish us to enter the world of land purchase and individual tenure then give us the means to do so, pay us and treat us fairly and give us good land.

Conclusion

In the confrontation of African witnesses with the Commission a number

[1] Evidence of John Kapuya and others, ZAH 1/1/4, pp. 1556–9.
[2] Evidence of Matthew Zwimba, ZAH 1/1/3, p. 1216.

of things had become much clearer than they had been before. It was plain to many people that the Commission was not ready to accept that communal agriculture could be economically productive or that it was socially desirable. It was plain that a fundamentally economic and political attitude was being taken by the Commission and that the various claims that could be made in the name of social justice – such as very much lower prices for land sold to Africans – would not be accepted. It was clear that the Commission thought in terms of balancing political forces rather than in terms of justice between the races. Various suggestions which might have done something to correct the existing imbalance – such as Matabese's suggestion that Africans should be given special purchase areas but that Europeans should not, or Sinyanga's suggestion that large-scale European land holding should be prohibited – would clearly be ignored by the Commission. After their appearance before the Commission most of the leaders and members of the associations realized that the best they could hope for was a fair apportionment of the unalienated land and fair provision for African residence near the towns. Many witnesses had spoken against the idea of a segregation bargain but it would be upon the fairness of that bargain that the Commission's report would be judged.

But there were also many who had appeared before the Commission, and more still who had not, for whom the issues were still obscured. In many rural areas the Commission's visit had created expectations that its report could not possibly fulfil. Despite everything said by the Commissioners the prevailing impression left was that more land would become available to Africans soon. Despite everything chiefs did not despair of getting additions to the Reserves or recovering lost tribal lands. And balanced against all these vague aspirations there was a general fatalism. Many agreed with Jio, the Ndau builder. 'In my heart I feel assured that the white people will not rejoice at the natives being now liberated because now the animals will escape.'[1]

The Commission's report was eagerly awaited. But before we can go on to examine that report and African reaction to it, we must seek for the one African voice that was not heard before the Commission – that of the industrial worker. For this voice was raised in the 1920s and the organization created to express it had something to say about the Carter Commission report when the time came.

[1] Evidence of Jio, ZAH 1/1/4, p. 1516.

SEVEN

The Mining Compounds and the Industrial and Commercial Workers Union

Organizations like the Rhodesian Bantu Voters' Association or the Rhodesian Native Association often spoke for the interests of those of their members who lived in towns but they seldom spoke for the interests of urban workers as such. Few of the leaders of these associations were drawn from the groups which were so active in forming the Northern Rhodesian Welfare Associations – the foremen and clerks and storemen of the mining compounds and other industrial concerns. In Southern Rhodesia leadership was in the hands of Native Department or commercial employees, mission teachers, the landleasing or landowning farmer. These men did not share an employer in common with large numbers of unskilled or semi-skilled workers nor have a common interest with them in demanding better wages or better working conditions; rather they came into contact with the African workers either as agents of white authority or as employers themselves. A man like Reverend Makgatho, with his secure Ethiopian church base at Riverside, was unusual in his ability to build up a 'connection' among the Bulawayo population independent of white authority. It was perhaps no accident that his son, Zacharia, was the only one of the active participants in the political associations who also took a leading role in the emergence of trade union activity.

The Southern Rhodesian political associations were particularly remote from the working population of the large mining compounds and from the workers at the great Wankie coalfields, who were in many ways in the best position for combined industrial action. In these key centres of industrial activity, where the workers lived together in management controlled compounds and fairly rapidly developed a sense of common interest, the great majority of the men employed were drawn from Nyasaland, Northern Rhodesia or Portuguese East Africa. Throughout the 1920s the proportion of indigenous Africans in employment in Southern Rhodesia was steadily rising but this rise was not reflected in the mines. The number of Southern

Rhodesian Africans employed on the mines in 1924 was 11,133; in 1930 it was 11,644. In 1924 Southern Rhodesian Africans provided 26·9 per cent of the mining labour force; in 1930 they provided 25·7 per cent. The highest percentage reached in this period was in 1928 when Rhodesian Africans constituted 29 per cent of the mining labour force. Moreover the Southern Rhodesian labourers tended to be employed on the many very small mines, where the workers lived in almost village conditions with their wives and families. The labour force of the large mines was overwhelmingly recruited from Nyasaland, Northern Rhodesia and Mozambique. So also were the élite positions – the mine clerks, the store-keepers, foremen, and so forth. Such jobs tended to be filled by the 'proto-intellectuals' of Nyasaland, men who formed a self-conscious élite, maintaining contact with each other from mine to mine but not attempting to establish contact with indigenous political movements. These men were far from cut off from the currents of African political consciousness and were in touch with developments in Nyasaland and in South Africa. But they were not in touch with the RBVA or the RNA and these associations did not penetrate the mine compounds, where, in any event, the management kept a tight control over any formally organized activity.

The situation was different in Bulawayo and Salisbury. In these towns the urban members of the associations lived in municipal locations along with thousands of African workers, drawn both from Southern Rhodesia and from far outside its borders. The African working population of these towns was growing rapidly. While the total labour force on the mines hardly increased in size between 1911 and 1930, remaining constant at about 40,000, the African working population of Bulawayo increased from some 5,000 in 1911 to some 10,500 in 1926 and to some 16,000 in 1931. In that year Salisbury had some 15,000 Africans in employment. A much larger proportion of these urban workers were indigenous Africans than was the case on the mines. During the 1920s the pressure of population on African land, the increase of African cash needs, the virtual collapse of African commercial agriculture as a means of raising money, all resulted in a great increase in the number of Shona and Ndebele men seeking work.

In 1924 there were some 38,700 Southern Rhodesian Africans employed in work other than mining: by 1928 there were some 70,572. By 1928 significantly more than half the African employees outside the mines were from Southern Rhodesia itself. Very many of these men were employed in European agriculture but at least an equal number sought work in domestic service, as messengers in offices and stores, as workers on the railways, and so on.[1]

The urban members of the associations shared with these workers common grievances about living conditions even if not about working conditions. But even there the sort of people who were prominent in the associations had spent a good deal of time in the past endeavouring to distinguish themselves from the bewildered migrant labour that poured in and out of the towns. The various associations made considerable and not unsuccessful attempts to appeal to and speak for a wider audience, but these attempts were directed towards the African cultivator in the Reserves or on unalienated lands. The associations were much more concerned with things like dipping fees, de-stocking, land shortage than they were with urban wage rates or the conditions of work for unskilled labour in the towns.

It was true, of course, that there was then no sort of clear-cut division as far as Southern Rhodesian Africans themselves were concerned between the cultivators in the Reserves and the workers in the towns. The urban labour force was still overwhelmingly short-term and unskilled, made up of men who had come into town from the Reserves and who would return from the town to them. In 1929 the Chief Native Commissioner estimated that there were only 15,857 Africans in the whole colony who could be described as 'urbanized' in the sense of having severed their commitment to tribal life and having sunk their roots in the towns. 98·4 per cent of the African population, in his view, were still fundamentally tribesmen and peasants. One of the problems of trade unionism when it did begin in Rhodesia was that to the urban workers as well as to the political associations such matters as dipping and de-stocking often seemed more important than the conditions of life and work in town. Nevertheless, if the worker was still very much also a tribesman and cultivator he did have interests as a *worker*. And these interests required to be articulated if African politics in Southern Rhodesia were to be either representative or effective.

Indeed, it is possible to go further. Already to some observers, both white and black, it seemed in the 1920s that only through the organization and expression of urban grievances could African politics become dynamic. The élite of the associations was too small and too dependent upon the Europeans; the rural areas were bewildered and usually passive, their spasms of millenarian enthusiasm impossible to harness. The great new fact, so it was believed, was the coming into existence of an African working

---

[1] These statistics are drawn from the *Official Year Book of the Colony of Southern Rhodesia* No. 2, 1930, and the *Official Year Book of the Colony of Southern Rhodesia* No. 3, 1932.

population – though not yet a working class – which was gathered together in the key economic and administrative centres of Southern Rhodesia and which might make a decisive impact upon them.

Combination in the Mining Compounds

At the beginning of the 1920s, however, there were few evidences of any effective articulation of the hopes, fears and grievances of the workers. There had been no strikes in the period before the First World War – the characteristic expression of discontent in those days was 'desertion' rather than combination. But in the 1920s various forms of combination began to grow up. Both in the mining compounds and in Bulawayo and Salisbury there was expression through deeds or words of the discontent of the workers.

In the mining compounds combination did not take the form of explicit industrial or political organization. Even when the new trade union movement developed in Bulawayo and Salisbury at the end of the 1920s it was no more successful than the RBVA or the RNA in penetrating the compounds, though it certainly tried harder to do so. Throughout the 1920s and 1930s the mines remained cut off from the industrial and political activity of the rest of Southern Rhodesia. In many ways, indeed, the history of the African Voice on the mines of Southern Rhodesia is part of the history of African politics in Northern Rhodesia, Nyasaland and South Africa rather than part of the political history of Southern Rhodesia itself. Nevertheless the developments on the mines, and especially the Shamva strike of 1927, had repercussions far outside them and must be treated in any account of Southern Rhodesian African politics.

What happened on the mines in Southern Rhodesia during the 1914–18 war and in the 1920s was very similar to what happened on the Copperbelt in the 1930s. The miners developed among themselves forms of social, religious and recreational organization which were not primarily intended to further political or industrial purposes. But when the moment came for action or protest these organizations were inevitably drawn in since they provided the means of communication and sometimes the symbols of authority. In the Copperbelt riots of 1935 it was untrue to say that the trouble had been *caused* by the existence and influence of the Watch Tower movement or the Beni dance societies; but there is no doubt from the evidence given to the Russell Commission that both Watch Tower and Beni were involved once the trouble began and helped to give it what structure it possessed. In the same way with the Shamva strike of 1927, or with the recurrent unrest at Wankie, the existence of Watch Tower, of dance societies, of tribal welfare and burial groups, helped to make more or less co-ordinated protest possible.

As early as 1919 the potentialities for co-ordinated action by African miners were revealed.

'Recently the native employees of a large mine,' reported the Chief Native Commissioner, 'determined to effect a reduction in the extortionate prices charged by certain local shopkeepers. Their first plan of campaign was to picket and forcibly prevent any natives from entering the stores in question. When, however, it was explained to them that this action was illegal, they at once withdrew their pickets and thereupon ordered a boycott. The success with which this was attended testifies to the thoroughness of their organization which embraces natives of many different tribes and tongues. The leaders influence and control the rest by means of harangues and debates, and by circularizing them with notices, pamphlets and other propagandist literature. These are signs of the times.'[1]

We possess a good deal of information about the various groupings which made co-ordination of this sort possible. Both the mining companies and the government were nervous about possible strike action and watched the compounds very closely. Thus in the early 1920s there was a scare about 'drilling in the compounds' when it was reported that miners were arming themselves and engaging in formal military exercises. On investigation it was found that miners were in fact indulging in the competitive dances of the Beni societies, which took the form of elaborate imitations of European military procedure and which had been carried south by disbanded soldiers and migrant labour from their East African place of origin. When this had been discovered, however, the authorities in Southern Rhodesia were no more certain than those in the north whether the Beni societies were to be regarded with suspicion or not. It was impossible to suppress this form of popular entertainment and yet in Southern Rhodesia, as on the Copperbelt in 1935, it was sometimes suspected that the hierarchy of ranks in the Beni societies was being used for the transmission of orders.

It was similarly difficult to determine what should be the official attitude to the various 'tribal' associations, burial societies, and so on that sprang up on the mines. In 1922 the Southern Rhodesian Chamber of Mines inquired of the Government whether they were to regard such societies as a prelude to trade unionism. The Compound Manager at Wankie said in 1923 that he had already experienced a strike 'due to the activities of a native society'

[1] Chief Native Commissioner's Report for 1919, *Southern Rhodesia : Departmental Reports : Native Affairs : 1900/01–1923.*

and that he feared further such protest. The Chief Native Commissioner reassured the mineowners that the Native Department had been unable to detect in the friendly societies any 'ulterior political design . . . and I am not aware that they have adopted the principles of trade unionism to any large extent'. But he added that 'natives in this territory have heard of the trade union movements in the south, and there is no reason for believing that this side will not develop in the course of time'. Once again it was impossible to suppress these 'mutual benefit societies', which provided the mine worker with some sort of security and once again the mine owners and managers were right to suppose that this sort of combination was potentially dangerous.[1]

Watch Tower on the Mines

But by far the greatest suspicion was directed towards the Church of the Watch Tower. The Watch Tower movement originated in Nyasaland in the years before the First World War. It was brought there by a remarkable and embittered convert of the Scottish mission, Elliot Kenan Kamwana, who had broken away from his teachers at Livingstonia and gone to South Africa in search of a more radical and less hypocritical creed. This he found in the teachings of the American Watch Tower Bible and Tract Society which had set up a base in Cape Town. Kamwana seized upon the predictions of millenarian upheaval, of the overthrow of the imperial powers, of the saving of the faithful remnant. These interpretations of the Bible seemed to prove the truth of his suspicion that the missionaries had been holding something back and they lent themselves ideally to the idea that unlettered Africans, through superior faith, could survive the disaster in which members of the organized churches were bound to perish. Kamwana created a mass movement among the Tonga on his return and appealed powerfully also to what Professor Shepperson has called the 'proto-intellectuals' of Nyasaland. Although Kamwana was arrested and deported his movement had taken deep roots. A number of his followers – Kenanites, as they called themselves – went south to Southern Rhodesia in search of work and thus carried the ideas of Kamwana's Watch Tower to the Rhodesian mining compounds.

The most important of these Nyasa Kenanites were the 'proto-intellectuals', employed as supervisors, clerks, cooks and so on. They were able to add to their memories of Kamwana's teaching the regular inspiration of Watch Tower Bible and Tract Society pamphlets to which they subscribed and which they read in English. Such men were convinced of the value of

[1] CNC to Secretary, Rhodesia Chamber of Mines, 1 September 1922, N 3/21/4.

their secret knowledge not only in spiritual but in educational terms. The Watch Tower members at Shamva mine believed that 'they are better informed and that other natives cannot follow their ideas on religion'. A Watch Tower preacher at Shamva informed a messenger sent to spy on him that if he read the literature of the movement he 'could leave his work and go on to do something better'. To them the movement combined the advantage of access to white knowledge with a total freedom from white control. 'The white people did not want natives to become clerks because they were afraid of the natives getting up in the world,' said a Yao preacher at Wankie. 'There was a white man in Cape Town who would send some books and letters to him from which he would teach the natives.' A typical figure of this sort of Watch Tower élite was Richard Kalinde, supervisor of the grain store and kitchen at Shamva mine, described by his employers as 'thoroughly honest and reliable . . . He reads a great deal, mostly books from America on the Life of Christ and religious matters.' Kalinde was one of the main figures of mine compound Watch Tower. In 1923 he provided the authorities with a list of members in the compounds along the Bulawayo-Salisbury road. In all there were then 173 members, of whom 171 were Nyasas of Kalinde's type. The root cause of the movement, thought the Native Commissioner, Mazoe, in the same year was 'the spread of education of a fairly high standard in Nyasaland leading to a desire for control by their own people in religious matters.'[1]

It did not please the authorities that the Nyasa 'proto-intellectuals' of the different mines were thus in contact with each other. But the real anxiety arose when Watch Tower teachings began to spread. For a long time there was no question of them spreading to the indigenous African population. 'The Church of the Watch Tower,' it was reported in the early 1920s, 'has not hitherto attempted any propaganda amongst the Mashona natives against whom there appears to be an underlying hostility.' It was not until the end of the 1920s, as we shall see in another chapter, that Watch Tower began to spread into the Reserves. Much earlier than that, however, the Nyasa adherents had begun to teach their faith to mine workers from Northern Rhodesia. 'Their doctrines have shown no marked tendency to spread among the indigenous population,' it was reported in 1923. 'On the other hand they appeal strongly to the mixed mining natives.'[2]

[1] Assistant N. C. Shamva to N. C. Mazoe, 14 June and 18 December 1922; N. C. Wankie to S/N/Bulawayo, 31 August 1923; N 3/5/8; Assistant N. C. Shabani to N. C. Belingwe, 11 October 1928, S 84/A/293; report by N. C. Mazoe, 1923, N3/5/6.
[2] N. C. Mazoe to S/N/Salisbury, 18 June 1923, N 3/5/8; S/N/Bulawayo to CNC, 4 December 1923, S 84/A/293.

The mines in Southern Rhodesia formed, in fact, a most important link in the complex chain of Watch Tower influence in Central Africa. It was through them that Watch Tower reached Northern Rhodesia. The first great mass outbreak of Watch Tower millenarianism in Northern Rhodesia was triggered by the deportation of mine-worker adherents of the faith from Southern Rhodesia in 1917. Thereafter Wankie colliery in particular became a great centre of migrant Northern Rhodesian Watch Tower. By 1923 the Watch Tower congregation there had built up to several hundred. When the main preacher was deported in November of that year he was seen off by a crowd of more than a thousand workers, and the Native Commissioner believed that there would have been a demonstration of protest had not the men been warned that the Globe and Phoenix Mine had recently sacked forty men for Watch Tower membership. Despite the attempts to suppress the movement at Wankie it continued to grow. By the end of the 1920s membership could be counted in thousands. And from Wankie workers returned especially to Bembaland to give fresh impetus to the movement there.[1]

These Northern Rhodesian converts were altogether more turbulent and formidable than the Richard Kalindes. Two examples of the sort of men who were being caught up in the movement in the Southern Rhodesian mines may be illuminating. One of them was the leading figure of the first outburst of Watch Tower in Northern Rhodesia, Hanoc Sindano. Sindano was born in Tanganyika and went south in search of work. 'In 1905 I went with two white men with cattle to Southern Rhodesia. I stayed four years at Enkeldoorn, one year at Que Que, two years at Gatooma and for a short period at lots of other Bomas. At first as a youngster I worked at herding fowls but afterwards as an underground miner. I entered the Church of the Watch Tower at Que Que . . . I have been in the Presbyterian Church, Seventh Day Adventist Church, Wesleyan Church and Watch Tower Church at Que Que, Gadzima, and Gwelo and at the Church of the Watch Tower at Cape Town.' The ideas picked up by Sindano from Nyasa teachers in the Que Que mine were explosive ones. 'If we pray very hard with all our hearts,' Robert Rotberg quotes him as telling his Northern Rhodesian flock, 'God will hear our prayer and will clear all the Europeans back home to England and everything will be ours, and we will be as rich as they are.' Or again, 'God only is to be respected and obeyed, nobody else on earth has any right to it; no more the European than the native chiefs. The English have no right whatsoever in the

[1] N. C. Wankie to S/N/Bulawayo, 30 November 1923, S 84/A/293.

country, they are committing injustice against the natives in pretending to have rights.'[1]

The second example is that of Henry Chibangwa, another migrant mine worker and deportee from Southern Rhodesia. In the early 1930s Chibangwa set up 'a certain organization of Awemba speaking people' at Luanshya. 'He said that he would represent their case to the Governor about their wages. As to why their wages were cut down during the depression, and why their wages should be cut when the Government did not cut the wages of their native employees. They collected about five pounds for him and he went to Livingstone. He came back and said that the Governor had told him that he would listen to these complaints at Luanshya. When the Governor came to Luanshya he did not welcome this man's representations because it was found that he had been deported from Southern Rhodesia, having made troubles there. This man was a member of the Watch Tower. When the Governor came he had a flag on which were Biblical quotations about Jesus coming to rule the earth. When the Governor saw this he did not welcome his representations but other native societies' representations were welcomed. When Henry found that his representation was denied he preached to the people that he had powers superior to those of administrative officers. He preached in the town location and in the mine compound that they must get back their wages which had been cut down during the depression.'[2]

It was this sort of connection between Watch Tower and industrial action that the Southern Rhodesian authorities most feared. When they first discovered Watch Tower in 1917 drastic action was taken. All known Watch Tower adherents were dismissed from their jobs and deported to Northern Rhodesia or Nyasaland. After the War, when Watch Tower reappeared, attitudes towards it were less extreme. The central administration decided that it should be watched but not suppressed and treatment of its adherents depended very much on the attitude of the local Native Commissioner or Compound Manager. In general Compound Managers were deeply suspicious of the movement. At Wankie, for instance, the Manager was convinced in 1923 that the Watch Tower adherents were 'using religion as a cloak to some extent for the purposes of a Labour Organization which he fears will sooner or later lead to trouble'. By August of that year he

---

[1] For Sindano see files N 3/5/8 and RC 3/9/5/29; Robert Rotberg, *The Rise of Nationalism in Central Africa: The Making of Malawi and Zambia, 1873–1964*, Harvard, 1965, pp. 135 and 138.

[2] Evidence of Sam Kawinga Kamchacha Mwase, 2 September 1935, *Northern Rhodesia Copperbelt Disturbances Commission, Russel 1935 Report, Despatch and Evidence.*

'seemed to apprehend dangers of native association or combination for strike purposes'. In November the Nyasa leader of the Wankie movement was deported. At Que Que the 'Compound Manager seized certain books the members of the Watch Tower Society had sent for . . . On the natives remonstrating they were signed off and a rumour was spread to the effect that no Christians were wanted there – only pagans and Mahommedans.' At Shamva in the middle 1920s the Manager took a different view, as he regarded his Watch Tower employees as outstandingly good workers. His tolerance was resented by other Managers and there was no doubt an element of pleasure mixed with their consternation when the Shamva mine workers struck in 1927. After that strike a number of Shamva Watch Tower leaders were deported to the north, among them Lefati Mwambula who was to become a leading figure in the Jehovah's Witnesses movement in Northern Rhodesia.[1]

The Shamva strike of 1927
This Shamva strike came as the climax of labour unrest and management fears. It was sudden, it was more or less complete and it was apparently well organized. It involved some three-and-a-half thousand mineworkers, nearly all from the north. It was said, and no doubt truly, that the dance societies, the mutual aid associations and Watch Tower were all involved in its co-ordination. The Government reacted strongly. At the insistence of the Governor and the Commandant of the Defence Force police were rushed to Shamva on lorries. Before long the strike collapsed. Twenty-two ringleaders were deported, and the remainder went back to work.

But the event created a great impression on both blacks and whites. A Rhodesian writer, Rawdon Hoare, tells us that 'the general strike at the Shamva mine caused great uneasiness among far-seeing Rhodesians. In the towns – particularly in Salisbury – there are in existence small bodies of intelligent natives who continually present grievances – in a quite constitutional manner – to the Chief Native Commissioner. Today they are satisfied with the reasoning of authority. But how long will it last, when the indefinite educational policy is advancing the native mind, without the necessary groundwork by which he can be made to see the reasoning of common sense? There is little doubt that these kindly formations will in the future – and not very distant future – blaze into labour Unions.' Characteristically Hoare blamed the missionaries, whose negrophile zeal

[1] N. C. Wankie to S/N/Bulawayo, 21 May and 31 August 1923, N 3/5/8; N. C. Wankie to S/N/Bulawayo, 30 November 1923; Memorandum by Compound Manager, Shamva, November 1923, S 84/A/259.

was carrying them away on 'the waves of fanaticism, waves that will eventually dash them against the rocks of Bolshevism and strikes.'[1]

The Establishment of the Rhodesian ICU

Hoare was right in one respect. 1927 and 1928 did see the blazing up of a Labour Union and one, incidentally, as critical of the missionaries as Hoare himself. But he was wrong to suppose that such a Union was likely to emerge from the 'kindly formations' of the élite. Instead it came as quite a new phenomenon on the Rhodesian scene – as a radical working man's organization, critical of the timidity of the élite. This new body was the Independent Industrial and Commercial Workers Union of Rhodesia which developed not in the mining compounds but in Bulawayo and Salisbury.

These towns provided an industrial environment very different from Wankie or the other mining centres. On the one hand it was certainly more difficult to organize a general strike there than it had been at Shamva mine. At Shamva the workers shared a single employer and lived in a single compound and were, moreover, drawn from relatively few areas in Northern Rhodesia and Nyasaland. In Bulawayo or in Salisbury there were many more workers engaged in a wide variety of jobs and drawn from all over Southern Rhodesia as well as other parts of central and southern Africa. In such a situation neither tribal nor 'mutual aid' societies nor the Watch Tower movement could provide an adequate organizational framework.

Tribal and regional 'mutual aid' societies existed in both Bulawayo and Salisbury in the 1920s. In Salisbury there were a variety of Nyasa societies – more than half the Salisbury African labour force was said to be Nyasa. In Bulawayo groups like the Bulawayo Location Mozambique Club and the Northern Rhodesian Bantu Association were recognized by the Municipality. The Lozi, Bemba and other tribal groupings possessed their own associations. Similar groupings developed among the Ndebele and Shona workers in the 1920s. They became in Clyde Mitchell's words, 'an integral part of the urban social structure'. Particularly common was the tribal burial society in which members paid a monthly contribution and were in return entitled to 'financial and social assistance if they are bereaved and also to certain benefits if they should become destitute'. These societies gave a measure of security to men in a very insecure situation. But except in those rare cases when workers in a particular industry or trade were overwhelmingly drawn from the same territory, region or tribe these societies

[1] Rawdon Hoare, *Rhodesian Mosaic*, London, 1934, pp. 61–2.

could not help to produce united industrial action in Bulawayo or Salisbury. In these towns, in fact, tribal societies were regarded as contributing to African disunity. They were blamed for the inter-tribal and inter-territorial tension, which expressed itself most spectacularly in the great Christmas faction fights in the Bulawayo locations. In Shamva co-operation between Bemba miners and Tonga clerks might produce coherent industrial action. But in Salisbury the divisive effects of the various Nyasa societies were strongly criticized by the leaders of the new Industrial and Commercial Workers Union.[1]

Similarly there were Watch Tower preachers active in Bulawayo in the later 1920s as well as the Ethiopian preachers already described. But there was little prospect of such men being able to bring together significant numbers of the 'proto-intellectuals' and of the workers as the Watch Tower movement did at Wankie, especially since Watch Tower had not yet made much impression on Rhodesian Africans themselves. What was needed in Bulawayo and Salisbury, or so thought the founders of the ICU, was a secular and pan-tribal organization.

It was easier to set up such an organization in Bulawayo and Salisbury than in the mining compounds, where the tight policing and control would have made it impossible. Thus it was in Bulawayo that the Rhodesian ICU first appeared. It took its inspiration, of course, from the Industrial and Commercial Workers Union of South Africa and from its great Nyasa leader, Clemens Kadalie. Kadalie was at this time probably the most famous of all Nyasalanders. His movement was the most striking of all South African mass movements in the twentieth century, even though it was past its prime in 1927. For years Kadalie and his followers had challenged both the white establishment and the élite leadership of Congress in South Africa, and for years the authorities in Rhodesia had feared the spread of Kadalie's influence to that territory.

They had good reasons to do so. In the first place there was the predicament of the Southern Rhodesian African workers and their growing consciousness of it. In the 1920s, as we have seen, the numbers of Southern Rhodesian Africans seeking work greatly increased. The African population became increasingly dependent upon wage labour to meet its cash needs. Thus where wages had accounted for only 31·4 per cent of Southern Rhodesian African cash earnings in 1903 they came to account for some 80 per cent by the end of the 1920s. But this 'dependence of the African peasant on the sale of labour' was accompanied by a steady decline in real wages from the 1920s onwards. Workers on the mines or in domestic service were

[1] J. Clyde Mitchell, *The Kalela Dance*, Manchester, 1956.

F

not too badly off since food and accommodation was provided. Worst hit were workers in Bulawayo and Salisbury who had to meet the cost of food and rent out of their low wages. The average wage for an unskilled adult worker in the towns was thirty shillings a month without food and shelter, and the rates charged for inadequate accommodation took a high proportion of this. It was not surprising that Rhodesian African workers who had been to South Africa and were aware of the operation of the ICU there should hope for an extension of its activities northwards. Thus in 1927 the Annual Congress of the ICU in South Africa received this cable: 'We Rhodesia workers are looking forward to the Congress to do something towards ramification of the ICU in Rhodesia at an early date.'[1]

In the second place Kadalie himself was deeply and personally interested in industrial conditions in Southern Rhodesia. Immediately before his arrival in South Africa in 1918 and his rapid emergence as leader of the ICU Kadalie had worked in various places in Rhodesia, including the mining compounds. His account of these Rhodesian experiences is well worth quoting here since it helps to link the conditions in the compounds to the trade union movement that developed in Bulawayo and Salisbury.

'At the Shamva Mine I worked as a clerk at first in the compound office. From there I was transferred to the General Manager's office to perform the same sort of work . . . It was here that I first experienced the effect of the colour bar. A European female typist . . . could not tolerate seeing me in the same office at my desk doing the same clerical work as herself. . . . (later) I went to Umvuma, near Fort Victoria, where I was taken on in the Compound Manager's office of the Falcon Mines. Here I had another very bitter experience. Wherever I was employed the mine authorities recognized my intelligence to be above the average of my fellow Africans. Thus I had some advantage over them. The compound manager was cruel. . . . This man used to get up at about 4 a.m. daily in order to send out various shifts. Every meaning he sjambokked the African miners. . . . The African clerks in the compound office, too, sometimes had a dose of his sjambok. . . . My presence on the South African political scene was a mystery to many, including officialdom. Of the three of us who gave ICU evidence before the Commission [the South African Wages Commission of 1925] A. W. G. Champion was known to have worked as a clerk on the mines. My connection with the mines was obscure to many. Before I came to the Union, I had worked as a clerk in two leading mines in Southern Rhodesia, where I watched the evils of the recruiting system. I resolved not to continue to be employed

[1] G. Arrighi, 'Labour Supplies in Historical Perspective'.

in mine compounds. It should be added that it was the systematic torture of the African people in Southern Rhodesia that kindled the spirit of revolt in me.'

Kadalie resolved to respond to the Rhodesian invitation and to send an ICU organizer to Bulawayo, where he had himself worked as a clerk in 1916 and 1917 and where he boasted of having 'organized some social activities among the African community, which were characterized as revolutionary by many people.' The impact of his ICU organizer, Robert Sambo, were to be characterized as revolutionary by many more people. Sambo was a remarkable man who later became the intellectual force behind one of the most interesting of Nyasaland's independent churches, the African National Church. He was from the same part of Nyasaland as Kadalie and knew him well. He was a forceful speaker and was concerned not only with urban wages and conditions but also with the treatment of rural wage labourers on European farms. Of all the African spokesmen in Southern Rhodesia in the 1920s he probably had the broadest conception of the African political struggle and the soundest understanding of the way in which the rural, the urban, the religious and the intellectual grievances of Africans were related to each other. In the late summer of 1927 Sambo began to hold meetings in Bulawayo to call for the formation of a Rhodesian branch of the ICU. He was assisted by a fellow Nyasa, John Mphamba. Reverend Makgatho's son, Zacharia, soon joined them and numbers of other Rhodesian Africans rallied to the idea of the ICU. The administration watched these developments with alarm and in the autumn of 1927 they pounced. Sambo was arrested and deported back to South Africa 'where he continued his connection with Clements Kadalie and the ICU'.

The protests that followed his deportation must have shown the Rhodesian administration that it was dealing with a new sort of movement. Kadalie at once raised the matter with the Secretary of State for the Colonies. Questions were raised in the House of Commons. Protests were even made at the 1928 meeting of the Southern Rhodesian Missionary Conference where John White described the deportation as deeply embittering to African feelings. Sambo himself took the matter up with the Nyasaland government, in a letter of great interest.

'He wrote about the Rhodesian Government, the part Nyasaland natives had played in building up the farming and mining industries of Rhodesia. He mentioned Kadalie, the House of Commons, the Labour Party, quoted the pay of labourers in Southern Rhodesia and gave his view of the conditions then prevailing on the farms in Southern Rhodesia. He concluded by remarking, "Unless natives are set on a better footing there will often be unrest and as a result we shall look to England and the League of Nations for help rather than our local authorities."'

Kadalie wrote direct to the government of Southern Rhodesia. 'He accused the Government of constituting themselves into prosecutor, judge and jury and in the best traditions of a capitalist's democracy the world over, and that free speech in Southern Rhodesia was non-existent as in other parts of the British Empire.' This was language to which the Southern Rhodesian government was little used. They were little used also to the defiance with which Kadalie ended. 'In spite of your ban we shall find means, as we have done in the past, to get our message to our fellow workers, and we shall find men and women in your colony to raise and uphold the banner of freedom from all forms of oppression.'[1]

Men and women *were* found in Southern Rhodesia. Some of them were still Nyasas, like Mphamba himself who continued to play an important part in the ICU until his departure for Nyasaland in July 1929. But more importantly many of the men who actually set up and led the Rhodesian ICU were Ndebele and Shona workers. Despite its origin the Rhodesian ICU rapidly acquired an indigenous voice. One of these men was Thomas Sikaleni Mazula, the first Chairman of the Rhodesian ICU. Mazula was employed by the government as a Messenger-Interpreter. He was given the choice of resigning either from his job or from the ICU chairmanship. Greatly to the surprise of the administration he chose to resign his job and carry on with his ICU work. Mazula continued to be a leading figure in the ICU until 1929 in which year he was demanding 'free, compulsory and undenominational education' and parliamentary representation for Africans.[2]

Three other Rhodesian Africans emerged as more important in the long run. One of these was S. Masoja Ndlovu, General Secretary of the ICU in 1929, another was Charles Mzingeli, Organizing Secretary in Salisbury, a third was Job Dumbutshena, who was responsible for attempting to spread the movement to the mining towns and compounds. They made a formidable combination. By 1929 the ICU was strong enough to begin to campaign vigorously in Bulawayo and to expand to other urban centres. By June 1929 a Salisbury branch had been established. By early 1930 Dumbutshena was addressing meetings in Gatooma, Shabani, Gwelo and

---

[1] These summaries of Sambo's and Kadalie's protests are taken from, 'Historical Survey of Native Controlled Missions operating in Nyasaland', December 1940, Zomba Archives.

[2] For Mazula see file S 84/A/154.

Que-Que and Masoja Ndlovu was making the first contacts in the Reserves. By Easter 1931 the ICU was able to hold its first Congress in Bulawayo.

Activities of the ICU in 1929 and 1930

By far the best way to capture the flavour of this remarkable movement is to quote from the CID reports which are preserved in the Native Department files in the National Archives, Salisbury. (ICU speakers often made references to the white detectives who attended their meetings. They called the CID reports 'our newspaper' because through them the government would become aware of the feelings of the people. They thanked the government with a mixture of irony and sincerity for sending white detectives, whose reports were likely to be more accurate than those of the ill-educated African police. Charles Mzingeli later recorded that one of the reasons that made him join the ICU was the evidence provided by these white detectives that the movement really worried the administration.) Very full reports exist for 1929 and 1930 since the ICU held public meetings on Saturdays and Sundays every week and these meetings were recorded at length. 1929 and early 1930 were in any case months of special ferment in urban and industrial politics. Early in 1929 white railway workers in Bulawayo went on strike. For a moment the possibility of a serious clash between them and the middle class Special Constables seemed real. Africans watched with fascination. As Rawdon Hoare tells us, the whites were very much aware of their audience of 'grinning and inquisitive natives'. 'What about the natives if the white population starts rioting? What about the Matabele? Remember Bulawayo is now the railway head-quarters . . . It is not such a long time since 1896. There are hundreds of Matabele living who remember the rising quite well. And, after all, it was the Matabele who started the Mashona rebellion, so there is no reason why riotous "whites" shouldn't cause grave discontent among the native tribes. When all's said and done we are only a handful among an immense native population.' In this sort of atmosphere the ICU meetings of 1929 and early 1930 took place.[1]

Let us begin with a meeting held on 29 June 1929 in Bulawayo location which was addressed among other speakers by John Mphamba. There was an audience of ninety.

James Mhaso: 'You will all understand that a man who is hungry will never be quiet . . . We want the Government to understand that the native is starving . . . We ask the Government to give us sufficient pay, but we do not want the same pay as Europeans. We will be obedient but

[1] Hoare, *Rhodesian Mosaic*, pp. 190–6.

we must complain. We criticize the Government because there should be proper pay for married men. We have a lot of taxes; we pay rent at the location, and also go to the Beer Hall; and we will do that until we die. This is a trap made by the Government. If you brew beer today, and are found in possession of it, you are arrested. It is the same beer as the Government makes in the beer halls. . . . When I heard the Police were stopping beer outside, I thought the Government were going to do something good instead of giving us a Beer Hall.

If the white people did not believe in uplifting the native they should have left us in darkness. We are workers suffering. You must all understand that. Your perspiration is counted out for nothing. Everything is worked by natives. You are digging gold out of the earth and are making holes in mines. That is the work of natives, working with pick and shovel. All roads are made by natives but if you walk there you are arrested. Natives sweep the pavements but are not allowed to walk on them. All big houses are built by natives. You must all understand that. One day the road will tell you that it was made by natives.

We were all made by God and God has given us minds to think. We have been given talents but we do nothing with them. The ministers were sent here by God to help us but they do not do so. Why did the ministers tell us that God said that if we want life we must dig in the ground? A minister can buy a motor car but if a native buys a motor car they think it is wrong. The ministers do not want the natives educated today.'

At the end of his speech Mhaso reported on the progress made in founding other branches:

James Mhaso: 'They will stop us this time, but presently they will not stop us because we are always telling the truth. We are a people. We have been educated.'

John Mphamba: 'A person who has gone to the Native Department today must have seen the native clerks there. They must take off their hats and boots. The Native Commissioner said that this is to show them different from him . . . . The Native Commissioner is the one who is pulling you back. He is dragging you down. He makes you say, "Inkosi". Who is going to be the "Inkosi"? What is God? When we first saw the Europeans we thought they had come to pull us out of darkness. While I was in school in Blantyre, there was a rule that scholars should not put on a hat or smoke like white men.

Let the people unite and tell the Government that we thank him for what he has done for us, and then tell him that the white men have come to this country for money. If Lobengula had wanted to he would have

called every nation to help him. He did not. That is why he was conquered. In Somaliland they are still fighting. That is because they are
united. Let us be united.'
Mphamba also discussed the European strike. He alleged that the white
labour leaders had betrayed their men:

John Mphamba : 'Mr Bowden is working for the King now . . . One day
I saw Mr Bowden at the Market. There was a strike there. After the
Police had arrested Mr Keller, Mr Keller returned and then came on the
side of the Police. He told all his men to stop the strike.'

Peter Mfulu : 'You see you cannot conquer the white people because
they are united. If you fight one white man the whole group will come
upon you. Do not say "I am a Blantyrer or a Sindebele". Then we shall
obtain our country. There is plenty of gold, silver and cotton. I am sure
if today they could give us what money we want we can do all that they
are doing. The native could do all that white men can do without their
assistance if only he had money . . . Let us claim our own stores so that
they can see we are civilized. You Matabele do not want to uplift yourselves . . . Today Masoja is going to Gatooma to open a new office. Our
Head Office will be in Salisbury. Be careful that the Mashonas do not
take this from your hands. They are united.'

John Mphamba : 'Men of Africa and the ICU. Unity is strength. By
you men with this constitution of the ICU we are going to win our
salvation . . . The ICU is not talking lies. This constitution was written
by a man of understanding. Why are you black people asleep? Wake up
and come to see your true God. The white man has brought another
God. That God is money. Everyone is praying to money. If money
is our God let us get money. I do not want to go to Europe for it. It is in
this ground.'

[Mphamba then referred to police threats to deport him to Nyasaland;]
'because I wanted the ICU to come into Rhodesia. I was going to fight in
the Police Station for the ICU. I thought you men would follow me.
Now is your time to wake up. I do not want you to think of assegais but
with words . . . I bring the ICU to all you, to fight for you . . . We are
treated like dogs. That is why the ICU is fighting. ICU does not want
these passes or searching in the location.'

[Mphamba explained that the ICU had demanded a Wage Board and
what a Wage Board was:] 'The Government is going to put every wage
up as a law. If the Government is going to say that everyone must start
with £5 according to his working and if someone is going to put on your
situpa (pass) £5 and if you are discharged to go to another place that man

must give you the same £5 ... Mr Keller and Mr Davies wanted a Wages Board for every white man. We are going to fight for both peoples. There is one God and we have one King.'

Gibson Tawako: 'In Nyasaland and Zululand there are new laws. If there are going to be chiefs they must be educated. There is a great difference between the old and the new. I am not separating you young men into tribes ... Our prophets were killed for speaking truth. Today it is the ICU ... They told us to leave all our native customs and now they are going back on their word. We thought that there would be equal rights for every civilized man ... Today at the Native Commissioners someone said "If you take me into this job I will do everything that you say". This is killing the natives ... It is you who are pressing yourselves down.'[1]

Most of the basic ICU themes emerge from this meeting. The call for unity, the disillusionment with the failure of the white man to live up to his 'civilizing' professions, the demand for higher wages. It was the swan song of Mphamba who spoke only once more at an ICU meeting, on the next day, 30 June 1929. He made the same appeal for united action, quoted an ICU anthem, and made an attack on the Indian economic exploitation of Africans. As a result of his speech of 29 June with its open attack on the Native Department the authorities discussed either prosecuting or deporting him. 'It is a mistake to allow natives too much freedom of speech ... His utterances would not be of any consequence were they not addressed to an ignorant people who themselves would not publicly indulge in the vituperative language used by Mphamba. They expect conduct of Mphamba's sort to be followed by punishment.' In fact Mphamba soon left Rhodesia on his own accord. After his departure Masoja Ndlovu became without doubt the dominant figure in the Bulawayo ICU.

The meeting of 5 January 1930 provides a good example of his oratory. The meeting took place in the context of fierce tribal fighting that had broken out in the Bulawayo location over the Christmas holidays, fighting that seemed to make a mockery of the ICU's drive for unity.

Masoja: We come to the time and parting of the ways that all young men should understand that this movement is for every blackman. The Church tells you about heaven and the ICU tells you of the things of this world. Tomorrow there will be a great conference which will be held in East London where young men will think of the scheme which will save Africans. I hear some of you saying that the ICU caused the trouble. The

[1] Report by Inspector Caryer on ICU meeting of 29 June 1929, S 84/A/300. I understand that this file has now been withdrawn and is not available for inspection.

ICU is not only for Matabele; it's a movement for the Africans. The people who started the confusion are uneducated people who do not think before they fight. Now, gentlemen, we fight for one thing, unity. I beseech you gentlemen to stop this nonsense. The ICU is the Gospel of peace because it unites different tribes. If you were all members of the ICU you would not have fought. . . . Now go back to your houses and be peaceful, as you should be under the British flag that teaches freedom and peace. Go back, do not fight, this movement is a Christian movement, you are Africans and we preach to you to be of one party. We are all under the British flag whether Mashona or Matabele. We are fighting for peace but not with our fists.[1]'

The same message was hammered home by Mzingeli in Salisbury. The ICU branch there had taken root. 'Salisbury town and vicinity is a most promising field for the ICU,' wrote the Native Commissioner, Salisbury, in December 1929, 'crowded as it is with natives who have much spare time on their hands and with no recreation other than idle chatter. It is only a matter of time before meetings to bait the Government will become the most popular form of entertainment to the native youth of Salisbury . . . The activities of the ICU should be nipped in the bud or trouble will ensue.' In Salisbury Mzingeli, himself a native of the Plumtree area and thus a symbol of the supra-provincial character of the ICU, tried hard to create a nationwide race or class consciousness among the 'native youth'. On 5 January he also spoke of the fighting in Bulawayo:

'It is a pity, the trouble in Bulawayo. The Northern and Matabele natives against the Mzezuru and the Manyika. Some have gone to hospital and some have been arrested for fighting between themselves. I wish the people who caused this should be sent to prison and given twenty-five cuts. . . . Instead of uniting they are dividing themselves. I beg every one of you not to take part in any fighting. Do not think of any Colour Bar against yourselves. The gospel of the ICU is not against anyone.'[2]

On the other hand various people *were* against the ICU. As it increased its influence, it alarmed other Africans whose leadership was being challenged. Mzingeli on 5 January attacked 'the well paid natives who are against the ICU'. He also attacked the Tonga and other tribal societies of Salisbury. 'Some natives are against the ICU, they will follow these useless societies. If anyone is against the ICU I challenge him to give the reasons. These false societies have been here for years. They have done nothing.'

[1] Report on ICU meeting in Bulawayo of 5 January 1930, S 84/A/300.
[2] Report of the ICU meeting in Salisbury of 5 January 1930, S 84/A/300.

And at a meeting in Bulawayo on 11 January 1930 a fascinating debate broke out between Masoja Ndlovu and a 'loyalist' critic.

This meeting had been called to tackle the issue of conditions in the Bulawayo locations. 'What is wrong with the Mayor and the Town Council and what is right with them?' asked the posters advertising the meeting. 'We the people of the Bantu race sincerely ask the European race what is wrong with the town council concerning the Bulawayo location?' An audience of some 300 turned up to 'hear the cock crow for the good of humanity under the indaba tree'. Masoja Ndlovu began the cock-cry:

'We are citizens of this town but we have no privileges in our location. Join the movement and we will cry, we will not let the Council rest or the Government rest; the Imperial Government must hear. We must have rights in this location . . . our own councillors, inspectors and guards. We are no longer the natives of fifty years ago . . . we want our rights. There are over 7000 in this location with no voice. Christ gave you this country and you must realize it. We are the suffering class and as long as you are a native you must realize that . . . We are all of one class and we must come together and unite.'

He then put to the meeting the following resolution: 'We, the Bantu people living under the Municipal Council, of Bulawayo, strongly protest against the fact that in the black area of Bulawayo no privileges are given us.'

Before a vote could be taken, however, Solomon, a location policeman, interrupted the proceedings. 'Your Secretary is talking to blocks of wood,' he said scornfully. 'Could one of you tell me what he has said? Some of the police have had twenty years' service and even yet they do not know all about the law, law is not easy to understand.' Solomon then referred to one of the Rhodesian heroes of the South African ICU, Masabalala, who had been leader of the ICU branch in Port Elizabeth and whose arrest in 1920 had triggered off riotous protests in which twenty-one Africans were killed by gun-fire.

'You remember Masabalala who was detained by the CID. He created such a disturbance that he cost the Government £40,000 and seventy lives were lost. When he got here he was not allowed to see his family and was made to report to the CID every four hours. I told him to leave my room because I was disgusted. You must think for yourselves,' Solomon exhorted. 'I was born in Rhodesia and am a servant of the Government and I challenge any of you to come against it. I was in Johannesburg when two Europeans were shot for making misleading statements, they were shot for going against the British flag . . . Don't follow agitators unless you have studied things for yourselves.'

Solomon's interjection was effective. One of the weaknesses of the Rhodesian ICU was a general fear of being involved in such a clash with the police. ICU speakers were always careful to emphasize that violence was no part of the policy of the movement. Masoja Ndlovu managed to deal with Solomon on 11 January. He was 'a tool of the capitalist class. He will shoot you any time that the capitalists tell him to do so . . . We will not be discouraged by our brother, he will come to us when he is in want.' Masoja's resolution was carried by over 200 votes. But it is clear that he took Solomon's challenge seriously. His speech the next day was a vindication of his whole position, cast in those terms which often gave the ICU something of the atmosphere of an independent church. 'A vision had come to him in his sleep last night in which it was apparent that the work he was doing was a right and just work. He spoke of Moses and Martin Luther saying what great men they were and that other great men must follow in their footsteps.' Solomon, Masoja said, was typical of the traitors who were always at hand to betray great men. 'He had been educated by the missionaries, probably in the Union, and had returned to betray us.' At the end he came back to the justifying realities of his audience's predicament. 'It is a wonder to me that you are not all thieves,' he told them. 'You get thirty shillings per month and out of this you have to pay eighteen shillings rent, leaving twelve shillings. How do you live?'[1]

By the beginning of 1930, then, the ICU was under a general attack. The Native Administration were planning to withdraw town passes from its leaders, the Roman Catholic church was threatening excommunication for anyone who joined it, African ministers of religion and government employees were warning that its agitation would lead to trouble. Masoja's response was defiant. 'You young men are too contented,' he told a meeting on 20 January. 'Those who leave this country say that it is Hell here and won't come back . . . You must not think that angels will come to the Europeans and tell them to give you more wages. No, we must agitate . . . By next week I am going out into the country to visit the chiefs and organize outside. We will organize from one end of the country to the other and make the Government wake up.'[2]

In the next two months Masoja Ndlovu and especially Job Dumbutshena were very active in carrying the ICU gospel to the Reserves and to the

---

[1] Reports of ICU meetings of 11 and 12 January 1930, S 84/A/300.
[2] Report of ICU meeting of 20 January 1930, S 84/A/300.

mining compounds. Masoja spoke at a meeting in chief Ngundu's kraal in the Gwanda district on 28 March 1930. He showed that he was able to appeal to rural as well as to urban audiences.

'Natives must protest against their cattle being killed on outbreak of disease. The Government wants natives to throw their cattle into the river and the natives say nothing. The Government tells the natives that their cattle can be cured by shooting, that shooting is a good medicine for their cattle. Natives know that it is wrong and should complain to the Government. The life of a native depends on his cattle. All good land is taken by the Europeans and the natives are being driven into the hills and the mopani veld where only animals can live. The Reserves are not fit to live in, the land there is no good and there is no natural supply of water. There is not enough room in the Reserves for all the natives . . . Natives belonged to the Government and any complaints must be laid before the Government. If that is not done the Government remains unaware of their grievances. He stated that he is not fighting the Government, having no gun, and that it is his work to lay native grievances openly before the Government.'[1]

Meanwhile Dumbutshena was having a difficult and frustrating time attempting to link the ICU movement with the closed world of the mining compounds. In March he reported back to a Bulawayo meeting. In Gatooma he had found people afraid to join the ICU because there was a rumour that all ICU men were 'to be branded on the forehead'. He tackled the Native Commissioner and the CID about it but they denied responsibility. He was warned not to try to enter the Cam and Motor mine. When he arrived there he was ordered off by the General Manager and taken away by African constables. The latter told him that it was feared that he was intending to organize a strike. He gave an undertaking that he would not do so and was allowed to see round the compound. He discovered that rent was charged for accommodation there and that a miner who earned twenty-five shillings a month paid five shillings rent. (This revelation brought cries of 'Shame' from a Bulawayo audience). The African miners then gathered around him. 'They said they could not go to visit the town. If a man went away from the mine without a pass he was arrested and fined seven shillings and six pence by the Magistrate; and when he returned to the compound he was fined another seven shillings and six pence by the mine authorities.' Their talk was interrupted by the arrival of the Manager who finally turned Job out. 'The mine is rotten inside,' declared Job later, 'that is why they did not want me in the compound. And that Native Com-

[1] Report of a meeting on 28 March 1930, S 84/A/301.

missioner, Gatooma, thinks the natives are dogs. He persecuted and tormented me.'

The Native Commissioner brought a case against Job for non-payment of tax and ordered him to walk to Hartley to appear in court. Members of the ICU in Gatooma collected enough money to pay his train fare. Job appeared in court before the Magistrate, who 'took me by the arm and said that he wanted to hear about the ICU and called all the chiefs around. Machayangombe, the paramount chief, was there. Mr Bibra said to him, "What shall I do with this man?" He replied that he wanted me to be arrested. I said that Machayangombe was dreaming and that the post of paramount chief should not be given to an old man who was dreaming and not educated.'[1]

It will have become obvious by now that there was considerable drama and excitement in the career of the ICU in 1929 and 1930. Its leaders were saying things hitherto unsaid and showing a boldness hitherto unknown. The confrontation of paramount Mashiangombi, a successor albeit a 'loyalist' one of the great rebel leader of 1896, with the intransigent Job Dumbutshena was something of a portent. There were many Africans and some whites who hoped that it portended a radical new energy entering the African politics of Rhodesia. One such white was the missionary A. S. Cripps. Cripps had hitherto shown little confidence in the ability of African organizations to defend African interests. On land and other matters he had worked by himself or through the Southern Rhodesia Missionary Conference rather than in alliance with the Rhodesian Bantu Voters' Association or the Rhodesian Native Association. Such bodies were altogether too élitist for him. But by the end of the 1920s he had become totally disillusioned with the Missionary Conference. He greatly admired Kadalie with whom he was in regular correspondence. And he saw great potentialities in the Rhodesian ICU. 'May it not be that the ICU may be chosen to take that protagonist's place in our crusade from which the Inter-Denominational Missionary Conference . . . has been abdicating?' he asked John White in October 1930. Other missionaries were outraged by a body which had launched such violent attacks on them. 'God created Africa as a nation,' cried Masoja Ndlovu, 'and your salvation as Africans is in your own hands. The time for praying is past. The things to which we are entitled do not come to us by waiting – the churches fail to assist us. We will have our own African Church in the future.' But Cripps accepted the justice of the ICU's criticisms and shared what he called their 'fierce find-you-out resentment' against the Rhodesian churches. He persuaded old

[1] Report of a meeting on 16 March 1930, S 84/A/300.

John White to meet Masoja Ndlovu and other ICU leaders in Bulawayo and planned to join the movement himself. 'When are you and I going to throw ourselves into Independent ICU,' he wrote to White in October 1930, 'not counting the cost in one way, though counting it in another? May God guide us!' They must be 'fanatical allies as well as candid friends' of the ICU. In December 1930 Cripps planned to walk to Bulawayo to take part in the first Congress of the ICU and thus attempt to secure 'Freedom of Speech by Forlorn Hope tactics'. In March 1931 he was urging White to try to secure a passport to enable Kadalie himself to attend this Congress – 'a forlorn hope job but another stage passed in our attempt to habituate the old régime with the idea of a Progressive Native Africa.'

In the end neither Cripps nor White were at the Easter Congress. But Cripps received reports of its proceedings which he thought 'fairly practical'. He put the ICU into contact with the Aborigines Protection Society in London. He canvassed wider clerical support for this 'Young Africa' movement. The ICU, wrote Cripps, 'was bruised reed and smoking flax' but it might be a real agency for the achievement of 'a Progressive Native Africa'.[1]

Another European who showed interest and sympathy with the ICU was the white Labour leader, Bowden. He even created some stir by addressing an ICU meeting in March 1930. 'I am a working man. I have to stand on a ladder and write signs. I painted a sign for the natives – look at it over there on the Coloured Persons' Dance Hall for everyone to see it. They paid me well for it. Today a native came to me and asked me to teach him God's truth. I am going to help that native. I am going to write a sign for him . . . You want better conditions and you'll only get it by organizing. Strength – think – see – hear – taste and feel it and then you'll win.' This speech aroused momentary hopes of a workers' alliance. On 29 March 1930 an African ICU speaker said that the Rhodesian Labour Party was 'similar in its aims and aspirations' and that the authorities suspected "the two parties of associating with each other for the mutual benefit of the workers".[2]

Bowden's speech was very much a flash in the pan. The chance of a united working class movement, if it had ever existed, was passing away as the white establishment came to terms with white workers. It was a dream to which Charles Mzingeli and others would return in later years but it had little reality in the 1930s and less thereafter. Nor were Cripps' hopes of arousing widespread sympathy for the ICU realizable. Nevertheless, the

---

[1] These paragraphs are based on a series of letter from Cripps to White in file CR 4/5/1.

[2] Report of Speech by Bowden, 15 March 1930, S 84/A/300.

interest shown in the movement by men as different as Bowden and Cripps demonstrates that the ICU had made its mark as something new in African politics. Clearly it was indeed the voice of radical discontent. But what were its potentialities of actual achievement?

The Weaknesses of the ICU
It is possible to see even in the reports of the ICU meetings themselves that the movement had serious weaknesses. There were four main ones: financial weakness; the disunity of the ICU in South Africa; the unreadiness for action of the African labour force in Rhodesia; and as a consequence of all these the failure of the leadership to work out an effective strategy of action.

Financial weakness was endemic to African organizations in Rhodesia at this period. As the Native Affairs Department Report for 1930 somewhat smugly noted, most 'antagonistic native associations' were 'wrecked on the rocks of finance'. The ICU was no exception. Workers' wages were very low. It was very difficult to collect money for a workers' movement. Time after time CID accounts of ICU meetings tell us that sums like three shillings or two shillings were raised from meetings attended by 150 or 100 people. On 2 February 1930 a Salisbury meeting attended by seventy people gave a total of ninepence to the collection. Even these small sums were begrudged. 'I have been told,' said Masoja Ndlovu on 16 February 1930, 'that some of our members may demand the return of their subscription if we fail to obtain better conditions for them. Does a native expect the return of the money he pays to the churches who promise him a paradise which he has not yet attained?' Various devices were attempted to put the ICU on a secure financial basis so that Ndlovu and Mzingeli and Dumbutshena could be employed as full-time organizers. Thus in January 1930 a private meeting of members of the ICU was held in Masoja's hut and it was decided that a member of the ICU was to apply for a general dealer's licence. 'If granted all members of the organization were to be warned to deal solely with him. The profits so obtained were to be placed of the credit of the ICU.' Neither this nor any other solution was successful and both Ndlovu and Mzingeli faced great difficulties in maintaining themselves.

In theory the Rhodesian ICU was supposed to pass twenty per cent of its exiguous funds to the parent body in South Africa. In fact its difficulties were compounded by the fact that the parent body was by 1930 split into a number of bitterly contesting factions. 'O that the New Africans were more at unity among themselves!' wrote Cripps, adding optimistically that he hoped 'to recommend to Clemens Kadalie the intensive study of Psalm 133 for the Crusaders of the New Africa'. The Rhodesian ICU, so earnestly calling for unity, were embarrassed by these divisions. Speakers were apt to be asked by sceptical members of their audience which ICU they belonged to. Usually the answer was that they followed Kadalie but there are some signs of restiveness with this subordination to an increasingly ineffective South African movement. 'We are in the Rhodesian ICU,' said Masoja Ndlovu on 1 March 1930, 'and we do not want any advice from Clements Kadalie. We are thinking for ourselves. The salvation of Rhodesia rests with my people and not with those in the Union. I am going to organize. We call our society the Independent ICU.'

But cutting themselves off from the ailing parent body was no way to find fresh energy. The main problem of the Rhodesian ICU was that it could not discover how to tap in Rhodesia the sort of readiness to protest that Kadalie had found in South Africa. ICU speakers constantly bewailed the timidity of their Rhodesian audiences. Masoja Ndlovu, for instance, spoke on 8 February 1930 about the refusal of more politically sophisticated Rhodesians in the Union to return to help in the cause and the failure of Rhodesian workers in the colony to take it up with any vigour:

'Walking about in the streets will never help you Africans – a lot of our friends are in the Union and will not come back until conditions have changed. They should come and help us work for our own salvation and talk to the Europeans. We do not want you to fight but we must ask for better conditions . . . If they do not want us to join the Communist Party and other parties not friendly to the Government they must treat us better . . . Look at the white people in Rhodesia today and read of how they started to come to Africa, and how they were drowned at sea and died on the land. Yet they did not stop and now they have mastered the whole world. I am fighting the capitalists for you. You cannot blame the white man. Blame yourselves for you are sleeping while I am fighting the cause for freedom.'

At the same meeting another speaker recounted how he was asked in South Africa 'if there was any native in Rhodesia with a bold heart. So I told him we are all afraid of being locked up.'[1]

'The ICU says you are cowards,' Job Dumbutshena told his Bulawayo audience. But clearly cowardice was not the explanation of the disinterest or the reluctance of the African worker in Rhodesia. It was rather that the ICU was a 'precocious' movement, to quote Professor Hooker's description. 'The ICU is for proletarian people,' said Mzingeli in Salisbury. 'We are the

[1] Reports of ICU meetings, S 84/A/300.

proletarian people.' Yet there was no proletariat in the classic sense of the word; no working class distinct from the tribesman or the peasant farmer. The ICU itself was far from being a workers' movement pure and simple. It varied in its appeals from an appeal to class to an appeal to territorial identity to an appeal to race. Sometimes the ICU was seen as the brotherhood of the poor, sometimes the poor were identified with Africans as a whole. 'We are not oppressed because we are Christians but because we are black.' More rarely the movement was seen as standing for the rights of workers, whether white or black. Sometimes the enemy was the whites as a whole, sometimes it was the capitalists. It was never easy to tell whether more prosperous Africans were to be regarded as class enemies or traitors to their race or part of a united African brotherhood.

The ICU itself was effective in terms of exhortation, stimulation, education. But it was not effective in terms of organization. It did not really function as a Trade Union at all. Its forum was the public square rather than the workshop. Its members were recruited from workers as most broadly defined. It could not organize with the effect of a movement based on common membership of a single trade or common employment by a single employer. It was no accident that it was the undramatic and little observed Bantu Benefit Transport Society, a mutual aid association of goods-shed workers which coexisted with the ICU in the 1920s, that survived to take the leading role in the great 1946 strike rather than the more flamboyant ICU.

In any case the 1920s and 30s were not favourable to effective organization. There was too much African labour and it was too little skilled. If a strike could be organized it could be easily broken merely by signing off the strikers and signing on hungry unemployed. The workers were exploited, said Peter Mfulu in Bulawayo, because so many Africans were brought in from the north and from Portuguese East Africa. 'If you look for a job today the mistress tells you that she will give you ten shillings a month because she knows that there are a lot of natives.'

The ICU leaders realized all this. For Masoja Ndlovu, for instance, strike action was very much something for the future rather than the present. 'Join the movement. We do not believe in strikes because we know that if you strike the white people will shoot you . . . One of these days the white people will make a strike and then we will also do so. When you are organized then you must join in . . . In South Africa they can strike because they are organized but we have to lay our grievances to Parliament.' Masoja and the others criticized the political associations for expecting that angels would change white hearts but they foreswore any more vigorous action themselves, including even the most peaceful strike action. Essentially they were reduced to the same appeal as that of the associations – raise funds, show your support and we will speak for you.

Sometimes, as for example when Job Dumbutshena was speaking in the delicate environment of the Que Que mining compound, the appeal sounded as deferential as the RBVA itself. 'You must satisfy your masters. We are not telling you to strike or fight. We only want you to work well, and to do what you are told and not to be cheeky to your masters . . . If we cry to them enough and without any fighting or trouble they will help us and we will be alright. We have quite a lot of white people who love us and if we can work together we will all be happy and our grievances will be settled.' Masoja in Bulawayo spoke with a different voice. 'If the Government try to pass any repressive laws this year we will make a Hell of a row. It is no use trying to stop the grass growing and we will be heard all over the world.' But basically he was saying the same thing. There was no-one else in the world in a position to put pressure on the Rhodesian administration to do what the ICU wanted them to do. Masoja could really only achieve anything in the unlikely event of there being enough 'white people who love us'.

Faced with this problem the ICU leaders did their best. They claimed that their protests had been responsible for the appointment of commissions of inquiry and that through them the workers' voice was being heard. But the claims were not very convincing. While Government favoured the Rhodesia Native Association and at least replied to the RBVA, ICU representations were met with a deliberate policy of disdainful silence. 'What they want is publicity and Government recognition of the fact that they are active agents,' minuted the Chief Native Commissioner. 'They prefer anything to the silence which confronts them.' It was not cowardice but also realism which held men back from committing themselves and their precious money to total support of the ICU.

Finally the ICU failed to make effective contact with the workers on the mines or with agricultural labourers on European farms. After Sambo's deportation the ICU leaders showed no interest in the situation of the farm labourers. They showed a good deal of interest in the mining compounds, as Dumbutshena's tour demonstrates, but they did not succeed in recruiting members or in setting up branches there. This lack of contact between the trade union and political movements of Bulawayo and Salisbury and the workers on the mines and farms continued into the 1950s and 1960s. Mine workers became more sophisticated and politically conscious. Nyasa clerks in this later period tended to belong to the Nyasaland Congress movement, while Bemba and other Northern Rhodesian miners tended to belong to the Northern Rhodesian Congress movement. Men of this sort were responsible for some effective industrial action after the Second World War including a large scale Wankie strike. But there was minimal involvement in the Southern Rhodesian trade unions or political parties. In much the same way the ideas of radical politics, which deeply penetrated the Reserves in the 1950s and 60s, made no impression on the labour force in the European farming areas.

For all its courage and excitement, then, the ICU could not do more in the late 1920s and early 1930s than express the things that the Rhodesian African worker was feeling. By the middle thirties it had fallen apart as a result of its contradictions and weaknesses and of government repression. Both Ndlovu and Mzingeli were prosecuted and imprisoned for short periods. Meanwhile the financial situation grew worse. In South Africa the movement had collapsed and by 1936 the ICU had ceased to exist in Rhodesia. It was to be ten years before whites were again faced with a radical industrial challenge.

The ICU and Later African Politics

But it would not be fair to end this chapter on a note of unrelieved failure. If the ICU was not the progenitor of an effective trade union movement it was in some sense the forerunner of the mass nationalist parties of the 1950s which used the same techniques – the boldly advertised mass meeting, the slogan, the anthem to close the meeting. To anyone who attended the meetings of Congress or of the National Democratic Party in the late 1950s and early 1960s there are striking echoes of theme and treatment in the records of ICU meetings of thirty years earlier. The ICU, indeed, was much more like the modern Congress-type mass organization in its urban manifestations than it was like a trade union. In this, too, it was precocious and premature. But if the times were not ripe for such a movement it made a deep and lasting impression on those who observed it. Nathan Shamuyarira tells us how the 'dauntless courage' of Masoja Ndlovu was remarked and remembered even by people who found themselves unable to emulate it. A number of people came to regard the ICU as marking in some sense the birth of radical politics in Southern Rhodesia.

An interesting involuntary expression of this is provided by a letter written to the Aborigines Protection Society in 1946 by Father Robert Baker, priest in charge of St Augustine's Mission, Penhalonga. Baker wrote in alarm at a speech made in Umtali by Edgar Whitehead in which Whitehead threatened to move legislation to prevent the registration of any further African voters, on the grounds that the 'native branch' of the Labour Party 'had awakened an interest in politics in certain native groups, notably those who lived in towns and did not in any way represent the opinions of the vast majority'. 'Having been in the Colony for thirty years,' wrote Baker, 'I doubt whether the formation of that branch has awakened an interest in politics in certain native groups. It existed before. Years ago I heard a native outside a store on the borders of a Reserve saying that Kadalie was the man for the Africans. The speaker was a native who had been to work in the coal mines in Natal, and had never been a Rhodesian town-dweller.'[1]

When the whole question of industrial action and organization was re-opened after the 1945 strike it seemed natural for Africans in Salisbury to revive the ICU. So in January 1946 representatives of the Salisbury African waiters, drivers, railway workers, of the headquarters branch of the Labour Party, of 'an African Burial Society' and of the Mount Darwin association combined to convene a public meeting at which Charles Mzingeli was the main speaker. At the end of the meeting it was resolved to create the Reformed Industrial and Commercial Workers Union. This body, which had no connections in South Africa, dominated the political life of the Salisbury African townships until the rise of the radical nationalist movement some ten years later.

Moreover, the young men who came into the ICU in the late 1920s were in many cases to have a long political life, linking in important ways the politics of the 1920s to those of the 1950s. One such man was Mzingeli himself, another was Masoja Ndlovu. The subsequent careers of these two men, indeed, admirably illustrate the complex and often contradictory tendencies of the ICU. Masoja Ndlovu has followed through the radical, nationalist, 'populist' tendencies of the movement which link it, as we have seen, with modern mass nationalism. Thus he became an office holder in the revived African National Congress of 1957 and was among those detained in Khami prison in the Southern Rhodesian emergency of 1959. Mzingeli, on the other hand, followed through the trade union, working class solidarity potentialities of the ICU. Before the emergence of the Reformed ICU in 1946 he had been the leading African figure in an attempt to work with progressive white labour and to establish an African branch of the Rhodesian Labour Party. Turning away from this to lead the RICU he continued to draw his inspiration from international working class parallels, staging for instance, a great May Day procession in the streets of Harare

[1] Baker to Secretary, APS, 15 April 1946, Rhodes House, Oxford, APS papers, G 495.

every year. The Africanist and nationalist inspiration which caught up Ndlovu was resisted by Mzingeli. One of the first acts of the young men who built up the early nationalist movements was to launch an attack on Mzingeli's influence and upon a position which they felt was anachronistic and irrelevant. So in a fascinating and complex way conflicts which were merely implicit in the old ICU resulted in Ndlovu and Mzingeli moving in diametrically opposed directions – Masoja to the restriction area and the detention camp, Mzingeli, outraged and uncomprehending at the nationalist movement, tragically ending his long career working with its white opponents.

EIGHT

The ICU
and the Associations
after the Carter Commission

OPPOSITION AND
ATTEMPTS AT UNITY

Industrial workers had not been represented in the evidence given to the Carter Commission. The formation of the ICU, however, ensured that their voices would be vociferously heard among the other African reactions to the report of the Commission after its publication in 1926.

Most commentators on Land Apportionment have accepted the justice of the Commission's own summary of African opinion. 'The overwhelming majority of those who understand the question are in favour of existing law being amended and of the establishment of separate areas in which each of the two races, black and white respectively, should be permitted to acquire interest in land. Missionaries, farmers and town-dwellers, the officials of the Native Department, the Natives in the out-districts and the Reserves, so far as they can grasp the subject, and the more advanced Natives are, generally speaking, all of one mind on this subject.' Historians have said that the Land Apportionment proposals of the Commission were acceptable to Africans and to white spokesmen on behalf of Africans: the attack on segregation, it is said, and the repudiation of the Land Apportionment Act came as a much later development.

An examination both of the proposals of the Carter Commission and of articulate African reaction to them suggests that these views are mistaken. In the first place, the recommendations of the Commission clearly fell very far short of what many African witnesses had asked for. This was most obviously so with the amount of land allocated for African purchase. Before the Commission's report whites already held some thirty-one million acres of land. The Reserves already accounted for some twenty-one-and-a-half million acres. Unalienated land amounted to forty-three-and-a-half million acres. The Commission suggested that some seven million acres of unalienated land should be set aside for 'Native Purchase'; some seventeen-

and-a-half million acres for purchase by Europeans; and the remaining nineteen million acres, largely waterless and infertile, should be left unassigned. Some African witnesses had suggested that Africans should be allocated five-eighths of the unalienated land. Very many had suggested that they should be allocated half.

African witnesses had asked that Native Purchase land should be good land, close enough to the communications network to make competitive commercial agriculture possible. These conditions were not met by the areas suggested for Native Purchase. African witnesses had suggested that within the new Native Purchase Areas land should be held on the same terms as Europeans owned land. They had suggested that there should be no limit set on the amount of land an African could own. The Commission recommended a top limit of one thousand acres for Native Purchase farms. Moreover, they could not be mortgaged or sub-let and title to them was provisional upon satisfactory development. No limitation on the size of holdings was suggested for Europeans.

African witnesses had urged that some satisfactory provision should be made for African economic enterprise in the urban areas. The Commission recommended that special townships might be set up in the Reserves where African craftsmen, and men with the skills of modern education, might serve the needs of the tribesmen. Given the disparity between what articulate Africans were prepared to accept as a segregation bargain and what they were offered it would be surprising if the Commissions' proposals commanded universal African support.

The Carter recommendations have been favourably received by historians, however. Philip Mason tells us that the proposals were 'not a harsh division as between conqueror and conquered'; Gann that they 'provided Africans with an area only slightly smaller than the whole of England. The indigenous folk, in terms of land, thus fared a great deal better than the Red Indians of North America, the Maori of New Zealand or the Araucanians of Chile.'

Such comparisons were very far from the minds of those Africans who had most eagerly heralded the appointment of the Carter Commission. Garner Sojini, who had thanked the Rhodesian Government for appointing the Commission, and Martha Ngano who had claimed that its appointment was the work of the RBVA both came to repudiate the report and its recommendations. The political associations condemned the report and called for a fresh inquiry. The ICU condemned the report. There can be little doubt from the evidence that the consensus of those Africans who were articulate on the matter was overwhelmingly hostile to the Land

Apportionment Bill which emerged from the Rhodesian Government's adoption of the Carter report.

Nor was this merely a matter of lack of realism on the part of infant African organizations. The missionaries and philanthropists who had welcomed the Commission's appointment condemned its report. Others who repudiated the recommendations of the Commission were Cripps and White, whose assent to the principle of segregation had done a great deal to bring the Commission about, and John Harris of the Aborigines Protection Society, who had lobbied year in, year out, for Native Purchase areas.

Why, then, was there such a general repudiation of the report by those 'who understood the question'? It was not, of course, in most cases because the report recommended segregation. There were some Africans who doggedly persisted in their dislike for the whole segregation principle but most African politicians were prepared to accept it in exchange for a fair bargain. But the bargain offered did not seem to be fair. This was certainly the conclusion reached by Cripps and White. Cripps had hoped that 'an equitable compromise' might result from the interacting pressures of 'those who are genuinely keen on Native Development' and the 'quasi-repressionists, apprehensive that Clause 43 may prove eventually to be in its working not a mere pious recommendation or aspiration but a living and expansive reality.' But as he scrutinized the report he became convinced that it gave too much to the white settlers, 'the Gods of the Rhodesian Gallery'. 'There are fine things in the Report,' he wrote to Bishop Paget, 'and there's a jolly enough tone in some places – but there are surely lots of things in it that ought not to go through without some chivalrous efforts on our part to better them.'[1]

By the time of the Southern Rhodesia Missionary Conference meeting in 1926 Cripps and White had resolved to attempt to persuade their colleagues to reject the report. In 1924 White had told the Conference that 'speaking as they were for the native people they were taking upon themselves a most solemn responsibility. The natives were not able to appreciate the significance of the move, nor could they understand all that was involved. It was for the missionaries who perceived the meaning to go guardedly. They wanted the natives to get land and have individual holdings,' but they 'must take care that the natives received something commensurate with the sacrifice they were being called upon to make'. Now, in 1926 White contrasted the thirty-seven per cent share allocated overall to Africans with the sixty-two per cent allocated to Europeans. 'It did not seem a fair division.' The recommended Native Purchase Areas, moreover, fell into 'inferior

[1] Cripps to Paget, 8 April 1926, ANG 1/1/9.

granite soil in which the Reserves are situated today. On the other hand the white area was enlarged where the soil was richer.'[1]

Cripps and White could not carry their colleagues with them. Many missionaries feared that the final legislation would be even less generous than the Carter report and wanted to lend their support to the Commission proposals. All White and Cripps could achieve was a recommendation that the unassigned nineteen million acres should be immediately divided between Europeans and Africans; a recommendation to which White himself said little significance could be attached since the land in question was fly-infested, waterless and sandy. The two men came to regret bitterly their earlier advocacy of the segregation bargain.

So, too, did John Harris of the Aborigines Protection Society. He also found it much easier to sell the idea that possessory segregation could be accepted in return for a just settlement than he did to ensure that the settlement *was* just. The support of the principle by the APS had been of much importance in moving the British Government to appoint the Commission. APS criticisms of the details of the report moved the British Government hardly at all. Yet Harris and his colleagues felt strongly that the bargain suggested was totally unfair. In June 1926 Harris and Buxton wrote to the Colonial Secretary to say that the suggested allocation of land 'would be a monstrously disproportionate proposition to say nothing of its inadequacy as a recompense to the Natives for the surrender of existing rights to purchase land which is anywhere available'. They urged the British Government to insist upon 'a reasonable and equitable division'; to recognize the importance to Africans of the right of communal purchase and title; to declare the unassigned nineteen million acres as Crown Land so as 'to ensure against the alienation' of these lands in future. A year later they were asserting that acceptance of the Commission's proposals would be 'a step fatal to native welfare'. In June 1929, when the Land Apportionment Bill was before the Labour Government for approval, Harris wrote to *The Manchester Guardian* that the decision was an 'Acid Test' of Labour's Imperial policy. If the bill went through 'the land policy of South Africa will be extended right up to the Zambezi today and beyond it tomorrow'. But no major changes were made in the Rhodesian proposals.[2]

Land Apportionment, in short, was something of a watershed for white radicals. The whites 'who perceived the meaning' had not done very well

---

[1] *Proceedings of the Southern Rhodesia Missionary Conference*, 1924 and 1926.

[2] Harris and Buxton to Colonial Secretary, 7 June 1926; same to same, 12 July 1927; Harris to Editor *Manchester Guardian* 27 June 1929; Rhodes House, Oxford, APS papers, file G 167.

for their African charges. Cripps and White came to feel that the Missionary Conference had abdicated its responsibilities. Cripps hoped that the ICU might emerge as a more effective spokesman of black interests. Harris bemoaned the lack of a strong African voice in Southern Rhodesia without which it was so difficult for whites to serve African interests.

It was, of course, true that there was no single strong and effective African voice. But Africans *were* saying things about Land Apportionment. It is not unimportant to establish what these things were.

The Rhodesian Bantu Voters' Association and the Carter Commission Report

Even after the their experiences as witnesses the leaders of the RBVA remained hopeful of the outcome of the Carter Commission's inquiries. Their annual general meeting of July 1925 took a studiously moderate line. They asked for the creation of a standing multi-racial affairs commission and for the abolition of passes. They returned to the subject of miscegenation which, through the presence of coloured children in African compounds, was producing 'what might well be called a White Peril'. But after the publication of the Carter Report things changed. In May 1926 the general meeting flared out in resolutions repudiating and condemning the Carter findings and recommendations. The meeting complained that the Commission had misunderstood the evidence. It held that African and missionary witnesses had been against 'districtal segregation'. It rejected the bargain offered by the Commission. And it concluded first with a statement of policy and desire and then with a reminder of that other attempted bargain – between African voters and the Responsible Government party – which was now shown so clearly to have been abortive. The meeting resolved:

'That the aim of all evidence given by the Bantus and Ministers were more or less in favour of the Colony being divided into two parts to enjoy the privileges of Clause 43, Government Gazette No. 27 (Extraordinary) of 1922 dated the 19 January, a part of which the Responsible Government was assigned.

His Majesty's loyal subjects have fervently followed the Government's platform for justice irrespective of colour and creed, etc, etc, as stated during the opening stages of the Responsible Government Campaign.'[1]

These protests, thought the Chief Native Commissioner, were indicative 'of the dissent of the numerically small progressive section of natives from the differentiation caused by segregation'. It later became clear that the

[1] Resolutions of the RBVA, 24 and 25 May 1926, S 84/A/260.

Native Department were disturbed by the opposition of 'the numerically small progressive section of natives' (going so far as to recommend that they all be moved to Northern Rhodesia) but they played the resolutions of the RBVA down. The RBVA was 'in no way representative of the bulk of the Native population'. Garner Sojini, its President, had only 'a scattered following of Fingos and Xosas in the Gwelo district. He does not represent, in any shape or form, any section of the indigenous people.' Such an estimate of the RBVA was rather disingenuous considering the alarm caused in 1924 and 1925 by its activities in the rural areas of Matabeleland.[1]

The Gwelo Native Welfare Association and the Carter Commission Report

The opposition of the GNWA could hardly be dismissed in quite the same way. What worried the administration about this organization was precisely that the land issue gave it a great boost, bringing together within it the educated Christian converts who had begun it and the chiefs and people of the surrounding areas.

The Carter Commission's visit to Gwelo and Selukwe had created a general anticipation that in one way or another more land would be provided for African occupation. Even when the report was published it was not at first condemned by the leaders of the Gwelo Native Welfare Association. Its Secretary, Alfred Maliwa Figode, adopted the strategy of calling for action in the Gwelo district to implement the general recommendations of the report. The Commissioners had not included land bordering on the Lower Gwelo Reserve among the areas recommended to be set aside for Native Purchase. But the land was good and much coveted by Gwelo Africans. Maliwa organized local rural opinion behind a request that it be set aside for African purchase. On 28 May a meeting of chiefs and headmen was held in the Seventh Day Adventist Hall, Lower Gwelo Reserve, 'to discuss the question of asking the Government to throw open some of the land adjoining the Lower Gwelo Reserve on the North East so as to enable Natives to purchase farms in accordance with the recommendations contained in the Land Commission's report'. Maliwa addressed this meeting and also a further gathering at Selukwe. On 20 June a much larger meeting of chiefs and people took place. 'Maliwa acted as the spokesman and addressed a large crowd. Chief Lukubula would have nothing to do with the matter and said that he was not prepared to support the proposal of ground being allocated for Native Areas adjoining the Lower Gwelo

[1] CNC to Secretary, Premier, 25 June 1926, S 84/A/260.

Reserve. The younger generation was very keen and it was agreed that the Native Commissioner, Gwelo, be interviewed.'[1]

Maliwa's initial strategy failed. The Native Department refused to consider the allocation of the land. At a general meeting in Gwelo on July 1926 the Southern Rhodesia Native Welfare Association, as it had now become, moved into a complete repudiation of the Carter recommendations. The meeting was attended by chiefs Mkoba, Malisa, and Gambiza, by the representative of chief Siwuntula and by six headmen, as well as by the educated members of the association and many other people. This unusually representative gathering passed a series of resolutions:

'Minutes and resolutions:

1 We record the minutes and resolutions passed by the Association in its meeting met on 12 July 1926 at Gwelo. The Delegates from various places attended. The subject was to discuss the contents of the Land Commission's Report.

2 Whereas pending thorough investigations in this connection the Association could not agree with the Report, as shown in the Map annexed.

3 The evidence of the Bantus and Chiefs etc: was in the really meaning of cutting the Colony in two equally divisions between Black and White to conserve the right and in wish of our Native people.

4 Whereas Association resoluted to ask the Honourable Government to issue a fresh Land Commission to inquire into this Land question fairly.

5 Taking into consideration the valuation of justice as against the British rule and principles.

6 Your humble Servants have followed the Government Platform for justice irrespective of tribes and status.

7 In conclusion your humble Servants hope the Honourable Government will take this matter into his kind consideration and to act so as to put us right in this difficulty.'[2]

It is obvious that these resolutions were strongly influenced by those passed by the annual general meeting of the RBVA in May 1926. But the presence of the chiefs and headmen made them less easy to dismiss. Later in 1927 a chief actually became President of the Native Welfare Association. This was Gwebu, a young Ndebele chief, who had worked in Cape Town and come into contact there with radical South African politics. In 1924 he had announced his intention of returning to Rhodesia as a representative of the South African National Congress and with the purpose of setting up a

[1] Acting NC, Gwelo, to S/N/Bulawayo, 28 June 1926, S 84/A/260.
[2] Rhodes House, Oxford, Aborigines Protection Society papers, G 166.

Rhodesian branch. Permission to do so was, of course, refused but Gwebu returned home anyway and took up his chiefly duties in the Inyatini section of Umzingwani. Gwebu, minuted the Chief Native Commissioner, 'is one of our young Matabele chiefs. Another young chief, Ngungumbana is also a member of the Association. It is natural for these young chiefs who have attained to some degree of education to take a lively interest in a matter of such importance to the Natives as the Land question.' Gwebu's presidency increased the influence of the association among the Ndebele. Meanwhile Maliwa Figode continued to work among his Shona kinsfolk and with the educated of Gwelo township. 'The Secretary is very active and preaches his propaganda at the kraals in the Reserves and elsewhere in the district and appears to have a fairly strong educated following.'[1]

In February 1927 the Welfare Association held a big general meeting under the chairmanship of Gwebu in 'the English Church (Native) Gwelo'. The meeting endorsed the resolutions of July 1926, repeating their rejection of the Carter Report and calling for another inquiry, and adding a number of other pertinent points, in particular calling for attention to the problem of African 'squatters' on land which would be declared European under the Bill. For some reason these February resolutions attracted wide notice. In April they were printed in *The Gwelo Times* in a tidied-up version. This version was sent by Cripps to the Aborigines Protection Society so that they could demonstrate African opposition to the recommendations of the Carter Commission.

And Cripps himself quoted the resolutions on the very last page in his *An Africa for Africans: A Plea on behalf of Territorial Segregation Areas* which was published later in 1927. *An Africa for Africans* has often been cited as proof of Cripps' total commitment to the ideal of segregation and hence to the land apportionment policy. But the book is also a trenchant criticism of the Carter Commission proposals. Cripps argued that if segregation was to be tried it should be tried properly; that Africans should be given large consolidated areas of good land; that the Imperial Government should finance the expropriation of European-held land needed to realize this instead of accepting 'a mere second-class makeshift scheme with an illusory attraction of cheapness' such as was recommended by the Commission; that communal tenure should be allowed in the new areas; that easy purchase terms be made available; and that labourers on European farms and workers in the towns should be allowed to lease land. Cripps' view of the segregation bargain – and that of many Africans – was summed

[1] CNC to Secretary, Premier, 27 April 1927; N. C. Gwelo to S/N/Bulawayo, 24 April 1927; S 84/A/260.

up in his text from Zechariah: 'And I said unto them, If ye think good, give me my price, and if not forbear.'

In his After-Word Cripps called upon the Welfare Association Resolutions to support his arguments.

'This book has asked attention for the Native African's point of view. It seems right, then, in discussing an African Land Question to allow an African Welfare Association to have the last word in its pages.

The general secretary (A. M. Zigode) of the Southern Rhodesia Native Welfare Association states "that the following resolutions were passed for submission to the Government at a recent conference held in Gwelo":

1 That in connection with the Native Land Bill the Association could not agree with the report of the Commission, pending thorough investigation.

2 That the Bantu chiefs, in their evidence, had really meant cutting the Colony into two equal portions for black and white.

3 That the Government be asked to appoint a fresh Land Commission.

4 That the British act and principle lays down fair play as between the races – equal justice, equal opportunity to rise, and equal right to this common land.

5 That most of the farms in the new proposed area for natives are quite dry and very unfertile, and the area in question would be far too small for the natives concerned.

6 That the difficulty of the whole matter is the unsatisfactory position with regard to native squatters; this is a Bill to make provision for the settlement of the native squatters' question by providing land on a place to which they may go, if they are removed from the farms where they are now.

7 That parliament has no right to deprive the natives of the land, under Clause 43, Government Gazette Extraordinary, dated 18 January 1922.'[1]

The Government also paid attention to the Welfare Association. 'I think this Association is one that needs careful watching,' minuted Sir Charles Coghlan, 'and reports should be made of its doings to headquarters as occasion arises.' Occasion arose several times in 1927. The Welfare Association built up close connections with African politicians in Bulawayo. By the middle of the year leaders of the RBVA like Zacharia Magkatho and Martha Ngano were playing a key role in the deliberations of the Welfare Association. Fortified by these connections and its continuing influence in the rural areas of Gwelo and Selukwe, the Welfare Association planned for

[1] A. S. Cripps, *An Africa for Africans. A Plea on behalf of Territorial Segregation Areas and of their Freedom in a South African Colony*, London, 1927, p. 200.

July 1927 its most ambitious meeting yet. Its purpose was to discuss the Land Apportionment Bill, the Education Bill and the Native Councils Bill; and to set up an Executive Committee to follow through its decisions. The Native Commissioner expected 'a large gathering including not only educated but kraal natives and possibly a few chiefs and headmen both from this district and the areas around Bulawayo'.[1]

This July meeting was the high point of the Association's activities. It was attended by some 150 people. Gwebu was there, so were chief Majinkila of Umzingwani, chief Malisa's son, Mazembe, and chief Gambiza. 'Educated natives from Bulawayo, Gwelo district and one or two from Inyati formed the majority and were much in evidence.' There were 'several prominent and respectable native teachers, notably Mfazi Ngano'. It was, in fact, an impressive assembly of Ndebele and Shona chiefs, Ndebele and Shona progressives, and 'alien native' leaders.

This meeting discussed the land question at length. A member of the Legislative Assembly, Danziger, who was opposing the Land Apportionment Bill there and arguing as an alternative the case for total segregation whereby 'all the Natives of the Colony should be given one compact and separate area', was asked to explain his plan to them. A committee of nine was elected to develop and represent the Welfare Association's land policy. It reflected the composition of the meeting as a whole, containing some Bulawayo members and some Gwelo members, some chiefly members and some progressive, some Ndebele members and some Shona.

Out of this committee emerged a series of resolutions. Most of them were identical to the resolutions of February: the Welfare Association was repeating the objections it had made against the Carter Report and applying them now to the Land Apportionment Bill. In addition there were some organizational recommendations designed to transform the Welfare Association into an effective provincial or even national body. The new name of African Welfare Association was chosen. It was agreed to appoint a paid organizing Secretary, each branch to raise ten shillings towards his salary. The individual membership subscription was raised to ten shillings a year. A Savings Bank account was opened. And the Government was asked 'whether there is any objection on the part of the Government to natives born in the Union, Northern Rhodesia or adjacent territories being members and office bearers of this Association, or if the Government desires that the Association should be confined to natives born in the Colony'.[2]

---

[1] Coghlan to CNC, 28 April 1927; N. C. Gwelo to S/N/Bulawayo, 27 June 1927; S 84/A/260.

[2] Resolutions, July 1927, S 84/A/260.

It was all a long way from the modest Gwelo Native Welfare Association of 1924. The Rhodesian Government thought that it was too long a way. In August 1927 they replied that 'the Association is not regarded as one under Government recognition'. Meanwhile the Native Commissioner in Gwelo had taken steps to break up a potentially dangerous alliance between the educated and the chiefs and headmen. It was his own belief that the educated leaders were using the chiefs as cat's-paws and committing them to statements that they did not understand. He alleged that the resolutions issued by the committee of nine had not been passed at the meeting which elected them. This was true but they were the same resolutions as those passed at the two previous meetings of the Association. 'This Association, in so far as chief Fish (Gwebu), Maliwa and others of its ringleaders are concerned, is a Society which conducts its business and propaganda in what is little removed from a private if not seditious atmosphere,' he wrote. He called in the local chiefs and told them that they were being misrepresented; he warned them that he had been compelled to report to Government that his confidence in the Association had been shaken. And he warned the Association itself that, 'I will not allow chief Fish, Maliwa or any of these people to hold meetings in Gwelo while I am in charge of the Native Affairs in this District.'

All this was enough to frighten off the chiefs and headmen and to sever the frail link between them and the Gwelo and Bulawayo progressives. 'Your confidence in the people was perfectly justified,' the chiefs hastened to assure the Native Commissioner. 'It is not in the people but in these strangers, the ringleaders, that you have been deceived ... We do not want to have anything more to do with them. They misrepresent us and they will lead us into trouble. Why should our affairs be interfered with by these people? Let them attend to their own business and leave us to attend to ours.'[1]

Maliwa was not frightened off. He denied that the chiefs and people had been misrepresented. There *was* general opposition to the Land Apportionment Bill even if the Native Department could frighten the chiefs into repudiating it. Maliwa was determined that this opposition should continue to be expressed. Despite the Native Commissioner's renewed warning that he would only permit meetings 'under the chairmanship of the Native Commissioner', Maliwa defied this illegal prohibition and called a meeting for December. 'An official wish,' wrote the indignant Commissioner, 'is, of course, usually regarded by the ordinary native as an order, but that the

[1] N. C. Gwelo to S/N/Bulawayo, 30 July 1927, S 84/A/260.

Secretary is not an ordinary native is pretty clear from the letter attached from which it will be seen that he says (ignoring my wishes) that he is convening another meeting.' The Commissioner toyed with the idea of prosecuting Maliwa 'for the passively contumacious manner in which my wishes have been ignored'. This turned out not to be necessary. In October Maliwa was 'required by his employers to serve either them or the Association'.[1]

The December meeting was attended by only twenty people. No chiefs, headmen or 'kraal natives' were present. Maliwa gave in his resignation. The land issue was not discussed. Official action had broken the back of the movement. Still, its career between early 1926 and December 1927 reveals a great deal about African reaction to the Carter Commission report and the policy of Land Apportionment – the early hopes that it would mean additional land where the tribesmen wanted it; the later disillusionment and the rejection of the report because of the smallness of the quantity and the badness of the quality of the land actually offered; the realization of the progressives that the policy was not conceived in the interests of improved farming but as a means of clearing 'squatters' from the European farms; the call for a new inquiry and the call for British justice to express itself by imposing an equal division between black and white. In this year-and-a-half the Welfare Association brought together an impressively wide cross-section of the African people of Matabeleland. The Native Commissioner, Gwelo, thought that the rural members were 'an assemblage of dupes', but it is at least possible that the Native Welfare Association provided one of the few means of expression for rural disillusionment as well as for the disillusionment of the progressives.

The ICU and Land Apportionment

At any rate it is clear that the leaders of the workers were as hostile to the land apportionment proposals as the leaders of the RBVA and the Welfare Association. The ICU often discussed land questions. Its style was different, of course. ICU speeches tended to be very generalized statements on inequality rather than specific criticism of the Commission report or the subsequent legislation. 'When Lobengula came here,' said Mfulu in Bulawayo, 'he did not go to the mountains. He stayed here in this fertile country where good crops are easily grown. This is your country.' 'The ground you till is absolutely worthless,' said Tengapi, 'the ground that was never tilled by anyone. The best part of the land is taken by Mr Whiteman and you are not allowed to plough there so we have to run away and go to

[1] N. C. Gwelo to S/N/Bulawayo, 3 October 1927; 30 December 1927, S 84/A/260.

G

work for the white man.' Masoja Ndlovu raised in a similarly general way the issue of land purchase. 'Every day new immigrants are coming from Europe and if you do not agitate for higher pay and try to buy yourself some ground, then you will all find yourselves in the Kalahari desert.'[1]

Masoja was sufficiently concerned about the Land Apportionment Bill, however, to take a leading role in a general meeting of associations organized by the RBVA for July 1929. There was nothing surprising about his readiness to work with the RBVA in this way. Kadalie had very often collaborated with Professor Jabavu in South Africa, though both Kadalie and Jabavu disliked Congress. In the same way it seems that in Southern Rhodesia the ICU and the RBVA found it easy enough to work together but that both were suspicious of the Rhodesia Native Association. Masoja took the chair on the second day of this combined meeting and together with Wesley Sojini of the RBVA dominated the proceedings.

Between them the two men scrutinized in turn all the native legislation of the Responsible Government politicians. Led by them the meeting voted unanimously against the proposed new Native Councils Bill. 'Natives should draft the Native Councils Bill to their own choosing and enjoyment.' 'Africans,' proclaimed Masoja, 'do not want the Native Commissioner to be the Chairman of the Native Councils, he is a European, how can he understand the domestic affairs of natives? Only a native can do this.' The meeting condemned government education policy. 'Why should our children always be sent to the missionaries?' asked Masoja. 'Do we not pay taxes to the Government? Then we want a Government school, we want to see something for our money, we want proper schooling for our children.'

Finally this 'Congress' of associations voted unanimously to repudiate the Land Apportionment Bill, then before the Southern Rhodesian Assembly.

Wesley Sojini: 'It is the resolution of this Congress not to accept it. You all know that from 1925 it was suggested that the land be proportioned into land for the black man and land for the white man. Some of you gave evidence at the Commission. This bill is now before the House of Assembly. This bill does not show any security for the native land. This is against our evidence. The evidence given by the natives was that land should be halved, the black man to have one half and the white man the other half.'

Masoja Ndlovu: 'Let us tell the Government that this Bill is wrong. Our people have been driven to lands where they cannot live. Our

[1] CID reports of ICU meetings in 1930, S 84/A/300.

cattle die for the want of water. We are sent to a land of windmills. What can the people do if there is no wind? It was suggested to the Government that we should move to the Kalahari desert. This is no good. Let us tell the Government that the bill is no good. It is all for the white man. Rhodesia is big. Let them cut the land in half and let us live on one side and the white man on the other. If they cannot do this they should at least give us a place for Reserves where there is water.'[1]

The Associations and Attempts at Unity

This 'Congress' marked the culmination of the disillusionment of participant associations. The Land Commission, which they had regarded as their great opportunity, had resulted in legislation which they repudiated. The full Government programme of 'concessions' to Africans, intended by the new Prime Minister, Moffat, to fulfil the election pledges of the Responsible Government Party was totally unsatisfactory in their eyes. In particular Government was doing little or nothing to build up an educated and progressive élite. On the contrary, it became increasingly clear that educated Africans were not acceptable to Government as spokesmen for their people. 'An impression is abroad,' it was lamented at the 'Congress', 'that educated and progressive natives are not in favour in some quarters.' Yet what alternative to the policy of participation was there? Even at this embittered meeting, with the ICU stalwart Masoja Ndlovu in the chair, he could offer no more revolutionary counsel to the men of the associations than that 'if we talk sensibly as we have done today the Government will take notice of us'.

Yet there *was* one new note in Masoja's address. Government would take notice of the resolutions of this particular meeting because it brought together the RBVA, the ICU, the Native Welfare Association and perhaps other African organizations. 'Unity is strength.' Of course this was not Masoja's unique discovery. As they reacted to the Land Apportionment Bill and to the manifest failure of the participation strategy in the later 1920s, most of the leaders of the associations moved towards an attempt to create a more completely representative organization. If there was one effective territory-wide body, it was thought, Government would be unable to play off other organizations against it or to deny its right to speak for the people. The 'Congress' of 1929 was only one of a number of unity attempts.

Thus in 1926 Matabese, the new President of the Rhodesian Native Association, who had opposed possessory segregation before the Carter Commission, presented a new constitution to the Native Department and

[1] Report by Detective Inspector Watt, 14 July 1929, S 84/A/261.

sought permission to campaign in the Reserves. 'The ultimate object,' wrote the Acting Chief Native Commissioner, 'is to absorb all other Native Associations and to form, from the Rhodesia Native Association so strengthened, a Native Advisory Council. This council would be the official mouthpiece of the Native population, both indigenous and non-indigenous. Should this object be attained the organization would supplant the existing system of representation of indigenes by Chiefs and Headmen.' Again, in December 1927, when Maliwa's enforced resignation from the African Welfare Association in Gwelo brought home to that body its own weakness, 'it was decided to abandon the title of African Native Welfare Association and to revert to the title of the Southern Rhodesia Native Welfare Association and it was also resolved that the latter Association be amalgamated with what is called the Southern Rhodesia Native Association'. So far as I know neither of these intentions was realized. The RNA certainly did not assimilate all other associations and the Welfare Association kept its own identity. But the impulse towards unity and effectiveness is plain.[1]

In 1929, as we have seen, there was a movement towards an even more ambitious grouping which would include representatives of the industrial workers as well as the leaders of the associations. In July the 'Congress' of associations met in Bulawayo under RBVA patronage and the chairmanship of Masoja Ndlovu. Later in the year Martha Ngano attended a meeting in Salisbury on behalf of the RBVA where she discussed with delegates of the ICU, the Bantu Benefit Transport Society, the Southern Rhodesia Native Welfare Association and the Southern Rhodesian Association the possibility of forming a permanent Congress movement. These attempts were not successful either. According to Professor Hooker, the Salisbury attempt was defeated by the objections of the ICU and the Bantu Benefit Society, objections which arose essentially out of 'Matabele-Mashona differences'. It seems probable that what was really at the root of the ICU's objections was its old dislike of the Congress movement in South Africa and its suspicion of the élitism of the associations.[2]

Yet regionalism, if not tribalism, was undoubtedly also at the root of the problem of unity. In the late 1920s Southern Rhodesia had three associations, theoretically territory-wide in scope but in effect influential in one region only. On the face of it it might seem that an effective Congress movement could very well have been made up through a confederation of the RBVA, with its strength in Matabeleland, the Welfare Association,

[1] Minute by ACNC, 24 August 1926, S 84/A/260; N. C. Gwelo to S/N/Bulawayo, 30 December 1927, S 84/A/261.
[2] Hooker, 'Welfare Associations'.

with its strength in the Midlands, and the RNA, with its strength in Mashonaland. It was through this sort of confederation that the Congress movements in Nyasaland and Northern Rhodesia later developed. But it was not to be the path in Southern Rhodesia.

Perhaps the claim of each association to represent the whole territory made each reluctant to accept the claims of the others. Perhaps the extent to which they had tapped regional rural sentiment was an obstacle to unity. On the face of it, once again, the contacts which had been made between educated leaders and rural audiences around Bulawayo and Gwelo could have been a source of strength to any confederal Congress. But in practice it seems likely that at the end of the 1920s unity was possible only at the Christian élite level. At the end of the 1920s Shona farmers were still re-calling the Ndebele raids of the nineteenth century and using these memories to justify suspicions of Bulawayo politicians. The chiefs and headmen of the Gwelo district were frightened out of the Native Welfare Association when the Bulawayo progressives began to come into it. In Bulawayo itself Ndebele town dwellers responded to the increasing pres-sures of life in the towns by making Shona workers the scapegoats of urban violence and demanding separate Ndebele villages.

At any rate when the Bantu Congress did emerge in 1934 it did not arise out of any confederation of existing organizations, nor out of any alliance of progressives and peasant farmers and industrial workers. It sprang out of another and quite distinct body which had developed in the 1920s – the Southern Rhodesia Missionary Conference of Native Christians. At this indigenous Christian élite level unity was possible. And no doubt unity was an advance. Nevertheless, the Bantu Congress of the 1930s also lacked some of the assets of the associations of the 1920s. It was more moderate and respectful than they had been. It made less effective contact with other groups among the African population. During the 1930s the Congress stood for the aspiration towards territorial unity, but it was other bodies that spoke for the grievances of the less educated townsmen or the workers or the peasants. For example, in the 1920s the grievances of Ndebele town-dwellers and of Ndebele tribesmen had been briefly canalized away from intensely tribal forms of expressions by the influence of the RBVA and the ICU. In the 1930s, or so it appears, these grievances were expressed not through Congress but through the Matabele Home Society.

The move towards confederal unity failed, then. Disunited still, the associations could find no other answer to their dilemma. Official comments in the year that Land Apportionment was enacted displayed a confident assurance of their weakness. Their opposition to land policy and the government's Native policy as a whole could safely be ignored. 'There are many native associations in this town [Bulawayo]; most of them are harmless and ineffective. Even the ICU, whose leaders are more active and fluent than most, makes little if any headway . . . If they are treated with what appears to be beneficent indifference, they are apt to die of inanition.' 'They have nothing but the best intentions,' wrote Prime Minister Moffat, 'viz., a desire to help their people, but it is also fairly clear that they have the vaguest ideas as to how they can act . . . What they have in mind seems far beyond their powers. The new Native Welfare Societies composed of Europeans have much the same objects in view and are far better able to carry them out . . . I do not think they can do any real good. I do not think they really know what it is they want or how they are going to get it.' It was an unfair epitaph on a decade of political activity but in the year that Land Apportionment went through it was a fair reflection on the power of the settler government and the impotence of its critics.[1]

Yet the opposition of the articulate African politicians was not without some practical significance. In 1931, for example, Chief Native Commissioner Carbutt explained the almost total lack of applications for Native Purchase farms in Matabeleland as 'partly due to the unsuitability of the land . . . and partly to the opposition of Native Associations to the provisions of the Land Apportionment Act, who are advising Natives not to purchase land, which they contend already belongs to them.' In 1934 this same Chief Native Commissioner put up a scheme to Prime Minister Huggins for sending all educated Africans for whom there were no opportunities in an increasingly segregated Rhodesia up to Northern Rhodesia so that the government 'would be freed of the embarrassing necessity to consider native interests'. The Rhodesian authorities were not quite as unperturbed by 'progressive' opposition as they liked to make out.[2]

The Revival of Ndebele 'Nationality' Politics: the Matabele Home Society
It remains to complete this chapter by examining two organizations of the late 1920s which were to have a future of very different kinds – the Matabele Home Society and the Southern Rhodesia Missionary Conference of Native Christians.

We have seen how the RBVA and the ICU made contact with the traditions of Ndebele opposition and how in making contact they both influenced and were influenced by Ndebele politics. To take one example of

---

[1] Moffat to CNC, 24 February 1930, S 84/A/261.
[2] CNC to Secretary, Premier, 30 June 1931, S 138/21; memorandum by Carbutt, July 1934, D.O. 35/390. These examples are both cited by Dr Palmer.

many, the emphasis placed by both the RBVA and the ICU at the end of the 1920s on the desirability of one great coherent African area rather than the scattered Reserves and Native Purchase Areas was essentially an Ndebele emphasis. It was a return to the vision of Nyamanda and the movement for an Ndebele National Home and it could hardly have appealed very greatly to the Shona. But the two organizations also brought Ndebele feeling in touch with wider horizons and with 'modern' ideas of African politics.

Given the intense land grievances of the Ndebele, their sense of solidarity, their relatively long political experience, it might have been expected that they would have gone on from this basis to become the driving force of African nationalism in Rhodesia. It has not turned out in this way. If anything modern African nationalism has been characteristically a Shona phenomenon. For this there are very many reasons. One of them, perhaps a symptom rather than a reason, was the turning away of the Ndebele from associations like the RBVA and the ICU and their return to frankly 'nationality' or tribal politics. The Matabele Home Society is an instance of this very important Ndebele withdrawal.

The Matabele Home Society came to the notice of the Native Department in November 1929. In that month the officers of the Society submitted a copy of its Constitution.

'Matabele Home Society : Forwards

We crave the understanding of the reader of this our Constitution. We humbly beg to overlook all errors and omissions. It being our first endeavour to establish good fellowship among the black races and co-operation and understanding with the ruling race.

The Constitution – The Name of the Society shall be: Matabele Home Society.

1 The objects are to support and build up the fallen Nation (Natives) and develop their welfare on a civilized basis and act as a channel between the authorities throughout Matabeleland *socially and morally.*

2 The Society in its working shall organize throughout Matabeleland and secure the co-operation of all persons who have at heart the objects of humanity, and are interested in the welfare of the Black races, to enlighten and show the public our opinion on matters affecting the Natives, to assist home Natives by every legitimate means.'[1]

The officers of the Society were drawn partly from Ndebele town-dwellers and partly from the Kumalo pressure group for the restoration of

[1] Constitution of the Matabele Home Society, S 84/A/261.

the Ndebele monarchy. Its first Secretary was Baleni Zembi, who had been General Secretary of the Loyal Mandabele Patriotic Society in 1916. A leading member was the Wesleyan teacher, Ntando, who had been Nguboyena's host in 1908 and a member of Nyamanda's party in 1920. The Treasurer was Gula Kumalo, who in September 1929 had approached the Native Department with Ntando and others of the Kumalo clan asking that 'one of Lobengula's heirs be made chief', and that 'land be set apart so that the clan could live together and not be a scattered brotherhood as they now are'. 'All other Clans had their native head,' said the delegation. 'The Kumalos had none. Yes, they had the Native Commissioner and the Government, but that was not the same thing. No Clan that had ever existed had been expected to live without a Head for ever – without a Patriarch or guardian who shared their customs and their joys and bereavements, and who was their immemorial fire at which a Clan – and every Clan – warms its hands.'[1]

Thus, although the Chairman of the MHS, Magavu Sikosana, raised the issues of education, the franchise, representation in Parliament and other national issues at his meeting with the Minister of Native Affairs in December 1929, the three abiding concerns of the Society were the conditions of life for urban dwelling Ndebele, the attempt to restore the monarchy and the question of Ndebele land.

Now that Nyamanda was dead, the hopes of the monarchists were pinned either on the mentally ill Nguboyena or on Lobengula's grandson, Rhodes. In January 1931 the Matabele Home Society representative in Nyamandhlovu was collecting funds for 'further medical attention to Nguboyena Kumalo'. 'One now sees that the Kumalo clan (and the) Home Society run hand in glove,' minuted the Superintendent of Natives, Bulawayo. 'They are gradually exposing their hand.' Later Rhodes Lobengula was elected Secretary of the Society.

What was the significance of all this? The Native Department believed that agitation for a restoration of the monarchy was no longer central to the concerns of the Ndebele. 'The petition for a Lobengula chief which at one time, and for long, had a considerable body of influential men behind it, has probably ceased to be a living issue except in the minds of a limited circle of Nguboyena's relatives and other Kumalos who are not in office or in receipt of stipends or other Government benefits.' It was hard for anyone to imagine that the restoration of the monarchy and the national homelands was a practical possibility any longer. Nor could the Ndebele monarchy any longer be made a focus for the political aspirations of non-Ndebele progres-

[1] S/N/Bulawayo to CNC, 26 September 1929, S 84/A/262.

sives as had once been the case. The Matabele Home Society was perhaps essentially the movement of Ndebele town dwellers desperately in search of stability and status. The monarchy was the symbol of Ndebelehood, that intangible quality which distinguished them from other denizens of the towns.

Certainly the urban members of the Matabele Home Society were concerned to separate themselves from the 'alien' migrant labourers who flocked to Bulawayo. Thus in September 1930 Gula Kumalo and Jack Mabulo, representing the Society, met the Superintendent of Natives in Bulawayo, to seek special status for resident Ndebele.

Gula Kumalo : 'The Location is no longer a safe place to live in. I think we have mentioned the matter before today, but we want a location of our own under Government control to live in. There are too many factions or sections in the Town location. It is most dangerous to be out at night; if you visit a friend and are coming home you are liable to be attacked by these mouth-organ gangs – gangs of natives. Some may be Makalaka from Fort Victoria District, other Abanyika or Mashona natives – some even of the people of this land.

You see, there are a lot of people who have worked for years and whose families have grown up in Locations. They know nothing of living outside on farms and Reserves – they do not want land to plough but they want a good Location to live in. Inkosi, I ask you to have these villages for us workers of the towns. There are thousands ready to go into such villages of nice rooms. We would like to have the people that go into them picked out . . . Keep the villages for decent people, and anyone not keeping the rules of the village – put them out . . . These gangs are bad and there is ill feeling between tribes. The Fort Victoria Makalaka are the worst and it seems they will fight. We hear. We see. We will repeat to you anything we hear and so assist the Police. We do not want to be mixed up in these things.'[1]

Professor Hooker has described the Matabele Home Society as 'an illustration of a reactionary answer to European conquest'. Gann has described it as 'arch conservative'. In many ways these descriptions are obviously accurate. It is instructive, for example, to contrast the reactions of the ICU, the RBVA and the Matabele Home Society to the single problem of inter-tribal violence in the Bulawayo locations. The ICU condemned all parties to this violence, called on Africans to set aside tribal prejudices and to unite, and demanded African control of the location. Martha Ngano of the RBVA asked that areas be set aside for long-term

[1] S/N/Bulawayo to CNC, 24 September 1930, S 84/A/261.

residents, but she explicitly denied that she was doing so because of the violence and low living standards of the migrant labourers. She blamed the mismanagement and authoritarianism of the municipality for conditions in the location. The Matabele Home Society put the blame for urban violence squarely on the Shona migrants and demanded villages for Ndebele workers. In so far as people who had supported either the ICU or the RBVA came to support the Matabele Home Society it was clearly a backward step.

The Rhodesian administration was shrewd enough to see that the emergence of the Matabele Home Society weakened the thrust of African politics. Officials disliked the revival of the kingship demand. They refused to allow the Society permission to campaign in the Reserves. They found the capacity of the Society to achieve its stated aims so limited as to be 'pathetic'. They asserted that African grievances should be expressed through indunas or through the newly created Native Welfare Societies in the towns. But there was no desire to suppress the Society. 'It seems to me that the more of these Societies there are the better,' wrote the Superintendent of Natives, Bulawayo, 'for their jealousy of each other and lack of unanimity is a source of weakness to all of them.'[1]

The Southern Rhodesia Missionary Conference of Native Christians
We have seen that so far from African politics in Southern Rhodesia being slow to develop in comparison with territories to the north, developments tended to take place in Rhodesia much earlier. Southern Rhodesia had territorial African associations, an African trade union movement, a Congress movement, many years before these things developed in Northern Rhodesia or Nyasaland. But the reason for this was mainly that Southern Rhodesia was so close to South Africa. The idea of territory-wide political associations, the idea of African trade unionism, both came into Rhodesia from South Africa. And we have seen that many of the key leaders of these developments were either South Africans or men who had worked in South Africa.

One of the reasons why there was something of a crisis in Rhodesian African politics at the end of the 1920s was that there was a disparity between the sophisticated political techniques and assumptions introduced from the south and the more slowly maturing politics of the indigenous people. A parallel can be drawn in the field of religion. Ethiopianism was introduced into Southern Rhodesia at the end of the nineteenth century by South Africans but independent Christianity did not really

[1] S/N/Bulawayo to CNC, 30 November 1929, S 84/A/261.

begin to develop in Rhodesia until the end of the 1920s and the 1930s when internal conditions favourable to its growth had developed. This largely Shona independency was nothing like as coherent as Reverend Makgatho's Ethiopianism but it was much more significant because it had deep local roots.

Something of the same sort happened in politics. Associations modelled on the South African model had shot up in the 1920s and I have argued that they had many relevant things to say. Some of them succeeded in making contact with Rhodesian Africans at grass roots or dirt streets level. But they were undoubtedly weakened both by their dependence on the leadership of 'alien' Africans and by their application in Rhodesia of tactics which derived from the very different South African situation. The RBVA could not make the vote a substitute for the assegai in a country where there were so few voters, the ICU could not use the strike weapon, concepts of territorial unity ran into the realities of tribalism and regionalism. In many ways the political concepts of the 1920s were too sophisticated for political realities.

At the beginning of the 1930s these attempts had fairly obviously failed. Land Apportionment had been enacted, the ICU was collapsing, the leadership of the sort of élite that had dominated the RBVA was undermined. A man like Garner Sojini, who stood for the progressive large scale African farmer, freely competing with the whites on a basis of economic independence, was a totally unrealistic symbol for the 1930s. The Land Apportionment Act ruled out the development of any such class of Africans. The fierce economic competition of the depression period ruled out any revival of prosperous agriculture in the African areas. African politics in Southern Rhodesia entered a new phase. They became much more exclusively the business of the slowly maturing indigenous élite, the men of the Christian solution, who were at last ready to take the stage. There were still not very many of them. In 1928 there were 1,549 African schools of all classes and between two and three thousand African teachers. It was African clergy who took a political lead at the end of the 1920s with the formation of the Southern Rhodesia Missionary Conference of Christian Natives which was in many ways the progenitor of the Bantu Congress of the 1930s. But at the end of the 1920s there were still only a handful of African clergy. The two denominations which had progressed furthest in the production of an African ministry were the Anglicans and the Wesleyans. In 1930 there were seven African Anglican priests and twelve African Wesleyan ministers. There were no African Catholic priests or Dutch Reformed Church ministers. The Salvation Army, with its more democratic traditions, possessed as many as sixty-five 'commissioned native officers' but other than these there were only some two dozen African clergy in Southern Rhodesia.

Not surprisingly these men were in many ways less impressive as political leaders than their predecessors. They were less self confident, more overawed by white power and knowledge. They did not expect to be able to engage in free economic or other competition with the whites and they were readier to accept the newly erected framework of possessory segregation. Most were restrained by their obligations to their employers. But they had grown out of the Southern Rhodesian situation.

The initiative towards the creation of an African Christian body was taken by a group of Shona Methodist preachers and teachers in 1926. In that year they approached the Secretary of the Southern Rhodesia Missionary Conference with the suggestion that the European body recognize a 'Native Christian Congress'. In 1928 the constitution of the new organization was approved. This constitution gave tight control to the European missionaries. It was provided that the President of the European Conference or his deputy should always take the chair at meetings of the African Conference. The resolutions passed by the African ministers were not to be forwarded directly to Government but were to be tabled at the European Conference for its endorsement or otherwise. It was laid down that the African Conference could not 'discuss the constitution of any of the Churches represented, or any financial or other arrangements it may make with its agents or other workers'. Membership of the African Conference was of course restricted to African clergy of the recognized Mission churches. Thus although the Conference claimed to represent 'a large proportion of the Christian natives of Southern Rhodesia' it did not include old stalwarts like Reverend Makgatho or Matthew Zwimba, nor did it include the leaders of the mass movements of Zionist and Pentecostal independency which are described in the next chapter. In short the African Conference was very much under the paternal control and supervision of the European missionaries.

All this defined the kind of political position the Conference, and later the Bantu Congress, would take up. The Conference spoke in the name of a special African interest, the interest of what it described as 'the Christian and enlightened Natives of the Colony'. It called for an opportunity for its members to meet 'Royal or other highly placed Visitors'. It criticized the African police for being 'uneducated and non-Christian' and expressed regret that they did not try to copy the 'gentlemanly' behaviour of European police. The 'Christian and enlightened Natives of the Colony' spoke in a tone of respect and deference. They thanked the Governor, Sir Herbert Stanley, 'who has been the first to invite us as honoured guests to Government House. He shook hands with us, and we felt that he was indeed God's representative and a Father of the Africans.' They said that they found the Land Apportionment Act 'perfectly satisfactory'. They said that if 'natives were allowed to exercise the franchise . . . we strongly believe that native votes will always be exercised for European members'.[1]

At the same time the African Conference did take up political issues. It asked that Africans should be consulted about the proposals for amalgamation with Northern Rhodesia, it called for an African wage board and it protested against rumoured intentions to remove the African franchise. It was this combination that found fuller expression in the Bantu Congress. The Congress was led by the same men – Reverend Samkange and Reverend Rusiki. And the Bantu Congress inherited the basic target of the African Conference, what Reverend Samkange called 'a progressive Christian nation under His Majesty's Government, irrespective of race, colour and creed'.

[1] Gray, *The Two Nations*, pp. 163–4; *Proceedings of the Southern Rhodesia Missionary Conference*, 1930, 1932, 1934.

NINE

The Rural Areas
of Mashonaland

PASSIVITY AND MILLENARIANISM

We have been examining the growth and the disillusionment of the élite political associations, the emergence of the indigenous Christian élite, and the attempts by the ICU to speak for African workers. What, meanwhile, of the rural population of Rhodesia and especially of Mashonaland? Quite considerable numbers of the rural Ndebele were caught up in the various movements already discussed, especially the Matabele Home Movement. But very few Shona in the rural areas were involved in the RNA or in any other movement. At the end of the 1920s any observer would have said that the Shona tribesmen were of all Africans the least politicized. Yet later mass nationalism drew heavily on the grievances and the commitment of rural Mashonaland.

This change is, of course, largely to be explained in terms of developments subsequent to 1930. But it is worthwhile examining what evidence there is for the mood of the Shona rural areas in the late 1920s. In 1923, as we saw in Chapter One, the mood of the Shona peoples in Belingwe was characterized by passivity, fatalistic acceptance and despair. This was characteristic enough of the Shona rural areas as a whole throughout the 1920s. Before the First World War the Shona rural economy had functioned successfully and the great majority of Shona men had been able to operate as full-time cultivators and to preserve a significant independence. By the 1920s this had changed in all the ways we have seen. The rural economy ceased to produce and to market successfully a sizeable agricultural surplus; Shona men were compelled to enter the labour market in ever-increasing numbers and at a time when wages were low; prices for African produce and stock declined. The independence of the Shona cultivator was undermined; he had become more dependent upon a variety of European goods; he was becoming 'proletarianized'. So demoralization spread through the rural areas which had now lost their economic *raison d'etre* without regaining any political or religious viability. As more men were caught up in migrant labour so the communities of the Reserves began to suffer from the distortions of social relations and institutions which this drain of manpower produced. To all this the initial response was naturally enough one of fatalism and despair. The old responses were clearly invalid but nothing presented itself as a convincing new answer. Was there any movement out of passivity, towards a new commitment, in the 1920s?

The Christian Solution and the Reaction Against It

In 1925 one of the most intelligent and individual of Rhodesian Native Commissioners, Nielsen, addressed himself to the problem of the apathy of the Shona Reserves. In Gutu, he wrote, there were some 30,000 people living 'in a state of degradation which must be seen to be believed'. This degradation, Nielsen thought, was the result of a radical failure of white rule. 'We have destroyed, to a large extent, the social structure of the Natives, such as it was, and we have given them nothing in its stead. It is true that we have given them peace, but is that enough?' The rural African was presented with no goal, no opportunities, no stimuli. There was no point or possibility in striving after the old communal goals. The result was 'brutish stupor'. 'They live and multiply like the beasts of the field.' They drink excessively 'as the only means of diversion from the dullness of their present existence'. The only way out, thought Nielsen, was a massive campaign of education and of encouragement to Africans to acquire the franchise, enter competitive economic activity and so on. 'We must give them, on the one hand, the means to strengthen the will to live better and to rise higher . . . and on the other we must let these people cherish those aspirations for a place for themselves in the sun of Africa which will grow naturally out of their awakening consciousness.'

Nielsen's analysis was essentially the same as that of the leaders of the RBVA. So, too, was his remedy. Nielsen was in fact a friend of Martha Ngano. In 1925 he got himself into trouble for advising a group of African teachers in Shabani to invite Martha down to address them. 'He asked us if we knew what a 'vote' was and we said we did not. He said a 'vote' was to elect people to represent our wants to the Government and it would tend to raise us. He said there was a woman in Bulawayo . . . He said if we liked we could write to this woman to come and speak to us.' Nielsen told the teachers, or so they reported, that 'the chiefs knew nothing that the whites talked to them and they never disclosed their peoples' troubles and they were men who drank and were drunkards'. Taken to task by an outraged Native Department, Nielsen explained. He was faced everywhere by demoralization, drunkenness, despair, 'and what it bred by these, a kind of concerted, if not organized, passive resistance to the demands of Government, particularly to the demand for tax.' His whole intention and endeavour was to foster 'the right kind of pride' since only in this way could the rural deadlock be broken.[1]

In its way Nielsen's analysis of the rural position was acute: a loss of pride was certainly the malaise from which rural society was suffering. But his remedy had little chance of success. For this there were two reasons. The first lay in Government policy and in the whole political and economic atmosphere of Southern Rhodesia in the late 1920s. Government talked in terms of development for the Reserves and set up industrial and agricultural schools but the whole movement of official thought was away from any sort of competition between Africans and Europeans and towards the separate and unequal policy of possessory segregation. What this meant for the African rural areas comes poignantly out of a little sketch published in the 1925 *Native Affairs Department Annual* by P. H. Moyo, an instructor at Tjolotjo industrial school. Moyo tried to explore why it was that the African areas of Rhodesia were not developing, and why inadequate use was made of what training facilities did exist. The Gwaai Reserve was 'a vast mass of land with a fairly large population and a very good number of young men'. If only they would go to the industrial school for three years 'they would be capable of putting up beautiful buildings of two or three rooms amongst their own people in the reserves. So that in course of time there might be a native town in the reserves built by such young men.' Moyo blamed the failure to develop such a town or to develop effective agriculture fairly and squarely on the Ndebele inhabitants of the Gwaai Reserve. The old men thought only of cattle, wives and beer; the young men thought only of migrating to work in the cities. 'We are very illiterate and we lack *esprit de corps*.' But in his concluding paragraph this ardent ally of the white administration in the uphill task of modernizing the notorious Gwaai Reserve struck another note. 'It seems as if all the reserves are far from any European dwellings. A reserve such as the one I know, which is forty miles from a railway station, makes it more difficult for a poor native to send his goods by train. I think it will take some time for railway lines to run into the reserves.'[2]

Modernization which was based upon the illusions of African towns springing up in the Gwaii Reserve and of a thriving cotton export forty

---

[1] These paragraphs are based upon two uncatalogued files in the National Archives, Salisbury, relating to an official inquiry into Nielsen's conduct.

[2] P. H. Moyo, 'Native Life in the Reserves', *The Southern Rhodesian Native Affairs Department Annual* No. 3, December 1925.

miles from the line of rail was not going to do anything very effective to stem demoralization. And so far from wishing to produce more educated and alert Africans and to encourage them to take the local initiative themselves, the Native Department was decidedly embarrassed by the number that had already been produced. There was no chance whatsoever of the massive investment in education for which Nielsen called.

The second reason why Nielsen's remedy stood little chance of success was that in the late 1920s there was a widespread African reaction against the Christian élite solution. The mission churches, or some of them, had been working to create 'the right kind of pride' for years. Through conversion from paganism the rural African would be won to a new society with new ideals, to a new sense of self-respect. The Christian leaven would work against sloth and drunkenness and propagate the message of a new hope. We should not underestimate the extent to which this programme was successful. In many cases the Christian message and the Christian experience did have this sort of effect. It would be shallow in the extreme to write off the African catechists and teachers and ministers of this period merely as aspirants to élite status. In many of them there was a real sense of Christian self-respect. And this Christian self-respect led to political action. It emphasized discipline, industry, education, 'civilization' – the programme of the associations, of the Conference of Christian Natives and of the Bantu Congress.

It is only just to contrast Nielsen's picture of degradation and despair with the picture of the Chiota Reserve drawn by John White at the end of the 1930s.

'More than thirty years ago I passed through Chiota Reserve with a few Mashona companions; our approach to the villages was not hailed with any delight; we were an entirely foreign element to them. We found the villages in an indescribably dirty condition, the people practically unclad. At our approach, they ran away for shelter. The adults were suspicious, sullen, unfriendly; night was made hideous by their dances and drunken revelry . . . Before starting out for home at the beginning of last year, we went to bid farewell to our African friends. At every place the community welcomed us with shouts of pleasure. The middle-aged people were the youths and maidens of our first trip. We were friends and talked familiarly together. Services were conducted in the churches, which were generally full of people. They were now dressed in fairly good clothing and had a clean, tidy appearance. The villages now were mostly cleaned up and had altogether a better appearance. The houses were larger and more suited to civilized people. One could not but exclaim as one passed through this country, "What great things hath God wrought!"'

This transformation in Chiota had been brought about, White believed, by the influence of the near-by Waddilove mission station and school. 'In this company today there are four hundred students. They represent the most progressive section of the people . . . Some are candidates for our Ministry; forty are in training for our evangelistic work; some eighty more are taking a teachers' course adapted to their attainments and the needs of the country. The balance is composed of young men and women who have come to this centre that they may receive a fuller education than is possible in their own towns or villages.' These students were to be the leaders of their people. 'We are trying to open every door of opportunity they are capable of entering . . . You would see shops for carpentry, a spinning and weaving school for the girls. We make our own bricks, and the buildings are erected by our own people. We have a large farm on which we teach better methods of agriculture . . . all of our people are very keen on scholastic work.' Student teachers and evangelists carried these skills into the Reserve. And while they thus influenced tribal life they symbolized in themselves a new Christian principle of unity. 'There are about two hundred and fifty communicants. These represent half a dozen tribes at least, and two distinct nationalities. Together we kneel, black and white, Matabele and Mashona, Basuto and Batonga – tribes that a few years ago were in deadly feud with each other. Now we are all one in Jesus Christ.'

White was here stating the ideal that lay behind the formation of the Bantu Congress and the leadership of many of the men who had been produced by Waddilove. Despite their élitism such men were in natural contact with the numerous church members of the Reserves. They seemed to be the obvious intermediaries between the Shona and the whites. John White claimed that they were the vanguard of a new Southern Rhodesia. As a result of the Christian influence, 'at last, after his age-long sleep, the African is wide awake. Give your imaginations wings, and you can see him there. Personified, Africa is like a great giant. From a pit of dark and evil spirits and many abominations, he is trying to climb.' When John White's biographer, Andrews, was summing up the achievement of the African Christian converts in 1935 he claimed that this Christian leaven had 'helped to keep the Mashona race from sinking back into degradation and serfdom when all was hanging in the balance'.[1]

And yet 'while all was hanging in the balance' very many Shona were reacting against the Christian solution. For this there were many reasons.

[1] C. F. Andrews, *John White of Mashonaland*, London, 1935, pp. 149–51, 230–2.

One of them was the resentment against Christian élitism. Men like Frank Sixubu, the Zulu catechist who had become a prosperous Mashonaland landowner, or Aaron Jacha, the Native Purchase Area farmer and Waddilove pupil who led Congress, were only too obviously distinct from the great majority of the rural population who had no opportunity for this sort of self-improvement and who were experiencing instead a growing shortage of land and decline of agricultural prices. Allied to this was the feeling that the Christian élite solution had in itself failed; that the whites had not allowed even those who had broken through to the élite to enter into most of the opportunities of the modern world. There was no equivalent in the Southern Rhodesia of the 1920s to the cash crop farmers of Tanganyika or Uganda; no equivalent even to the opportunities open in Northern Rhodesia to educated Africans. Neither in the urban nor in the rural areas did education and espousal of the Christian values seem likely to lead to security or prosperity.

This was important since many Shona had turned originally to Christianity because of its assumed effectiveness in the new colonial world. Some individuals had experienced an overwhelming sense of personal salvation and reshaping. Shona rural society, in general, however, had admitted the Christian influence after the risings of 1896–7 because the old religious beliefs had manifestly failed in a contest of strength with the new. By the 1920s the instrumental efficacy of Christianity had come to be doubted. Very many Shona had come to share the views expressed at that time by a Manyika migrant to South Africa, John Chavafambira.

'We used to talk a lot about Christians. Even now we do. We don't think a lot of Christians. We don't believe in Jesus. We used to pray in olden times to our native God, Mwari, and to the *midzimu*, for rain. It always helped. Now we pray to Jesus and rain never comes. We have no corn, no land, nothing. We all hate the Christians; they talk, talk and nothing comes to us from it. I am only waiting to go home and learn how to pray to our God and will never pray to Jesus and won't be a Christian any more . . . The Christian priests are so bad that they are against native doctors and native medicines. When a missionary comes to our houses at home they chase him away. Nobody wants to talk to them. Why should they? The white people came to the country, it is the natives' country, took everything away from us – the land, the cattle, and made us work. We cannot move without a pass, have to pay taxes, and they have given us Jesus. We don't want him.'[1]

[1] Wulf Sachs, *Black Hamlet. The Mind of an African Negro revealed by psychoanalysis*, London, 1937, pp. 113–14.

If the progressive and modernizing road indicated by the RBVA was not open to them, if the Christian solution as offered by the missionaries had thus disillusioned them, what ways out of apathy and into self-respect were open to men like John Chavafambira? Some turned back to traditional religion but this was not really an effective solution because the Chavafambiras could not persuade themselves that it was still instrumental. To many it seemed that the answer lay in African – and Shona – adaptations of Christian concepts through the creation of independent African churches which would allow the ordinary man to regain a sense of purpose and modernizing achievement without losing a sense of community.

The late 1920s and early 1930s were the great founding age of Shona independency. First there was the outburst of rural Watch Tower in northern Mashonaland, then the spread of Zionism and the rise of the Vapostori movement. These movements soon involved many thousands of Shona and their hymns and prayers and gospels became a very important part of the African voice.

Watch Tower: the Teaching of Kunga

Watch Tower spread to the Shona rural areas at the end of the 1920s because it spoke the language of their dreams. As a European witness said in the different context of Copperbelt independency, 'natives are very fond of the book of Revelations – they are interested in dreams – they have dreams of their own.' The dream-fulfilling visions of Watch Tower emerge very clearly from CID reports of the preaching of one Kunga, a dedicated missionary of Kenan Kamwana's church, who came to Bulawayo in the 1920s 'teaching religion'. Kunga had been converted to Watch Tower in 1918 through visiting its leader in Nyasaland, Bennet Siyasi, then languishing in jail. 'Bennet told me to repent as the Kingdom of Heaven was near and that they were being kept in jail for the cause of Christ. I visited him frequently in jail and he taught me the words of the Bible and told me that if I was arrested I must not deny that I was a follower of Christ.' In 1919 Kunga came to work in the Rezende Mine in Penhalonga district, Rhodesia. 'I had a dream. I was preaching in the Rezende Compound and the natives there would not believe me and I was very troubled. At this time I had a dream and Gabriel spoke to me and told me that the natives there were no good and he told me to leave Penhalonga and go on to Bulawayo and preach to the natives there and save them.'[1]

Kunga began his Bulawayo ministry in 1923. In his own curious way he strove to engender a supernaturally supported self-confidence. 'In America

[1] Kunga's statement, 16 May 1923, N 3/5/8.

the natives are equal to the white man and that is why the English people in Rhodesia do not want an American type of religion in this country.' Americans were prevented from opening more Mission Stations 'as they are afraid we will become too clever and cease to work for them'. The King was really on the side of Africans. 'King George V tells the truth to the English but the people of this country do not abide by what he says but make their own laws. In 1912 the King wanted to come to Rhodesia to see the natives and change the law for them, but the white people of Southern Rhodesia sent him a message and told him not to come as there was too much sickness in the country and the King believed them and did not come.' But if white Rhodesians were thus able to frustrate such potential saviours as King George V and American Negro missionaries, they would not be able to avert the coming millennium. 'The time is at hand,' proclaimed Kunga, 'the end of the world is near. Goliath was a very strong man but David killed him. This will be the same with us and the white people. You must hold on fast and the kingdom is near . . . I want to preach to the natives so that when Jesus Christ comes he will find you all Christians . . . You must be strong as the world will shortly be changed and the white people that have high positions will be our servants in heaven.' In Kunga's teaching the time was very much at hand. He saw the crisis as coming 'some time between next September and November of this year' 1923, the moment in fact of the coming into power of the first settler government. It was to be triggered off by another great world war. 'When England was at war with Germany they promised the natives of this country that if we fought for England we would all be free men. Many of our people did fight and were killed and yet we are not free.' There were three nations in the world, Kunga claimed, which had never been defeated in war by the English – the Americans, the Belgians and the Portuguese. These would combine to 'fight England and win and then all we natives will be free . . . You must remain in your kraals – that is white against white. Only the fool native will go.' When the whites had torn themselves to pieces God would bring about the triumph of the meek, the humbled, the apparently powerless who in reality held the terrible power of faith and foreknowledge. 'The white men are jealous of me and Jesus is coming again and the world will be changed. The natives would then be in greater power and that is why the white people do not want me to preach.'[1]

Kunga was not very successful in Bulawayo because the administration moved in to prevent the spread of his influence amongst indigenous Africans. But it is easy to see the attraction of his doctrine. He was playing

[1] CID reports of Kunga's meetings of 5, 7, 14, 17, 20 and 29 June 1923, N 3/5/8.

on themes which had much meaning for Rhodesian Africans. The Manyika migrant in South Africa, John Chavafambira, was at about the same time retelling his dreams to a white doctor. He knew that better luck was coming for he dreamed that King George came to Johannesburg. 'Plenty whites and natives met him,' he described the dream, 'the big man, the big King. All very friendly, natives and whites. I was very surprised. They all shouted, "The King has come to help the people." All sang, blacks and whites. After this the King left us and went back to England.' Chavafambira dreamt too of entering the world of the American Negro. 'He would go to America. He would sing the Manyika songs. His voice was good and he could master the language. He would acquire great wealth, open a shop. He would buy a gramophone, a house, furniture, a motorcycle, no, a car!'[1]

The great problem for all African organizations was how to do something effective to change things. None of them had solved it. In the 1920s it seemed no more and no less practical to join Watch Tower and pray for the millenium then to join the RBVA or the ICU and to hope that whites would hear the African voice. Moreover Watch Tower teaching was at once strikingly similar to the prophecies of the mediums and the Mwari priests who had led the risings of 1896 and apparently superior to them in power. For Watch Tower claimed to possess the true secret and to mediate the true efficacy of Christianity. 'The white men are hiding the truth of the gospel and I give it to you quite openly.' The transformation of the world through spiritual forces – this was what so many Shona and Ndebele had banked on in 1896 and in a different way in their acceptance of mission Christianity and it was what some of them were ready to bank on again.

Administrative Attitudes towards Watch Tower

For some time before the first appearance of Watch Tower in the rural areas of Southern Rhodesia the administration had nervously anticipated its arrival. In 1923 a memorandum stimulated by the founding of the Rhodesian Bantu Voters' Association contrasted that organization with Watch Tower ideas from Nyasaland. Watch Tower, it said, 'was not founded upon an acceptance of a system of policy based upon European forms but is more distinctly African in its nature'. Its aims were vague, its structure imprecise. 'It is more, as it were, the reaction of the virile Central African Negroid to the impact of European ideas on tribal life and to the world war.' Southern Rhodesia, the memorandum contended, was the

[1] Sachs, *Black Hamlet*, p. 134.

meeting place of the two forces of South African racial solidarity as embodied in the RBVA and of Nyasa millenarianism. The situation had to be closely watched for as a result of this combination of influences 'native political movements' might take 'unexpected directions'. In 1924 the Chief Native Commissioner followed up this warning by requesting legislation to control preaching by Africans who were not under European supervision. 'This colony has been assailed by separatist bodies both from the south and the north,' he wrote. 'Those from the south have not thrived hitherto and it is the Watch Tower movement which, albeit its propaganda has been largely limited to northern natives, accentuates our need for protective steps. Our indigenous population will more than probably become increasingly receptive to such subversive ideas, to counter which the proposed legislation will undoubtedly assist us.'[1]

In the event the draft legislation was submitted to the Southern Rhodesia Missionary Conference in order that British objections might be forestalled. The Conference, led by Cripps and White, repudiated the draft and it was dropped by government. But the administrative scrutiny of Watch Tower did not relax. And then, in 1925, the Watch Tower movement spread to the Shona rural areas. For the next five or six years a constant battle was waged between Watch Tower preachers coming across the border from Northern Rhodesia or going into the Reserves from their places of employment in Southern Rhodesia, on the one hand, and the Native Department and the police on the other. The areas affected were the Urungwe, Sinoia and Sipolilo districts, an extensive belt of country north and north-west of Salisbury, straddling the main Salisbury-Lusaka road and accessible to Watch Tower preachers coming south from Northern Rhodesia over the Zambezi. The two periods of most intense activity were 1926 and from late 1928 into 1929.

The movement that resulted from this activity was very different from the Watch Tower cells in the mining compounds. It did not affect the proto-intellectuals of the Shona who were to be found at this time among those loyal to mission Christianity. But it did affect a wide range of other people in the Shona rural areas. Its first appearance in a district was often among those attending a small and remote kraal school or catechist's class in one of the Lomagundi villages – people who were aspirants after education and status at this very humble level but at the same time people who were not profitably part of the mission connection. Such people were often younger men or women but the evidence suggests that Watch Tower also appealed powerfully to the older members of Shona rural society even although it

[1] Correspondence on Watch Tower, N 3/5/8 and S 84/A/259.

was generally bitterly opposed by the chiefs. Clearly Watch Tower was attracting support for a variety of reasons and it is interesting to examine what they were.

Though it was much less prominent than in the Watch Tower cells in the mining compounds the desire for educational provision which would allow effective competition with the whites was an element in the Lomagundi movement, and presumably existed particularly in the ill-provided kraal schools. Thus a European resident in the area testified that Watch Tower preachers were telling the Shona 'that white people would not educate natives to any degree as they knew they would lose their dominance' and that missionary education was a device to keep them down. A Shona Watch Tower adherent testified that he had been told that when the great day came the whites would be swept away and 'when that was over we would go to school'. The frequent mentions of the sophisticated skills of the American Negroes was important in this connection. Among the other roles they were to play in the promised millennium was that of teacher. But it is important to realize that in effect Watch Tower influences in Lomagundi led to withdrawal from all existing educational facilities rather than any attempt to create new ones. The 'Ethiopian' African Methodist Episcopal Church, which shared the same suspicions of mission education, set up in Matabeleland its own admirable kraal schools. Men like Richard Kalinde were educating themselves in the compounds through their reading of the quite complex Watch Tower material in English which they obtained from Cape Town. But in Lomagundi educational improvements had to wait upon the millennium. 'You will go and tell Father Crane,' the men at Doma's kraal told an African teacher, 'that we will not be quick to see his teachers in the kraal.' But Father Crane's teachers were not replaced by any other teachers, and Crane himself believed that this attack on mission schools was supported especially by older people who disliked the social differentiation produced by western education.[1]

This sort of ambiguity was evident in many ways in the Lomagundi movement. Thus the movement appealed to Shona intransigents who longed to offer a challenge to the whites similar to that of 1896–7 but at the same time it appealed in terms which revealed a desire to share the material prosperity of the whites and a belief that in some way the whites would have to be overthrown through the use of forces which were modern in themselves. The appeal was no longer to Mwari, Chaminuka or Nehanda but to the God of the white man himself. The allies no longer looked among neighbouring African tribes but among the westernized American

[1] Evidence of Mureya, evidence of Walsh, January 1929, S 84/A/293.

Negro community. The miraculously provided weapons were no longer to be spears or even guns but aeroplanes.

'In about six months', so Shona tribesmen in Urungwe were reported to have been told by Watch Tower preachers in May 1929, 'a flight of aeroplanes will come from America – sent by a person who lives under the water there – manned by black people, who will make an aerial reconnaissance of the whole country. These negroes will recognize their own people and will then return to America. Shortly after this they will return and bring war in their train. The white people will then be driven out of the country and the natives will be freed from all taxes and European control. All those who have been dipped (baptized) will be rendered bullet proof thereby; any bullets striking them will be made harmless, merely flattening out and falling to the ground in coming into contact with one of the faithful.'[1]

In this promise of invulnerability, of course, the Watch Tower preachers were following the leaders of the 1896 risings. But in other ways, as the people of Lomagundi were only too well aware, the situation in the 1920s was very different. 'Given arms,' African labourers in Lomagundi said, 'the natives would beat the whites as they could stand more.' But the people were disarmed. 'We have no guns,' bemoaned Watch Tower folllowers in July 1929, 'therefore we are as children and must wait for the (supernatural) wind and aeroplanes from America which will rid us of the Europeans who are our oppressors.' A profound sense of the technical superiority of the whites was felt by almost all Shona at this time. One of John Chavafambira's dreams expressed very well the general fatalism about the possibility of ordinary protest or resistance. 'I saw plenty of our people with spears, singing and shouting. The white men came and laughed at us so much. They just stood and laughed. Then other white people came and killed all our people in twenty minutes.'[2]

Watch Tower teaching was important because it promised a supernatural way out of this situation of perpetual white superiority. It was hard to tell whether its influence would lead to active resistance in anticipation of the millennium or merely to preparation for an expectation of it; hard to tell whether its effect was more to harden and focus resentment or to allow it safe expression from the white point of view in terms of millennial dreams. 'The teachers do not only make the usual promises of wealth and the dis-

---

[1] Statement by Joe, 21 May 1929, cited in ANC Sinoia to NC Sinoia, 23 May 1929, S 84/A/293.
[2] ANC, Urungwe to NC Sinoia, 11 May 1929, S 84/A/293; Sachs, *Black Hamlet* p. 164.

appearance of the white people,' reported a 'loyal' African in May 1929, 'but talk of the oppression and troubles the white people have brought; that the natives are as good as the white people and should have everything they have. They say "If the white people had not taken our guns away and made us like women, we should have done some fighting long ago like they have in Nyasaland, but what can be done without guns? We are as women. You must dip and be ready for the day when some power will drive the white people out of the country, otherwise you will not have wealth" . . . Last month the teachers were supposed to be telling the natives that they would *see* what was going to happen this month . . . What do they think they can do? They have no guns. The Maswina listen too easily.'[1]

Watch Tower in Lomagundi, then, was partly an expression of resentment at what was seen as a conspiracy between the missionaries and other whites, partly an expression of a desire to overthrow white control, partly an expression of a desire to enter into and enjoy white wealth, partly an acceptance of the need to adopt new customs, partly an expression of desperate belief that the African people were not as it seemed deserted by the gods and incapable of influencing their own fate, but rather a chosen people entrusted with the true secret of the future.

In its own way Watch Tower inculcated pride and self respect. What was being built up in Lomagundi was a community of the faithful, expectant of the coming millennium, and observing its own rules of conduct so as to prepare the world for the Lord. Watch Tower teaching emphasized community and fraternity amongst believers. It was received in many places primarily as a means of eradicating witchcraft and Watch Tower baptism was thought of as making it impossible for the 'dipped' person ever again to bewitch or to be bewitched. Watch Tower believers were not separated from each other by education. Beer drinking was frowned upon. In short a real attempt was being made to re-structure demoralized rural society.

The fullest account we have of the Watch Tower communities of Lomagundi at the end of the 1920s was put together in January 1929 by the Native Commissioner, Sinoia. It is very unsympathetic, and some of its details are certainly inaccurate, but it is worth quoting extensively none the less.

'Towards the end of October I heard that the movement was again afoot, so I sent out and brought in about eighty men and women for investigation purposes and inquiries. It appears that on their return to their kraals the natives went through some sort of re-dipping to purify them

[1] Acting Assistant CNC to Acting CNC, 2 July 1929, S 84/A/293.

from their evil contact with the Native Commissioner, and the movement has been carried on quietly ever since.

The field of operation seems to be from the Dande River in the N. W. Sipolilo Reserve, westward across the Hunyani River north of the second fly fence to Doma. Thence in a milder degree from there to Angwa River. It has spread quite extensively west of the Angwa amongst Chanetsa's people . . . Many people including old men were dipped in a short period.

The sect is divided into six classes, as under:

1 MAPASTARA: are those who carry out the baptism ceremony and burial ceremonies. (The names of eight such officers are given in the report; only one is an 'alien native'; the other seven are residents of the Urungwe and Sipolilo districts).

2 ODARA: Giver of names to children born and names given soon after birth.

3 MADIKONI: visiting sick, praying at bedside, and burying dead.

4 MAPURUJARA: are those who have to see that kraals etc., are kept swept, are sent on errands and see that children have bodies kept clean.

5 MAPIRICHARA: youths who cut reeds for the coffins.

6 MAKRISTU: other members of the faith.

CEREMONIES

a BAPTISM – This is carried out at night in the vicinity of a pool, where fires are kindled around which the people emerging from the water sit. A Muwanga pole lighted at both ends is placed across the pool. In front of this, one behind the other, stand the officials. The convert is handed from one to the other till the last priest is reached. This priest has a red material spread on the water called a 'CHITAMBARA' (Kiswahili – a handkerchief). After prayers this is wrung out and kept. The convert on reaching the priest turns and faces backwards. He is then pushed under the water and quickly pulled out, led by one of the attendants by a side route, and sits by the fire. Names such as Yakobi, Josiah, Geni, Isaki, Egines, Roda, Ada, Grace, Jessie and Kate are given. Their respective totems have been supplanted by the single totem 'Israel' which is to be used to the exclusion of their real totems under ban of punishments.

Apparently each convert receives a small ticket, thus:

Zioni Mpatuke Amerika

(Name) GRACE

Signed by Dipper.

This ticket must be carefully guarded and secreted.

b GREETINGS – When people meet they are not to 'hombera' to each other but shake hands, addressing each other 'Chikonde amayi' if females, and 'Chikonde Baba' if males. Children, men, women, and even mothers-in-law are shaken by the hand by all and no modesty, as of old, is shown . . .

c SABBATH – Wednesday is the Watch Tower sabbath. No labour can be performed but must be dedicated to prayer . . .

d TABOOS – Zebra, Porcupine, Tortoise, Pig and Wart-Hog must not be eaten because persons not dipped will be turned into these. Shawe charms and ornaments and all medicinal charms are to be discarded. Bume beer only is to be imbibed. The dead are not to be mourned. Graves are to be kept up and constantly swept and the kraal site is to be free of all rubbish. People not dipped are to be shunned and referred to as 'SIADOMA' or more commonly 'NYOKA'. An Israel cannot eat food with a Nyoka or live close by one or come into bodily contact with one. Swearing at or striking one another is taboo.

e DEITIES – It is alleged they pray to Mwari but REYI, JOHN CHILEMBWE and MARIYA occupy a great place in all their beliefs.

f SONGS – These are all in an alien tongue of Chinyanga, Chisenga, and kindred tribes, not in Chishona. This suggests a strong northern influence. New songs are constantly added so the older ones are soon discarded. The words of the new ones are not easily recognizable. The songs can be sung by a whole congregation in an undertone.

g DEATHS – When a believer dies he is not bent up in the authordox (sic) Shona way but is laid out straight, reeds are cut, and he is placed in a wicker work coffin wrapped up in a blanket . . .

h BURIAL – A hole is dug in a selected flat place . . . The body is placed in the grave, prayers said and songs sung, then covered in . . .

i BELIEFS AND OBJECTS – It is believed that Reyi, John Chilembwe and Mariya will rise out of the water and come to the people in the 'Mbudzi' moon. They will give the people a potent to drink from a cup. This will send the recipient to sleep for seven days. When they awake they will be white and have amassed wealth. They will not need to work. If they work they will work for present whitemen and the whitemen will work for them. All people will be on an equal footing financially and socially. Those who have not dipped will die or turn into animals . . . To show that they have faith a fourth person whose name is not disclosed is to accompany those mentioned. This person will be covered in sores and will dip food into the sores and give the food to believers to eat. The eating of the contaminated food will prove their sincerity.

It is further alleged that books and literature will come this year and that this work comes from America.

Monogamy is preached, but I notice that several of the Deacons have two wives . . .

When the Mapastaka are asked why everything is kept so secret they assert that the originators of the movement instructed it to be kept from the white men because if known the adherents would be killed. As the movement is secretive and we have no information of its inner objects we must treat it with suspicion. Its popularity, its spread amongst the old people must be an indication that its objects must be congenial to native thought. Originally the wholesale departure of the whites was preached, owing to our intervention this policy has been modified to a socialistic alternative.'[1]

Watch Tower restructuring of society seems to have succeeded in creating united communities of the faithful. But it did so at the price of cutting the faithful off from the rest of Shona tribal society. Shona chiefs, whose authority was unrecognized by the movement, did their best to destroy it.

'My country is being destroyed by the Watch Tower movement,' complained Chief Bepura in January 1929. 'It comes from Blantyre and some of its emissaries came first to Dandara (Urungwe), then to Majinga, then to A. Louw's farm, then to my country. Makiyi came first with "London", both in Mr Howman's time. They brought the tidings that the white people would be taken by a great wind and that we Blacks would see our dead rise white and we ourselves would be white after we had baptized. There was to be a period of unconsciousness, then a miraculous and glorious resurrection in the month of the goat. Those who refused to be baptized were called "werayi". After this movement had subsided there was a recrudescence started by Mdapi and Chikowera, sons of Masoro of Bepura. I brought them in to Mr Hulley and told him this but they were released . . . After their release the whole District (Bepura's) began to dip.

New doctrines introduced include a change of greeting. This is now "Chikundano" . . . Our burial laws have also been altered and all our customs so that we older people who retain our old laws are apart now from those of my people who have dipped. They are shameless in their familiarity with their mother-in-laws and they do not even salute us their elders. They have been given European names and they say "Our King is now America". They say America is Black not White. We shall

[1] N. C. Sinoia to CNC, 3 January 1929, S 84/A/293.

take the white people's stores and we shall own them. We shall be the people who remain. This will be done in the month of the goat (November). When November came and nothing happened they said, "It will be next November". They say "Pakari", meaning "Haste the Day" ... Some of the people who are detained are merely dupes, others are dangerous and say, "Let us hold together. If we are killed by the whites let us die together." The movement is madness and is destroying my country.'[1]

This, then, was the character of the Watch Tower movement in Lomagundi. What was its significance? The administration puzzled over this question. Most members of the Native Department agreed that the movement had alarming political implications. At the lowest estimate it was held that 'from the native point of view the teaching of the Watch Tower, with its prophecies of the end of the white man's rule is insulting to the Government and therefore, for the sake of Native administration, such preaching should be treated as a crime'. At the worst there was 'the hidden suspicion that the movement is poisoning the native mind against the British and preparing a perfect ground for Bolschevism (sic) or kindred institutions'. The fullest statement of the need for adequate control was made by Bullock, then Native Commissioner, Sinoia. His annual report for 1958 recorded:

'I have to report a recrudescence of activity in the so-called Watch Tower movement. The movement seems to have gained strength and I regard as important the fact that the Acting Native Commissioner discovered in his investigations the basis of an organization – crude and almost ridiculous so far, but yet an organization. It is of importance also to note that the movement has made most headway in areas on the outskirts of civilization, and among tribes of Natives who are still almost quite unsophisticated and who live in wild country where there has been very little penetration by Christian missionaries. The result has been a restlessness which while not regarded as dangerous at present, yet may contain the seeds of disorder; and I am of the opinion that the time has come when some action should be taken. The ideal corrective would be an immediate planned and intensive campaign by some strongly organized church, having as its objective the conversion to Christianity of all Natives in the area affected and the establishment of regular Native Churches under the authority of a governing body. But is such a movement practicable and, if so, can it be carried out at an early date?

If not, then the Government may have to ask itself if the alternative measure – that is repressive legislation – is not indicated; and if the first

[1] Chief Bepura's statement, January 1929, S 84/A/293.

action should not be control of irresponsible preachers . . . A risk which is not obvious to all is to be apprehended. It is the danger which arises from the fact that in inferior societies the strange mental aberrations known as 'crowd states' are not controlled by the checks which exist in a developed social system, and that movements which commence in what may be exaltation of mind are prone to overrun the individual intention of the sane man in the mob and lead to disorderly actions . . . It is to be emphasized that the tribes affected by this movement have reached only the second stage of political evolution. There are, therefore, fundamental differences between their social structure and our own; e.g. they are in a state in which political and religious institutions have not yet been differentiated – life has not yet become institutionalized. Is it not then the case that the exercise of a form of liberty which may be rightly demanded in an advanced community may not be so justly claimed in a tribe whose social system differs from ours, especially in that very relevant aspect that political and religious groupings are not yet distinguished? That which is concerned with religion qua religion with us, is necessarily also political with them because of that difference.

From another point of view it may be said that there is no doubt that the social structure of Native societies must alter. But are we justified in allowing it to be suddenly changed, or even destroyed, by emotional excitation engendered by propaganda which is either malevolent or wildly irresponsible . . . Liberty of the individual and the right of free speech may not readily be tampered with, especially in religious matters – and indeed a clause in the Charter makes free all forms of religion which are in the interest of humanity. It is to be doubted, however, whether this Watch Tower excitation can be defined as truly religious. And does not History teach us that uncontrolled pseudo-religious gatherings are far from being beneficial to uncivilized Natives? It is enough to mention Mwana Leza, Chilembwe, or the "Israelites" at Bulhoek: though a closer parallel may be found in the history of Hau Hauism or debased Christianity among the Maoris.'

Bullock urged that steps should at once be taken to introduce effective legislation to control Watch Tower preachers and that a Vagrancy Act 'which should cover a wide field and supersede the obsolescent Police Offences Act' should be passed. In addition there should be 'a short additional Native Schools Act' to control teaching and preaching in kraal schools. He envisaged a situation arising in which 'the clan system . . . assailed by Europeanized institutions' would prove quite inadequate to guarantee social or political control of the rural areas. In such a situation 'the provisions of the Vagrancy Acts or any other laws dealing with social disorders will not be enforceable for long in our vast areas except by the multiplication of Police or military forces in a system of direct rule. This is an eventuality which our line of Native Policy may lead us to face.'[1]

The necessity and difficulty of controlling the rural areas – now so much a preoccupation of Southern Rhodesian governments – was thus stated clearly in 1929 in response to the challenge of Watch Tower, the first of the twentieth century mass movements to demonstrate the collapse of chiefly power. It is an interesting coincidence that the Lomagundi areas penetrated by Watch Tower from across the Zambezi have also been the scene of a great deal of recent guerrilla activity. As we shall see the administration did indeed push through security legislation in the 1930s. But meanwhile, as Bullock remarked, 'some measure to cope with the Watch Tower activities is urgently required'. In the end Watch Tower was coped with by a show of strength – 'the multiplication of Police or military forces'. 'Alien native' preachers were arrested and deported. Regular patrols of the Reserves by Native Department Messengers were instituted, thereby driving Watch Tower ceremonies on to European farming land. And in June 1929 a mixed European and African police patrol was sent through the area. 'Mobility was clearly demonstrated,' minuted Bullock. 'It was considered desirable to show also efficiency in field work and the capability of European details to take independent action; in a word to show that Native agitators were mistaken in their allegations that our younger men would be helpless in the veld if deprived of Native guidance and assistance. I have reason to believe that a salutary object lesson was learned by the Natives of the areas patrolled and that doctrines subversive of authority have received a check.'[2]

These Native Department assessments of the significance of Watch Tower were sober in comparison to others made in the 1930s. In 1936, for instance, after Watch Tower had been condemned by the Commission of Inquiry into the Copperbelt riots, there was a debate in the Southern Rhodesian Legislative Assembly on the new Sedition Bill. It was generally agreed that Watch Tower and its influence at Wankie and on the mines was the best justification for the proposed legislation. Captain Downes assured the Assembly that Watch Tower was 'definitely revolutionary'. 'The Bible is definitely being used and being illustrated so that the ignorant native is getting a completely false impression with regard to his spiritual welfare and there is no doubt that in conjunction with this a whole system of

---

[1] NC Sinoia, Report for the year ending 31 December 1928, S 84/A/293.
[2] NC Sinoia to CNC, December 1929, S 84/A/293.

voodooism and witchcraft has grown up which extends from West Africa to East Africa and from Basutoland to Egypt. We know that it is waiting to come forward as soon as it can obtain the arms and ammunition. The arms and ammunition are actually on the horizon today . . . I maintain that with the Abyssinian War and the rifles coming into Africa and being undoubtedly carried in this direction the potentiality of this organization for mischief is infinitely greater today than in the past.'[1]

This vision of Watch Tower as a continent-wide revolutionary conspiracy, voicing 'a national spirit', was shared by radical left-wing commentators on the African scene. The great West Indian Pan-Africanist, C. L. R. James, for example, regarded Watch Tower activity in Central Africa as much more significant than the organized élite political parties of West Africa. West Africa, he wrote in 1938, was but 'the fringe' of the continent and the political parties did not express mass discontent. Watch Tower, on the other hand, revealed 'what is going on in the minds of the great masses of Africans'. Watch Tower, believed James, was a 'secret society'. 'Its influence is widely spread throughout Africa and . . . it is the most powerful revolutionary force in Africa today.' Through Watch Tower 'religion becomes a weapon in the class struggle'. 'Should world events give these people a chance they will destroy what has them by the throat as surely as the San Domingo blacks destroyed the French plantocracy . . . Such are the ideas moving in the minds of these African copper miners. They represent political realities and express political aspirations far more closely than programmes and policies of parties with millions of members, numerous journals and half a century of history behind them. Watch Tower is what the thinking native thinks and what he is prepared to die for. This apparent fanaticism is the best indication to the true feelings of many millions of Africans. They know what they want but they do not know what to do.'[2]

How, then, should we today assess the significance of a movement like Watch Tower in Lomagundi? We know for certain that Watch Tower was not a 'secret society' with co-ordinated branches throughout the continent or even throughout Central Africa. We know for certain that Watch Tower preachers and leaders were not transporting rifles into the Rhodesias. We rightly take much more seriously than did the Native Department the religious and sociological roots of Watch Tower and see its significance much more in religious and social terms than in political terms. Yet when

---

[1] Speech by Captain Downes, 28 April 1936, *Southern Rhodesian Legislative Assembly Debates*, vol. 16, Part I, p. 1115.
[2] C. L. R. James, *History of the Negro Revolt*, London, 1938.

H

all this is said was there not still a considerable political significance in the Lomagundi Watch Tower movement and one that can be expressed in much the terms used by C. L. R. James? If James thought Watch Tower more significant and representative than the whole formal West African political movement we may ask whether it was not more significant and representative than the polite political associations of Southern Rhodesia. Did not Watch Tower in Lomagundi reveal what was going on in the minds of the great mass of Africans in the rural areas of Rhodesia? Did it not in a real sense 'represent political realities and express political aspirations' in a situation in which only cataclysmic change could bring about African ability to control their own destiny? Above all, did not Watch Tower in Lomagundi reveal that the Shona knew what they wanted but that they did not yet know what to do?

To my mind this Watch Tower episode has a double significance in the history of African protest in Southern Rhodesia. In the first place it reveals that the Shona of Lomagundi were still thinking in terms of violent upheaval rather than of accommodation but that they were now ready and able to move out of their memories of the Shona past. In Watch Tower the Shona peoples of Lomagundi were accepting a Nyasa mythology. They were repudiating as no longer effective their secular traditional leaders and their traditional spiritual protective machinery. They were turning to a new millenarianism and adopting new customs and new ways of life. In this there was remote promise for the emergence of a mass nationalist movement, secular in intent but with millenarian implications, based upon the same essential proposition – 'We shall be the people who remain'. In the second place the Watch Tower episode is surely important to any attempt to recapture the African Voice in Southern Rhodesia. More convincingly than in the RBVA, more convincingly even than in the ICU, we hear the tones of bewilderment, bitterness, fatalism and desperate hope which was the characteristic response of the African masses in the 1920s.

This emerges most convincingly of all in a report from Lomagundi after the police patrol had frightened off the alien leaders of Watch Tower and the movement had been taken over by indigenous leaders in a brief revival. In this period Shona Watch Tower leaders developed their own refinements of Watch Tower doctrines. Thus in March 1931 Shona preachers in Urungwe were teaching that 'a big wind will come and sweep away Europeans and all Natives who have not been baptized; at the same time all Watch Tower believers will die and on the seventh day will rise from the dead and will then see all their relatives who have died in the past risen also; they will find in occupation of the country American Negroes who will rule it; these blacks are clever and enlightened people, far surpassing Europeans; all Watch Tower members will become wealthy and own such things as motor-cars and aeroplanes; great wealth will accrue to believers through the sale of their produce to the American blacks; for eggs one pound will be paid, for a fowl one pound and for a goat two pounds.'[1]

Even in their millenarian dreams the Shona of Lomagundi were not yet imagining themselves as rulers of a modern state system. A dramatic increase of agricultural prices was at that moment an apt symbol of paradise for them. The potentiality for the emergence of a mass territorial nationalist movement aiming at control by indigenous Africans was there but it was still a remote possibility. A good deal of time had still to pass before this could be conceived by the rural masses.

THE ZIONIST AND VAPOSTORI MOVEMENTS

Watch Tower, for all its interest, did not turn out to be as long-lived or deeply-rooted as other independent Christian movements of the late 1920s and early 1930s. Two of these in particular, Zionism in western Mashonaland and the Vapostori movement in eastern Mashonaland, were to develop into indigenous churches on a really large scale. The manner in which the Zionist and Vapostori churches came into being in Mashonaland and the reasons for which their influence spread throw considerable light on the Shona rural situation.

Thanks to the researches of Mr M. L. Daneel, whose work on these Shona independent churches is likely not only to fill in an important gap in the history of independency but also to raise questions of fundamental importance for its understanding throughout southern Africa, we know much more than we did about the early days of Zionism and the Vapostori movement. A full account must await publication of Mr Daneel's material but this chapter would be woefully incomplete without some reference to these remarkable churches.[2]

Zionism

We saw in an earlier chapter how Zionism was introduced into the rural areas of Matabeleland. But it was in Mashonaland, and particularly in

[1] ANC Urungwe to NC Lomagundi, 28 March 1931, S 138/226.

[2] Mr M. I. Daneel is working on the interaction of these churches and other independent church movements with traditional religion and mission Christianity and with local politics and society. I am very grateful indeed to him for making available to me the drafts of his chapters on the early history of Zionism and the Vapostori.

western Mashonaland, that the movement really took root. Zionism was introduced into western Mashonaland by a number of Dutch Reformed Church members who had gone to South Africa to work and there encountered Bishop Mhlangu's Zionist Apostolic Church or the Zionist Apostolic Faith Mission of Enginasi Lekhanyana. Characteristic of these men was Samuel Mutendi, a Rozwi from Bikita. Mutendi claimed descent from the Rozwi Mambos and experienced prophetic dreams and fits of spirit possession. Neither were sufficient to gain him prestige in the colonial world. He had become a member of the Dutch Reformed Church for whom he worked for some time as a kraal school assistant. He also worked as a policeman. But the road to further advancement in the service of mission or government seemed blocked. His fits of possession were interpreted by Dutch Reformed Church members as the results either of illness or of evil spirits. They made missionaries doubtful whether he should be allowed to continue to teach and preach. Mutendi himself was convinced that his fits were a sign of genuine spiritual gifts and in his situation of frustration dreamt of recognition of his spiritual gifts by the people of his area. In 1922 Mutendi journeyed south in order to earn money so that he could buy cattle. In Pretoria he encountered the Zion Apostolic Faith Mission. The Zionists laid emphasis upon the role of the Holy Spirit and upon the power granted to those who opened themselves to possession by it. Mutendi found himself at once at home, his gifts recognized. He was impressed by the efficiency of this wholly African church and the scope it gave for men of ability. He was impressed by the instrumental claims made by it and by its confidence in its ability to heal, to exorcise, to unite. In 1923 Mutendi was baptized in the local river Jordan and soon after was chosen to return to Rhodesia as an emissary of the church. 'Samuel came here carrying the Word only,' the scriptures of his Zion Christian Church tell us, 'without blankets or extra clothes . . . As Moses was afraid when he was *sent*, so he was very much afraid.'[1]

Although Mutendi at first met mockery he had no need to be afraid. He was returning to an area in which the Mwari cult had been very strong but where most men no longer found it possible to believe in its continued efficacy. Mutendi's Zionism held out the promise of being able to do what the Mwari cult had done – to cure, to bring fertility, to bring rain, to exorcize – and what mission Christianity could not do. But it also spoke with Christian authority in the name of the Holy Spirit and of the primitive church. It was very much a black man's church but it was by no means a

---

[1] The quotation is translated by Mr Daneel from the handbook of Mutendi's church, *Rungano*.

backward-looking church. Like Watch Tower it set out new command-
ments and demanded new manners. Its otherness from tribal life was
emphasized by the robes worn by its officers and members. All this made
an immediate appeal. By the end of the 1920s Mutendi had a large following. His homestead grew as he acquired wives and gifts and as a special
compound was built there to accommodate those who came to him for
relief. Zion City, as his kraal came to be called, soon stood as symbol of
African achievement. Mutendi's Zionism spread to the Gutu Reserve,
among many other places, where it combated the drunkenness, passivity
and despair which Nielsen had seen there through creating its own kind of
pride. Mutendi's activities, however, were looked upon with grave suspicion by the administration and the missionaries. The administration
believed that the outbreaks of excitement and enthusiasm characteristic of
the sect might lead to serious disorder and that Mutendi's authority undermined that of the chiefs. The missionaries found his Zion Christian Church
a rival not only to the Mwari cult, which Mutendi openly attacked, but
also to their own influence. In 1929 Mutendi was imprisoned for unlaw-
fully opening a school. For a period in the early 1930s the Zion Christian
Church was proscribed and services had to be held at night in the caves.

Despite this attempted suppression, however, Zionism had come to stay.
Gradually the hostility of the administration gave way to tolerance.
Mutendi and the other original leaders of Zionism continued to gain
followers. There were splits and secessions and ramifications. By the
1950s Zionism could count its followers in tens of thousands.

The Vapostori Movement

Even more successful than Zionism, and more of a peculiarly Shona
achievement was the Vapostori movement. This was the creation of
eastern Mashonaland and sprang particularly from the Manyika people. If
Zionism can be seen as meeting the needs of ex-adherents of the Mwari
cult the Vapostori movement can be seen as providing an indigenous
answer to the dilemma of John Chavafambira of Manyika. For the background against which the movement arose we may turn again to Chavafambira's biographer, Wulf Sachs.

In the mid 1930s Sachs accompanied his friend and patient, Chavafambira, on a visit to his home in Manicaland. It was an area in which, as
we have seen, bitterness and disillusionment with mission Christianity was
finding increasing expression. It was an area, also, in which confidence in
the older spiritual forces of the Shona world could not be easily revived;
in 1918, for example, the *ngangas* had expressed themselves as helpless to

combat the influenza epidemic then sweeping the Reserves. 'They told the people that the disease came from the white folk. It was not sent by the *midzimu*, or by the Mwari, but by the white people. So many were killed in the great war of the white people that the blood of the dead had caused this great sickness.' At the time of Sachs' visit the area was in a state of severe unrest because of the threat of the implementation of Land Apportionment. His account of it brings out all the elements of the Shona rural situation.

'To make matters worse, the tax collector chose this particular time to visit the district. He demanded all arrears of government tax, together with all outstanding rents, which must be paid to the landlords ... The inhabitants of the kraal were thunderstruck at having notices served on them to the effect that they and their families might be moved at any time to a Reserve in the mountains. The thing was incredible. Because of a depression that they could neither avert nor understand, it was possible that they might be removed from the land on which they had lived for centuries! Taken to a Reserve even now incapable of supporting its inhabitants . . . Ugly rumours started of a general revolt throughout Manyikaland. The stories of bloodshed in the Northern Rhodesian Copper mines served to give point to them . . . Everywhere the people clutched at any slender hope.

There was expectancy in the air. Everyone knew that something overwhelming was upon them; that their peaceful, ordered life, lived as their forefathers had prescribed, was to be shattered much as a hillside is dynamited by a railway gang. They had seen such an explosion. But afterwards, after the upheaval, what then? What was their future? Darkness, like a blanket, was choking them in its heavy folds. Who would read the riddle and lighten their darkness? Where could they go for a sign?

Rumours and stories multiplied – wild tales of thousands of natives killed and imprisoned because they refused to pay the tax. Young blood preached revolt, recalling feverish sagas of old wars against the whites, the foreigners, the aliens who seized the land of their forefathers.

But the excited voices were drowned by the increasing evidence cited by the more responsible members of the community who knew only too well the futility of using violence. They capped saga with saga. Had not the first Mutassa chief and his famous blacksmith, who forged magical weapons to destroy the Portuguese invaders from the sea, been betrayed to the whites? Chief, blacksmith, everyone had been slaughtered.

The Christian ministers, black and white, could not fail to note the

unrest and turmoil rife in their flocks. All the people were Christians now
and attended their churches more frequently in this time of stress. The
pastors warned them continually against violent measures, which would
react so surely on themselves . . .

The kraal stood shoulder to shoulder in its firm refusal to pay the
tax . . . Life in the kraal became paralysed. The lands were left untended.
Why till the fields that at any moment they might be ordered to leave?
It was fantastic. To leave the soil from which they had sprung, where the
stones, the trees, the flowers, the very blades of grass, spoke to each one
of his life, his childhood, his loves, his work! To tear them away would
be to leave a bleeding wound in them and in their land; to rend a man
from the land on which his ancestors had lived and in which his parents
were buried was to commit a crime screaming to heaven for vengeance.
For, in a world that was slipping from under their feet, protection and
succour could be sought only from these ancestors. In them they
resisted; to them they prayed.'[1]

In 'a world that was slipping from under their feet' very many Manyika
found in Christian independency the 'sign', the answer to the 'riddle'.
The great figure of Manyika independency was Muchabaya Ngomberume
of the Maranke Reserve, who took the name Johanne after his call to found
his own church. Muchabaya was baptized as a Methodist and learnt to read
and write in a Methodist school. He then went as a wage labourer to
Umtali. He had a long history of visions and of prophetic dreams which
culminated in July 1932 with the descent upon him of the Holy Spirit. In
the Apostolic testament, *Humbowe Hutswa Ve Wapostori* Muchabaya, now
Johanne, describes his vision.

'I was in a house which had been divided into two by the Holy Spirit.
In the house there were many ministers of the various churches. There
was a sudden lightening and a voice beckoned me to shout out loudly to
the people that the Kingdom of God had come and that they had to
accept God. The voice also said: You are blessed, son of Africa! I then
shouted loudly to the sleeping ministers of the churches, but they remained fast asleep.'

Johanne himself was given the following powers:

'You will have power to cure the sick by laying hands on them and by
consecrating water for them to drink; you will be able to drive away any
kind of *shavi* (evil spirit) through the laying on of hands; take the long
staff wherever you go for healing purposes; through your hands fertility
will come to the barren and when you step in fire you will not be burnt.

[1] Sachs, *Black Hamlet*, pp. 257–9.

When you lay hands on a new convert so that he can perform miracles, so be it. If you want him to have the Holy Spirit, so be it. If you want him to heal others, he will do so. If you want him to prophesy or to preach it will be so. Those who die after you have unfastened them will be saved, but those who die before you have done so will be judged by God.'[1]

Johanne's movement was rapidly successful. Obviously it contained an explicitly political and anti-European element. Salvation was to come from the Son of Africa, not from the sleeping ministers of the mission churches. At the close of the baptismal ceremonies of the new church the great Africanist hymn 'Ishe komborera Afrika' was sung. The Vapostori of Johanne Maranke were to be the saved remnant and to triumph over chiefs and mission converts and Europeans. All this made a ready appeal to the Manyika. The situation was much the same as that described by Dr Kingsley Garbett in his account of the influence of another eastern Shona Apostolic church, the church of Johannes Masowe, in the Korekore area. 'The Church had a simple and direct political appeal,' Kingsley Garbett tells us of the 1950s. 'It taught that the poverty of Africans was the result of the greed of the Europeans, who had received all their wealth from the technical knowledge made available to them through God whom they had now rejected. The Church promised that God would reward Africans in Heaven and that Europeans would be condemned to Hell. It also taught that at some time in the future technical knowledge would be made available to Africans through the Prophets. Thus the Masowe church offered an avenue for the expression of discontent and a rationalization for the poverty of the Valley Korekore.'[1]

But the Vapostori movement did not only offer this sort of rationalization for the state of Shona rural society. Through its emphasis upon healing and through its emphasis upon exorcism it offered a means of re-gaining community and unity within the Shona rural world. It thus undertook to perform something which the mission churches, with their refusal to accept the reality of witchcraft and their separation of men from the community through education, were manifestly not able to achieve.

Yet this restored unity was not to be achieved by a return to traditional customs. The Vapostori offered their own solutions to the problems of evil, misfortune, infertility and set their faces more rigorously against those who offered traditional solutions than did the mission Christians themselves. They also prohibited beer drinking and tobacco. Like the Loma-

---

[1] These extracts are translated by Mr Daneel.
[2] G. Kingsley Garbett, 'Prestige, Status and Power in a Modern Valley Korekore Chiefdom', *Africa* vol. XXXVIII, No. 3, July 1967.

gundi Watch Tower movement this was a restructuring of Shona rural society by the force of an African Christianity. To belong to the Vapostori involved a more radical break with the tribal past at the level of custom if not at the level of assumptions than to belong to the mission churches. Ndabaningi Sithole, in his remarkable biography of Obed Mutezo, writes of Obed's wife, Sarah, a Vapostori convert who had 'turned against many of the things and practices of her own people' because the Vapostori had taught her to 'live by faith in God'. Obed himself, a Methodist convert, had made no such conscious break with his own traditions.[1]

The Vapostori movement appealed to the Shona because it took seriously the fundamental notions of healing, prophecy and exorcism which had formed the basis of Shona traditional religion. At the same time, although the Vapostori were suspicious of mission education, they were committed to transforming change. The saved remnant were to be a new and worthier people. The Vapostori provided the discipline of faith and self-respect, and could in certain situations play a modernizing role.

For all these reasons the Vapostori movement grew strong. By 1940 there were more than one hundred *Pasika* sites, at which Vapostori adherents annually received the bread and wine from the hands of the founder. The movement spread into South Africa, into the Congo, into Malawi. By the 1950s there were over 50,000 adherents of Johanne's church and some 20,000 people annually attended the *Pasika* festival in Maranke itself. The various rebuffs and repressions which the movement experienced merely strengthened its convictions.

'All you who wear veils and white garments,' a Fort Victoria Vapostori leader told his flock in the 1960s, 'will not die a natural death. For all who believe that they are the Apostles of God will be killed. This is because our actions are not profitable to us on earth, but they will help us to enter heaven. Now people laugh at us because we have become a spectacle to angels and to men. We are fools for Christ's sake. Look at our founder, John Maranke. When he opened this church he was imprisoned and beaten. But he did not despair. We too are not afraid to die, because in Christ we have already overcome death. Many churches have been founded before ours, but no member of these churches has ever had to suffer for his faith as we. I am sorry for members of all other churches for they will go to hell. But Jesus Christ will help us to enter heaven.'[2]

---

[1] Ndabaningi Sithole, *Obed Mutezo, the Mudzimu-Christian Nationalist*, Nairobi, forthcoming.

[2] Sister Mary Aquina, 'The People of the Spirit', *Africa*, vol. XXXVIII, No. 2, April 1967.

I

Conclusion

The Zionist and Vapostori movements obviously expressed many of the emotions that were present in the Watch Tower flare up in Lomagundi. They were in the same way an articulation of the feelings of thousands of rural Shona. Their achievement was to institutionalize themselves; to make their more subdued millenarian message a source of long-term hope; to combine millenarianism with attempts at improvement. They represented one step further than Watch Tower along the road from the risings of 1896 to the emergence of modern mass nationalism.

Of course, taken by itself and without any reservations, this statement is too bald. Of course these movements were not primarily political. Of course movements of this sort are not merely some sort of intermediate stage which is replaced by modern mass nationalist parties. These churches co-exist with nationalism. Indeed, membership of churches of this kind may be positively incompatible with membership of a mass nationalist party – as membership of the Lenshina church in Zambia was incompatible with membership of UNIP. The nationalist party is in many ways a rival to such churches when it comes into existence. It is claiming the exclusive loyalty of the mass of Africans just as they do. The result may well be open hostility between two different sorts of appeal for faith. To the best of my knowledge this sort of rivalry has not developed in Southern Rhodesia and there are a good many examples of the sympathy felt by members of the Zionist and Vapostori churches for the modern nationalist movement. But it is not upon this sort of sympathy that I base the claim that the development of these churches was a landmark in political as well as in religious history. It is more a matter of concepts; of the succession of ideas about the Shona predicament.

The Christian élite leadership produced by Waddilove and other mission schools had, of course, their own ideas about the Shona predicament. These were obviously important in the development of African politics in Southern Rhodesia: the clear line of descent from the Bantu Congress of the 1930s to the revived Congress of the 1950s and its successor nationalist movements is plain. But these élite ideas about politics could never in themselves have produced the climate of nationalism. The concepts of the Shona independent churches were closer in many ways to that climate.

The Significance
of the African Voice

In the year 1930 the range of African protest in Southern Rhodesia was impressive. In that year the ICU was at the peak of its influence. There was further unrest at Wankie and in other mine compounds. The political associations were seeking to combine into one effective territorial organization while the Watch Tower movement was active in the rural areas of northern Mashonaland and the ground was ready for the spectacular flowering of the Zionist and Vapostori movements. It would have been difficult then to make the comparison so often made thirty years later between the passivity of Southern Rhodesian Africans and the activity of Northern Rhodesian Africans. 'As soon as you cross the bridge at the Falls,' Philip Mason noted in 1959, you hear 'the loud sound of African voices. In the South it is not easy to speak, with any certainty of African opinion; it is there but it does not show above the surface . . . All this is changed in the North: here one is at once aware that there is a vigorous African National Congress with a vocal leader . . . The sound of African voices, usually raised in protest or demand, is then the difference that strikes a student as soon as he crosses the Zambezi.' In 1930 the contrast would surely have been the other way. No African voices were as loud in 1930 as they were in 1959 but they were certainly much louder in Southern than in Northern Rhodesia.[1]

But what was the significance of this Southern Rhodesian African voice? The Reverend John White, that great missionary spokesman on behalf of the 'politically dumb' African people, had no doubts about the answer to this question. He believed that the various activities of the late 1920s were the infallible signs of a great movement of articulate nationalism.

'Historians of the future,' White told the Southern Rhodesia Missionary Conference in 1926, 'will describe the period in which we are now living as the era of African renaissance. In the case of some of us

[1] Philip Mason, *Year of Decision, Rhodesia and Nyasaland in 1960*, London, 1960, pp. 93–4.

here this awakening has synchronized with our missionary experience. Since I set foot in Africa over thirty years ago a profound change has taken place in the entire outlook of the native people of the sub-continent. Through the public press and by various other authors we are constantly being reminded of what is called the dawning Bantu race consciousness; of his restlessness under white dominion; of his dissatisfaction with his social, industrial and political status. To those who look below the surface these things are the symptoms of a profound psychological revolution that is silently, slowly but surely, going on. In short, we are witnessing a nation in its birth throes. At this racial awakening no-one can be surprised. For the African people to have remained stagnant under the circumstances would have proclaimed them less than human... Chief among these awakening messages we must place the message of the missionary. He tells them of privileges and responsibilities in a Kingdom in which all men have equal opportunity; of a Heavenly Father who has no favourites in His world-wide family; of a brotherhood that knows nothing of race or colour. Such teaching is bound to be revolutionary; it cannot be otherwise. Wherever we go, if we are true to our message, we are bound to turn the world upside down. But Christianity is by no means the only revolutionary force at work. The last fifty years has witnessed a great democratic uprising among the masses of Europe. They now vehemently deny the right of a few privileged persons to shape their destiny or say how they shall live. The news of what is taking place there filters through even to Africa, potently affecting the black masses of this Continent. If Europe's bottom dog may growl and shake himself, why not Africa's?

'This awakening, as all awakenings do, has raised a host of problems... The native, on his part, refuses to take things for granted. He cannot admit that he must remain in a state of childish tutelage for ever. He is not content with his position of a mere hewer of wood and drawer of water; he has resolved to fit himself to take his place in the skilled industries of the country; he questions whether it is fitting that he should have no word to say about the laws he is required to obey, the taxes he must pay, the education he must receive and the share he must have of the public services of his country. "Am I never," he asks, "to take any part in determining matters that so vitally affect me and my people; shall I always remain, with folded arms, a mere amused spectator of this momentous drama?"

'Anyone with insight into things may note a deep and growing discontent. They tell us with deference of their desires today; tomorrow they may speak in more vehement accents, and the whispers become a clamorous demand.'[1]

There is no doubt that in this great speech White was more perceptive than his alarmed audience. Yet to obtain a proper estimate of the significance of the Southern Rhodesian African protest of the 1920s we must balance White's testimony against that of a very different sort of witness. In 1935 a police official appeared before the Commission of Inquiry into the Copperbelt disturbances of that year. The witness, one Arthur Goslett, had served in the Southern Rhodesian police before moving to Northern Rhodesia and had had experience of dealing with the Bulawayo faction fights of 1929, 'the alien natives against the indigenous'. He now expounded to the Commission the difference between the two territories. 'The natives in Southern Rhodesia have far more respect for Government officials than they have in this country. There was one instance during the trouble in Bulawayo when three Europeans routed between 200 and 300 natives. I do not think that we could hope for the same success here. In Southern Rhodesia you might say that every inch of the territory is policed, you have regular patrols. The European police are always in touch with the natives and go among them and I think that has a certain beneficial effect. They see that they cannot get away with a crime, they are found out and brought to justice. Here it is only the line of rail really which is policed. The natives anywhere else never see a policeman. Crimes may be committed and never brought to justice . . . In Southern Rhodesia the Police perform many duties which are here considered to be the function of the Administrative Officer. There are adequate numbers to perform these duties and in this country it is not so. In Southern Rhodesia you are always among the natives, one might say you are in constant contact with their pulse, you can feel how they react to things, but here you never get amongst the natives.'[2]

These are the two poles between which African politics in Southern Rhodesia moved. On the one hand there was the greater provocation and the greater sophistication; on the other hand there was the greater control and the greater restraint. Partly because of the South African influence, partly because of the constant pressure of white society and the white economy, Africans in Southern Rhodesia became involved in formal political associations and trade union movements earlier than Africans in Northern Rhodesia. They appreciated at a much earlier date the need for

[1] Presidential address, *Proceedings of the SRMC*, 1926.
[2] Evidence of Arthur Houston Stanley Goslett 8 August 1935, *Northern Rhodesia Copperbelt Disturbances Commission : Russel 1935 Report, Despatch and Evidence.*

action at a territorial rather than a local level. But at the same time the very conditions that evoked this response also did much to weaken it. John White was right but so was Arthur Goslett. In Southern Rhodesia the Native Administration and the police and, more important than either, the tangible evidence of white supremacy *were* 'always among the natives'.

In the 1930s the balance seemed to tilt towards control and restraint. The associations of the 1920s had failed in their attempts to modify the Responsible Government system by working within it; where they had seemed to threaten a dangerous alliance between educated town-dwellers and tribesmen, as in Gwelo, the expression of disapproval by the authorities had sufficed to break it up. Firmer action was needed, and was taken, against the ICU and Watch Tower. Refusal or withdrawal of recognition; the dismissal of men from jobs; police patrols in Lomagundi; deportations; prosecutions brought against Masoja and Mzingeli; advice to chiefs not to mix themselves up with 'political agitators' – all this was enough at that period to ensure that the whispers did not become clamorous demands. In the 1930s, also, Government took fresh powers to deal with any further outbreaks of millenarian or industrial discontent. In 1936 although another Native Preachers Bill had to be withdrawn a Sedition Bill was passed. 'For want of such a measure,' said the Minister of Justice, 'we as a Colony have suffered too long the introduction and the spread of subversive and seditious propaganda and literature in this Colony, much of which unfortunately has taken root in the native mind. It may be difficult to eradicate the harm already done, but at any rate, it is high time that we provided some measure of restraint for the future.' The Minister quoted extensively from the Watch Tower Bible and Tract Society publications and told the Assembly of an unnamed African speaker who asked his audience:

'How are we going to succeed? When you natives unite, you will look for a leader who will speak to the officials. If you find one bee you can kill it easily, but you could not do the same with a bee-hive. You should first unite and ask for what you want. We do not want to do this like those in Northern Rhodesia (i.e. the Copperbelt strikers) who did not do it in a proper way. You will have to pay something, about 1s a month. This will be to support the people until I tell them to stop working at Umtali, Salisbury, Gatooma, Que Que, Gwelo and Bulawayo, because that is the only way we can do it.'

'It is unfair,' concluded the Minister, 'to leave the people to be agitated into strikes, which they do not understand at all and they may only bring upon themselves what has happened to the unfortunate natives in Northern Rhodesia; bloodshed, possibly, or at any rate civil commotion hitherto unknown in this Colony.' In the same year the Native Registration Act tightened up the whole system of control of movement of Africans within the Colony.[1]

In the 1930s, then, or at least after the ICU had collapsed, Africans continued to 'tell us with deference of their desires' through the Conference of Christian Natives or the Bantu Congress. The less deferential aspirations of many Shona found a half-disguised expression in the great movement of independent Christianity with its implicit challenge to the 'progressive Christian' ethic of Congress. The aspirations of many Ndebele found some sort of expression through the Matabele Home Society. But of the great movement that White heralded there was little sign.

Yet if the precocious political experiments of the 1920s were balanced by the restraining realities of the situation, in the same way the moderation and restraint of African political expression in the 1930s and early 1940s was accompanied by profounder movements of pressure and the provocation of the response to them. If the radicalism of the ICU was misleading so, too, was the calm of the 1930s.

For one thing, as we have already seen, the leadership of the 1930s – whether of the élite Congress or the independent churches – was an indigenous leadership rather than largely an alien one. For another thing the implications of the policies of Responsible Government were working themselves out. There was most importantly the operation of the Land Apportionment Act itself. As it turned out the criticisms which had been made of the Act by the associations proved justified. The amount of land allocated for Native Purchase under the Act had been calculated on the basis of certain assumptions about the size of the African population that would have to live in those areas as the result of overspill from the Reserves and the clearing of squatters from white areas. There were two flaws in these assumptions. One was that most of the squatters were not the sort of people who would be able to purchase land or to pass the qualifications required of Native Purchase farmers; if the Native Purchase Areas were indeed going to be developed as such there would be no resting place for the squatters there. The second miscalculation was that the numbers involved soon turned out to be much greater than the Commission had supposed.

In these circumstances the Land Apportionment policy hit at all African land interests. People who lived in the Reserves experienced an increasing land shortage and a consequent deterioration of land. Africans who lived in European areas faced eviction without adequate alternatives. Africans

[1] *Southern Rhodesian Legislative Assembly Debates* Vol. 16, Part 1, p. 1021 et seq.

who wanted to buy land and set up as progressive farmers were frustrated because much of the Native Purchase land was left unsurveyed and unallocated, largely because of the need to absorb evicted squatters somewhere.

It was not until the 1940s that large-scale movements of Africans off European land into the Reserves took place. But even in the 1930s the impact of the Land Apportionment policy was clear enough in some places. Roger Woods has written of an extreme case. In the Mount Darwin district at the end of the 1920s Korekore farmers were moved off land designated for Native Purchase. 'Under government orders they were forced from this area into the adjoining reserves.' But the land thus cleared lay fallow and unused for thirty years. It was not until 1954 that it was surveyed for settlement by Native Purchase Farmers and set up as the Chesa Native Purchase Area. It is not hard to imagine the feelings of the Korekore in the Reserve at the sight of this empty land.[1]

Evictions were felt more by the Shona than by the Ndebele. The rent agreements in central Matabeleland were maintained so that there was no major eviction from the old Ndebele heartland. There was no resistance to the displacements even in Mashonaland but there is no doubt that the implementation of the Act increased tensions and heightened radicalism amongst the Shona. This was all the more true because so few of the Shona had understood what the implications of Land Apportionment were going to be. The Gwelo Native Welfare Association might understand that the Act was mainly designed to deal with the problem of African 'squatters' but few of the rural Shona witnesses to the Carter Commission saw it in that way. To them it had seemed a question of *more* land for Africans even if the new land was put beyond the aspirations of most of them by its cost.

In the end the working out of the Act also involved a revolution in the Reserves, first in terms of agricultural methods and then in terms of the Government's efforts to introduce individual tenure under the Land Husbandry Act of 1951. Of course the problems of African land use in Southern Rhodesia were not created solely by the policy of possessory segregation and the detested enforcement of ridges and culling of cattle were not merely irritations and burdens for rural Africans but part of an effort to meet a rapidly increasing human and animal population. But the policy of possessory segregation meant that these attempts were bound to involve injustice and provoke resistance. Africans in the Reserves reacted to the Land Husbandry Act just as Nzimende had told the Carter Com-

[1] Roger Woods, 'The Dynamics of Land Settlement. Pointers from a Rhodesian land settlement scheme', unpublished seminar paper, Dar es Salaam, 1966.

mission in 1925 they would react to the introduction of individual tenure there. 'The moment a native buys land in the Reserve, which he cultivates, what is going to become of the Reserve?' asked Nzimende. 'What is going to become of the Reserve if the native is allowed to buy?' So Africans in the 1950s asked themselves what was going to become of the Reserves if people were allowed to have individual property rights there.

This question was asked particularly by Africans in the towns, for whom the availability of land in the Reserves was still in the 1950s their only real security. Lewis Gann tells us that on urban questions the Matabele Home Society, and one might add many of the African witnesses in 1925, 'saw the problem much more clearly' than the Carter Commission. The Commission 'looked upon the whole land problem in purely rural terms and . . . saw labour migrancy as part of the natural order of things. The whole question of African urbanization was therefore not squarely tackled at a time when the territory still had the opportunity – even in terms of a purely segregationist philosophy – to formulate a national policy for planning native townships which might be sufficiently accessible to white quarters to obviate transport problems and sufficiently attractive to promote the creation of a stable class of African urban householders.' As Bulawayo and Salisbury grew into large urban and industrial complexes the municipal provision of housing and facilities for Africans proved more and more inadequate.[1]

The grievances of a rootless urban working population were thus added to those of the tribesmen. The Rhodesian Government would have done well to have paid more attention to the criticism and requests of the associations. They would have done well also to confront the challenge posed by the ICU instead of merely suppressing it. The time was not ripe for strike action when the ICU was active but that did not mean that it never would be ripe or that strikes could be averted by passing the Sedition Act or by passing Industrial Conciliation legislation that defined white men only as workers. Slowly there grew up associations of workers in single industries which were better fitted than the ICU to speak effectively for the interests of the growing labour force in the towns.

Finally the Land Apportionment policy in its implementation did little enough to satisfy the progressive élite. Roger Woods describes what happened in the 1930s so far as the allocation of Native Purchase farms was concerned. 'The evidence is that "progressive natives" (i.e. those with capital) met nothing but frustration in trying to acquire land. By tying the pace of settlement to the speed of surveying the areas the Land Board had

[1] Gann, *A History of Southern Rhodesia*, pp. 281–2.

actually settled only 893 farmers by the outbreak of World War II. Another 409 persons had been approved as settled but had not been allocated land and an uncounted number had not been approved. It happened that many of the successful applicants in the thirties were retired BSA policemen, evangelists and teachers from Missions, and the odd "boss boys" from European farms and mines. Most of them were old and many had their origins in Nyasaland, Mozambique or South Africa and so the scheme enabled them to be rewarded for faithful service and gave them a stake in the country that they did not have or had lost. Many of these people had little or no recent experience in agriculture and the expectations of pockets of "highly productive Native farms providing an example to the adjoining reserves" were not fulfilled. These settlers simply subsisted in a manner identical to that of the reserves.' Clearly allocation of Native Purchase Area farms at this rate and in this sort of way was not going to create the large African middle class with a vested interest in the system which might have bought off progressive discontent. Even as late as 1963 only about one million of the seven million acres set aside for Native Purchase had been disposed of to individual farmers. In that year there were some 6,500 farmers but even this was a far cry from the effects which the Carter Commission had envisaged would flow from the segregation bargain.[1]

At the Southern Rhodesia Missionary Conference in 1934 the death of John White was mourned, and as if to retrospectively justify some of his warnings the Conference noted that the Land Apportionment Act seemed likely to 'work to the detriment of those it was actually intended to help. Natives were being squeezed out of their ancestral heritage and nobody knew where they would have to go. The Native Purchase Areas would only accommodate a limited number, and thousands would have to go to the Reserves.' As time went by the consequences of Land Apportionment did more than any other single factor to ensure that White's predictions were fulfilled and that Africans came to speak 'in more vehement accents' and the whispers became 'clamorous' demands.[2]

The clamour arose after the Second World War in a whole variety of outbursts. There were the strikes of 1945 and 1948, the revival of the Reformed ICU and the hey-day of African Trade Unionism; there was the fight against the Land Husbandry Act waged by Benjamin Burumbo and the African Workers' Voice Association; there was the founding of the City Youth League in Salisbury in 1955; there was the formation of the revived and militant Congress in 1957 and subsequently the successor nationalist

---

[1] Woods, 'The Dynamics of Land Settlement'.
[2] *Proceedings of the SRMC,* 1934.

organizations – the National Democratic Party, the Zimbabwe African People's Union. Some thirty years after White's Presidential address the spectacle of a nation in its birth-throes was obvious to very many people. In the late 1950s and early 1960s the various traditions of Southern Rhodesian African politics seemed to come together. The revived Congress, NDP, ZAPU inherited the central focus and the territorial claim of the old Bantu Congress and of the Associations; they adopted many of the methods and much of the rhetoric of the old ICU; they managed to reach the rural areas and tap rural discontents without losing their national character; they managed to draw upon the memories of the risings, the remaining veneration for traditional religion, the concepts of both the Mission churches and of independency. For a brief period the nationalist movements were inclusive of many separate and often rival traditions of African life in Rhodesia. The grievances of the cultivators in the Reserves, of the townsmen, of the frustrated 'progressives' combined to create what seemed to many observers a totally new movement, springing in the most surprising way out of African passivity and division.

This is no place to discuss in any detail the rise of mass nationalism in Southern Rhodesia – it requires a volume to itself. But no study of African politics up to 1930 can end without attempting some answer to the question of their significance in relation to the later nationalist movement. What were the links between the protests and experiments I have been describing and the articulate nationalist politics of thirty years later? Was there a single if mysterious process of growth and development? Was there a great current, often running underground, which issued in the nationalist movement? Or was the nationalist movement produced by the circumstances of the 1950s without reference to what had gone before?

I think that at the moment it is possible to give four answers to these questions. In the first place there are the specific links between the politics of the 1920s and the politics of the 1950s, some of which have already been mentioned. There is the revival of the Reformed ICU; the career of Mzingeli; the sudden return of old Masoja Ndlovu, who had been silent since the mid 1930s, to join the revived Congress movement in 1958. In a different context there is the political succession of the Nyandoro family; rebel leaders in 1896; protestants against destocking in the 1930s; culminating in George Nyandoro playing a leading role in the City Youth League, in Congress and its successor movements. Of course the pattern is not simple. We are not dealing with a monolithic movement of common interests. Some of the members of the old Bantu Congress, for example, came into the revived Congress of the 1950s and its successors. Thus Job

Dumbutshena, the old ICU stalwart and later a member of the Bantu Congress, came into the National Democratic Party. Other old members of the Bantu Congress still clung to the politics of élite participation rather than of mass protest and found themselves in the white-led United Rhodesia Party or the Central Africa Party. Mr Garfield Todd's Central Africa Party in particular inherited a good deal of the Christian progressive tradition of the 1930s. Similarly, some members of the Matabele Home Society found it easy to move into a national movement; others did not. It must be admitted also that few members of the mass nationalist parties thought of themselves as part of a great continuous tradition of protest; most thought of themselves as reacting against and repudiating older traditions of African politics. Yet even this reaction was part of a process which linked new and old.

In the second place there is what might be called the connection of predicament. Different in many ways as the two situations were, the nationalist parties of the 1950s shared a basic dilemma with the politicians and protesters of the 1920s. There was still the combination of provocation and control, of radicalism and restraint. It was sometimes possible to forget the strength of the white presence in Southern Rhodesia during the heady days of the break up of the Federation, when the nationalist movement seemed essentially similar to those in Northern Rhodesia and Nyasaland and seemed headed for the same triumphs. But the dilemma was still there. It was this essential situation that accounted for the fact that in between the outbursts of clamour and protest after the Second World War there came great stretches of participation politics. Between the 1948 strike and the founding of the City Youth League there stretched the years of 'Partnership', the revived attempt to work through use of the vote and dialogue with white politicians. It was this also that accounted for the fact that even at the peak of the outburst of protest, when the African movement was showing its greatest strength, there was the same fundamental uncertainty about tactics that the ICU, for example, had shown in the late 1920s.

Even today, now that the radical nationalists have opted out of the political tradition altogether and gone back to a policy of direct and violent confrontation in the guerrilla movement, they operate in a situation determined by the experiences and attitudes we have been discussing in this book. The guerrillas appeal back to the risings of 1896 and 1897 and call their movement after them. In trying to reach the mass of the people in the rural areas they have to combat the long decades of fatalistic acceptance of the superior military might of the whites. In trying to organize they face the problems of fragmentation created by the aftermath and suppression of the risings and by the implementation of possessory segregation. In 1896 the rebels lived along the main communication routes and side by side with the whites. Today the guerrillas have to move through white farm land in order to pass from reserve to reserve; the roads and railways run through white land; the towns and strategic centres are in white territory.

It is very important, indeed, not to forget this legacy of fragmentation. The centralizing tradition, which runs from the RBVA to the mass nationalist movements, is important. But so has been the reality of disintegration in a quite physical and geographical sense. Ndabaningi Sithole reminds us of this very effectively in his account of the first Congress meeting in Nyanyadzi settlement in south east Mashonaland in 1958. One of the Congress leaders, Peter Mtandwa, read from Ezekiel the passage about the scattered and dry bones:

'The hand of the Lord was upon me, and carried me out in the spirit of the Lord and set me down in the midst of the valley which was full of bones . . . and behold there were very many in the open valley; and, lo, they were very dry. And he said unto me, Son of man, can these bones live? And I answered, O, Lord God, thou knowest. And again he said unto me, Prophesy upon these bones and say unto them, O ye dry bones, hear the word of the Lord . . . So I prophesied as I was commanded: and as I prophesied, there was a noise, and behold a shaking, and the bones came together, bone to his bone.'

'This passage made a lot of meaning' to those who listened, writes Sithole. To them 'the dry bones were the Africans who were scattered all over Rhodesia and who had lost any political coherence since 1896. (They were) impressed by the fact that for the first time the Africans were moving up and down the country organizing the people to fight for their rights . . . Indeed, the dry bones of Zimbabwe were coming together and God was breathing the breath of life into them.'[1]

This passage conveys something of the feeling of novelty that the nationalist movement brought with it. But considerable though the achievements of the nationalist movement were they could not, of course, do anything about the geographical incoherence of the African areas of Southern Rhodesia. Nor were they any more successful than the movements of the 1920s had been in linking the Reserves to the white areas between them by establishing effective contact with the Nyasa and other 'alien' labourers on white farms.

Closely connected to this connection of predicament is the connection

[1] Sithole, *Obed Mutezo*.

through tactics. Although the African politics of the period 1890 to 1930 were on a small scale they ran through most of the tactics available to African movements in Southern Rhodesia. The tactic of armed resistance with Mapondera, the tactic of appeal to an outside tribunal with Nyamanda, the tactic of participation with the RBVA, the tactic of protest within the system rather than appeal outside it with the ICU, the tactic of basing a modern style movement on tribal nationality with the Matabele Home Society, the tactic of linking the concerns of the élite with the basic anxieties of the tribesman over land and cattle with Martha Ngano and the Southern Rhodesia Native Welfare Association, the tactic of calling upon the white man to live up to the implications of the Christian message and the civilizing mission with the Conference of Christian Natives and the Bantu Congress, the tactic of penetration from the north: all were tried and all failed.

The petition, the delegation, the statement to the press, the mass meeting, the slogan, the anthem – all these and more were features of African politics before 1930. At least until the guerrilla phase subsequent African politics did not produce new tactics or use new methods, though they employed the old ones much more effectively and on a much greater scale. An understanding of the limitations of the tactics employed by African movements before 1930 is no bad beginning for understanding the problems of mass nationalism in Southern Rhodesia.

Finally, and I think distinct from the other three, is the obvious but important fact that the phenomena which this book describes were part of the total African experience in Southern Rhodesia even if it cannot be shown that they flowed directly into or linked up with the later nationalist movement. That movement, like every other aspect of African life in the 1950s and 1960s was coloured by the quality of African life in the 1910s and 1920s. In the independent African states to the north of Southern Rhodesia scholars are coming to think about the African politics of earlier decades not so much in terms of the roots of nationalism but in terms of the roots of post-independence African politics. In Southern Rhodesia the situation has been and remains such that most African voices have been raised in protest against the colonial situation. But I hope it has been clear from this book that one cannot see African politics in Southern Rhodesia any more than in Kenya or Tanzania in terms of an undifferentiated black mass on the one hand and an undifferentiated white minority on the other. This book should really have been called *African Voices in Southern Rhodesia*. The voices recorded represented individuals and interests which were very different from each other. The existence of such differences and the emergence of interests and classes within the African population of Southern Rhodesia is a key determinant of contemporary African politics there. What we need is a social and economic history of the African population of Southern Rhodesia. Until we get it I hope that some at least of this book will suggest the complexity out of which nationalist politics have arisen.

Select Bibliography

Books and Articles

Alvord, E. D., *Agricultural demonstration work on Native Reserves*, Department of Native Development, Occasional Paper No. 3, Salisbury, 1930.

Andrews, C. F., *John White of Mashonaland*, London, 1935.

Aquina, Sister Mary, 'Christianity in a Rhodesian Tribal Trust Land', *African Social Research*, 1, 1966.

—— 'The People of the Spirit; An Independent Church in Rhodesia', *Africa*, vol. XXXVII, 1967.

—— 'Zionists in Rhodesia', *Africa*, vol. XXXIX, 1969.

—— *Chiefs and Councils in Rhodesia: Transition from Patriarchal to Bureaucratic Power*, London, forthcoming.

Arrighi, G., *The Political Economy of Rhodesia*, The Hague, 1967.

—— 'Labour supplies in historical perspective: the Rhodesian case', University College, Dar es Salaam, September 1967, mimeo.

Barrett, D. B., *Schism and Renewal: An Analysis of Six Thousand Contemporary Religious Movements*, Nairobi, 1968.

Benson, Mary, *The African Patriots: the story of the African National Congress of South Africa*, London, 1963.

Brown, K., *Land in Southern Rhodesia*, London, 1959.

Cripps, A. S., *An Africa for Africans: A Plea on behalf of Territorial Segregation Areas and of their Freedom in a South African Colony*, London, 1927.

Daneel, M. L., 'Shona independent churches and Ancestor Worship', *Workshop in Religious Research*, Nairobi, 1967, paper no. 50.

Farrant, Jean, *Mashonaland Martyr: Bernard Mizeki and the Pioneer Church*, Cape Town, 1966.

Gann, L. H., 'The Southern Rhodesian land apportionment act, 1930: an essay in trusteeship', *National Archives of Rhodesia and Nyasaland, Occasional Papers*, no. 1, June 1963.

—— *A History of Southern Rhodesia: Early Days to 1934*, London, 1965.

Gann, L. H. and Gelfand, M., *Huggins of Rhodesia: The Man and his Country*, London, 1964.

Garbett, G. Kingsley, 'Religious Aspects of Political Succession among the Valley Korekore', in *The Zambesian Past: Studies in Central African History*, eds. Eric Stokes and Richard Brown, Manchester, 1966.

—— 'Prestige, Status and Power in a Modern Valley Korekore Chiefdom', *Africa*, vol. XXXVIII, no. 3, 1967.

—— 'Spirit Mediums as Mediators in Korekore Society', in *Spirit Mediumship and Society in Africa*, eds. John Beattie and John Middleton, London, 1969.

Gray, R., *The Two Nations: Aspects of the Development of Race Relations in the Rhodesias and Nyasaland*, London, 1960.

Hoare, Rawdon, *Rhodesian Mosaic*, London, 1934.

Holleman, J. F., *Chief, Council and Commissioner: Some Problems of Government in Rhodesia*, Afrika Studiecentrum, Assen, 1969.

Hooker, J. R., 'Welfare Associations and other instruments of accommodation in the Rhodesias between the World Wars', *Comparative Studies in Society and History*, vol. 9, no. 1, 1966.

—— 'Witnesses and Watchtower in the Rhodesias and Nyasaland', *Journal of African History*, vol. 6, no. 1, 1965.

Jabavu, D. D. T., *The Life of John Tengo Jabavu, editor of 'Imvo Zabantsundu', 1884–1921*, Lovedale Institution Press, 1922.

James, C. L. R., *History of the Negro Revolt*, London, 1938.

Long, B. K., *Drummond Chaplin*, Oxford, 1941.

Mason, P., *Year of Decision: Rhodesia and Nyasaland in 1960*, London, 1960.

Mitchell, J. Clyde, *The Kalela Dance*, Manchester, 1956.

—— *Tribalism and the Plural Society*, London, 1960.

Mokwile, J. S., 'Native Ideals', *The Southern Rhodesian Native Affairs Department Annual*, no. 1, 1924.

Moyo, P. H., 'Native Life in the Reserves', *The Southern Rhodesian Native Affairs Department Annual*, no. 3, 1925.

Murphree, M. W., *Christianity and the Shona*, London, 1969.

Palley, C., *The Constitutional History and Law of Southern Rhodesia, 1888–1965, 1888–1965*, Oxford, 1966.

Palmer, R. H., *Aspects of Rhodesian Land Policy, 1890–1936*, The Central African Historical Association, Local Series 22, Salisbury, 1968.

—— 'War and Land in Rhodesia', University of East Africa, Social Science Council Conference, Nairobi, 1969.

Parker, F., *African Development and Education in Southern Rhodesia*, International education monographs, no. 2, Columbus, Ohio, 1960.

Ranger, T. O., *State and Church in Southern Rhodesia, 1919–1939*, Historical Association of Rhodesia and Nyasaland, Local Series 4, Salisbury, 1961.

—— 'The early history of independency in Southern Rhodesia', *Religion in*

Africa, ed. W. Montgomery Watt, Centre of African Studies, Edinburgh University, Edinburgh, 1964.

—— 'The last days of the empire of Mwene Mutapa', *Conference on the History of the Central African Peoples*, Lusaka, 1963.

—— 'The Ethiopian Episode in Barotseland, 1900–1905', *Rhodes Livingstone Journal*, no. 37, 1965.

—— 'African attempts to control education in East and Central Africa, 1900–1939', *Past and Present*, no. 32, 1965.

—— 'Traditional Authorities and the Rise of Modern Politics in Southern Rhodesia, 1898–1930', *The Zambesian Past: Studies in Central African History*, eds. Eric Stokes and Richard Brown, Manchester, 1966.

—— *Revolt in Southern Rhodesia, 1897: A Study in African Resistance*, London, 1967.

—— 'African Politics in twentieth-century Southern Rhodesia', in *Aspects of Central African History*, ed. T. O. Ranger, London, 1968.

—— 'Nationality and Nationalism: the case of Barotseland', *Journal of the Historical Society of Nigeria*, vol. 4, no. 2, 1968.

Rennie, J. K., 'Settlers and Missionaries in South Melsetter, 1893–1925', UCRN, Salisbury, 1966, mimeo.

Roder, W., 'The division of Land Resources in Southern Rhodesia', *Annals of the Association of American Geographers*, vol. 54, March 1964.

Rotberg, R. I., *The Rise of Nationalism in Central Africa: the making of Malawi and Zambia, 1873–1964*, Harvard, 1965.

Roux, E., *Time Longer Than Rope: A History of the Struggle of the Black Man for Freedom in South Africa*, Madison, 1964.

Sachs, W., *Black Hamlet: The Mind of an African Negro revealed by psychoanalysis*, London, 1937.

Shamuyarira, N., *Crisis in Rhodesia*, London, 1965.

Shepperson, G., 'Nyasaland and the Millenium', in *Millenial Dreams in Action*, ed. S. Thrupp, The Hague, 1962.

—— 'Church and Sect in Central Africa', *Rhodes Livingstone Journal*, no. 33, 1963.

—— 'Ethiopianism, Past and Present', in *Christianity in Tropical Africa*, ed. C. G. Baeta, International African Institute, 1968.

Shepperson, G. and Price, T., *Independent African: John Chilembwe*, Edinburgh, 1958.

Simons, H. J. and R. E., *Class and Colour in South Africa, 1850–1950*, London, 1969.

Sithole, N., *African Nationalism*, Cape Town, 1959.
—— *Obed Mutezo: the Mudzimu-Christian Nationalist*, Nairobi, forthcoming.
Smulders, W., 'Chief Chivero', *Jesuit Missions*, vol. XIV, no. 136, 1968.
Sundkler, Bengt, *Bantu Prophets in South Africa*, International African Institute, 1961.
Van Velsen, J., 'Trends in African Nationalism in Southern Rhodesia', *Kroniek van Afrika*, Leiden, June 1964.
—— 'Some early pressure groups in Malawi', in *The Zambesian Past: Studies in Central African History*, eds. Eric Stokes and Richard Brown, Manchester, 1966.
Wallis, J. P. R., *One Man's Hand: The Story of Sir Charles Coghlan and the Liberation of Southern Rhodesia*, London, 1950.
Walsh, Peter, 'The Origins of African Political Consciousness in South Africa', *Journal of Modern African Studies*, vol. 6, no. 4, 1969.
—— *The Rise of African Nationalism in South Africa*, forthcoming.
Woods, R., 'The Dynamics of Land Settlement: Pointers from a Rhodesian land settlement scheme', seminar paper, University College, Dar es Salaam, 1966, mimeo.
Yudelman, M., *Africans on the Land: Economic Problems of African Agricultural Development in Southern, Central and East Africa with Special Reference to Southern Rhodesia*, London, 1964.

Archival Sources

a) *National Archives of Rhodesia*:

The greater part of this book is based on material on file in the National Archives, Salisbury, where I worked between 1959 and 1963. A thirty year access rule operates in Southern Rhodesia and I was able to see material up to the early 1930s. A good part of the material listed below has been withdrawn from public access.

Files coded A relate to the office of the Administrator, the chief executive of the Colony under British South Africa Company rule. Files coded N relate to the Native Department; they also contain extensive reports by the Criminal Investigation Department, made available to the Native Department for its information. Police and CID files in general are not deposited in the National Archives and not available for consultation. Files coded S relate to the executive offices after the establishment of Responsible Government in 1923. I understand that these files have subsequently been re-coded. Files coded ZAH contain the very abundant evidence given to the Carter Commission in 1925. These are the four sources upon which I have drawn most abundantly.

In addition I have drawn upon one file coded CT which contains correspondence with the Cape Town office of the British South Africa Company; one file coded D, which contains material relating to the trial of Mapondera; one file coded L, which relates to applications by Africans to purchase or lease Company land; five volumes coded LO, which contain correspondence sent to the London Office of the Company; and two files coded RC, which contain material relating to the office of the Resident Commissioner.

In general, of course, this material is official in character but it does contain a good deal directly produced by Africans – petitions, minutes, intercepted correspondence, and so on.

The National Archives also possesses an extensive collection of privately donated manuscripts. Of these I have used one file coded ANG, which contains correspondence between A. S. Cripps and Bishop Paget; one file coded CR which contains correspondence between Cripps and John White; one file coded HA, which contains the correspondence of the missionary, Hale; and a file coded WI, which contains the notes of an interview with one of the Ndebele charged with the murder of whites in 1896.

Administrator's Office:

A 3/6/9	A 11/2/12/8
A 3/18/1 – 2	A 11/2/12/11
A 3/18/4	A 11/2/18/3
A 3/18/10–11	A 12/1/16
A 3/18/18/6	AM 2/1/7
A 3/18/24	

Native Department:

N 3/1/18	N 3/16/3
N 3/5/3	N 3/16/9
N 3/5/6	N 3/19/3
N 3/5/8	N 3/19/4
N 3/7/2	N 3/21/1
N 3/10/5	N 3/21/4
N 3/14/5	N 3/33/12

Executive offices after 1923:

S 84/A/154	S 84/A/300
S 84/A/259	S 84/A/301
S 84/A/260	S 84/A/293
S 84/A/261	S 138/21
S 84/A/262	S 138/226
S 84/A/264	

Evidence to the Carter Commission, 1925:

ZAH 1/1/1	ZAH 1/1/3
ZAH 1/1/2	ZAH 1/1/4

Cape Town correspondence:
CT 1/6/8

Mapondera Trial:
D 3/5/10

Land application file:
L 2/1/175

London Office correspondence:
LO 5/7/1–4

Resident Commissioner's office:

RC 3/3/8	RC 3/9/5/29

Private manuscript deposits:

ANG 1/1/9	HA 4/1/1
CR 4/5/1	WI 8/1/3

b) *Manuscripts deposited at Rhodes House, Oxford*

The library at Rhodes House has two major archival collections relevant to the theme of this book. One of these is the collection of the papers of Cecil John Rhodes himself. Of this extensive material I cite in this book only one file, file C.27, but I have found a great deal more than this invaluable for background.

The other major collection is the papers of the Anti-Slavery and Aborigines Protection Society. Richer still for Kenya and South Africa, these papers are rich enough for Southern Rhodesia to provide the back-bone of the doctoral thesis being prepared by Mrs Rachel Whitehead. I have used the following files of correspondence between the Secretary of the APS, John Harris, and a variety of people in Africa and Britain:

G 166

G 167

G 172

G 173

G 495

c) *National Archives of Malawi*

I have used a photo-copy of the invaluable 'Historical Survey of Native Controlled Missions operating in Nyasaland', drawn up in December 1940, and held by the National Archives, Zomba. I am grateful to Dr Roderick McDonald for making this available to me.

Index of Themes

Index of personal, national, tribal, organisational and place names

ST. MARY'S COLLEGE OF MARYLAND
ST. MARY'S CITY, MARYLAND

053200

DATE DUE			
JAN 18 78			
DEC 19 1976			

DT   **Ranger, Terence O.**   78
962   The African voice in
.42   Southern Rhodesia, 1898-1930
.R35
1970b   053200
                                        C21709